THE SPANISH CONQUEST

IN AMERICA,

AND ITS RELATION TO THE HISTORY OF SLAVERY AND TO THE GOVERNMENT OF COLONIES.

BY ARTHUR HELPS.

VOL. IV.

NEW YORK:
HARPER & BROTHERS, PUBLISHERS,
FRANKLIN SQUARE.
1868.

CONTENTS OF VOL. IV.

BOOK XVII.

THE FEUD BETWEEN THE PIZARROS AND THE ALMAGROS.

BOOK XVIII.

THE NEW LAWS.

BOOK XIX.

THE RECONQUEST OF PERU BY THE PRESIDENT GASCA.

BOOK XX.

THE PROTECTORS OF THE INDIANS: THEIR EFFORTS AND ACHIEVEMENTS.

CHAPTER VI.

BOOK XXI.

A GENERAL SURVEY OF SPANISH COLONIZATION IN AMERICA.

CHAPTER I.

CHAPTER II.

CHAPTER III.

CHAPTER IV.

CHAPTER V.

BOOK XVII.

THE FEUD BETWEEN THE PIZARROS AND THE ALMAGROS.

THE

SPANISH CONQUEST IN AMERICA.

CHAPTER I.

THE FEUD BETWEEN THE PIZARROS AND THE ALMAGROS.—ALVARADO'S ENTRANCE INTO PERU.—ALMAGRO PROCEEDS TO CONQUER CHILI.—FERNANDO PIZARRO TAKES THE COMMAND AT CUSCO.

WHEN the wild beasts of a forest have hunted down their prey, there comes the difficulty of tearing it into equal or rather into satisfying shares, which mostly ends in renewed bloodshed. Nor is the same stage of the proceedings less perilous to associates among the higher animals; and men, notwithstanding all their writings and agreements, rules, forms, and orders, are hardly restrained from flying at each other's throats when they come to the distribution of profits, honors, or rewards. The feud between the Pizarros and the Almagros, which forms the next great series of events in American history, is one of the most memorable quarrels in the world. Pizarro and Almagro were two rude, unlettered men, of questionable origin; but their disputes were of as much importance to mankind as almost any which occurred in that century, rich as it is in historical incident, except perhaps the long-continued quarrel between the Emperor Charles the Fifth and Francis the First.

Moreover, the European feud between these monarchs was important chiefly on account of its indirect consequences, inasmuch as it gave room for the Reformation to grow and establish itself; but this dire contest in America destroyed almost every person of any note who came within its influence, desolated the country where it originated, prevented the growth of colonization, and changed for the worse the whole course of legislation for the Spanish colonies. Its effects were distinctly visible for a century afterward, whereas the wars between France and Spain, though they seemed to be all-important at the time, did not leave any permanent mark upon either country.

There were no signs, however, of the depth and fatality of this feud between the Pizarros and Almagros at the period immediately succeeding the execution of Atahuallpa. That act of injustice having been perpetrated, Pizarro gave the royal *borla* to a brother of the late Inca, and set out from Cassamarca on his way to Cusco. It was now time to extend his conquests and to make himself master of the chief city in Peru. Accordingly, in company with his comrade Almagro and the new Inca, Pizarro quitted Cassamarca in the summer of 1553, having remained in that beautiful district seven months.

It is unnecessary to give any detailed account of the events of this journey. The hostile Indians, wherever met, were encountered and routed by the Spaniards, with the aid, as they imagined, of their tutelary saint, whose assistance, however, does not seem to have been much needed. The newly-appointed Inca died. The death of this prince has been attributed to the grief he felt at the depression of his royal race. It is said that after the *borla* had been placed upon him, he was no sooner out of Pizarro's presence than, tearing the regal emblem from his forehead, he threw it on the ground, and stamped upon it, declaring that he would not wear a thing which he regarded as a mark of his slavery and of his shame. His most devoted followers sought to conquer this resolution; but they did so in vain; and, giving way to unutterable disgust at his subservient position, he expired in two months' time after he had received the *borla* from the hands of the man who had conquered his people and taken away his brother's life.* Pizarro exceedingly regretted the death of this Inca, for it was very convenient to the Spanish conqueror to have at his beck a scion of the royal race, who must be submissive to him, but whose semblance of authority might prevent the Peruvians from attempting farther resistance.

Chilicuchima, the unfortunate general whom Ferdinand Pizarro had persuaded to accompany him to the Spanish quarters, became suspected of being in communication with the enemy, and was most unjustly condemned to be burnt by Pizarro. When the Spaniards approached the city of Cusco, they found that the Indians there were disposed to make a great resistance. But a brother of Guascar, named Manco

* "Les événements qui venaient de se passer avaient rempli son âme d'une si vive douleur, et il comprenait si bien les intentions secrètes de Pizarro, qu'il ne fut pas plutôt hors de sa présence, qu'arrachant de son front la houppe impériale, il la jeta à terre et la foula aux pieds avec mépris, en déclarant à ceux qui l'entouraient que jamais il ne porterait ces insignes qu'il regardait comme la marque de son esclavage et de sa honte. Les personnes qui lui étaient le plus dévouées essayèrent de le persuader. On employa les supplications et les larmes; mais tout fut inutile: car, continuant à mépriser la marque de sa dignité, et plongé dans la plus amère douleur, il mourut deux mois après son couronnement, victime de ses souffrances morales."—*Histoire du Royaume du Quito: par* Don Juan de Velasco. Ternaux-Compans. *Voyages*, tom. i., liv. iii., p. 377.

Inca, who held the chief authority in the place, and was accounted by the Cuscans as the reigning Inca, came out to meet Pizarro as a friend, in consequence of which the Spaniards entered "the great and holy city" of Cusco after a slight resistance, on the 15th of November, 1533.* Notwithstanding that Cusco had been rifled in the first instance by Pizarro's messengers, there still remained in that city great treasures, which, when divided into four hundred and eighty parts, gave, as some say, four thousand *pesos* to each Spaniard in the army. Among the spoil were ten or twelve statues of female figures, made of fine gold, as large as life, and "as beautiful and well wrought as if they had been alive."† This division having been accomplished, Pizarro attended to the affairs of religion. He caused the idols to be pulled down, placed crosses on all the highways, built a church, and then, with all due solemnities, in the presence of a notary and of fitting witnesses, took possession of the town "in the name of the invincible King of Castile and Leon, Don Carlos the First of that name."

The fierce and valorous captains who had fought under the banners of Atahuallpa did not remain indolent or pacific spectators of the Spanish conquest. The principal warriors among them were Quizquiz and Ruminavi. We can not enter into the obscure and confused operations by which these captains were destroyed. It will be sufficient to remark that all their efforts proved unavailing to stop the main current of the Spanish conquest of Peru, which, however,

* This was exactly a year after their entry into Cassamarca, which had taken place on the 15th of November, 1532.

† "E fra l'altre cose singolari, era veder . . . . . 10 ó 12 statue di donne, della grandezza delle donne di quel paese, tutte d'oro fino, cosi belle e ben fatte come se fossero vive."—*Relatione di* PERO SANCO. *Viaggi di* RAMUSIO.

was threatened from a different quarter in a very singular and unexpected manner.

One of the most renowned companions of Cortez in his conquest of New Spain was Pedro de Alvarado, the conqueror of Guatemala, and afterward the governor of that province, where he might have had sufficient occupation for the remainder of his life—enough, indeed, for many statesmen and many commanders. But the peculiar restlessness of Alvarado, and the difficulty for a man to leave off conquering who has once tasted the delight of conquest, tempted him now to farther enterprises. The report of the riches of Peru sped quickly from South America over the provinces of Spain, and was so attractive that Charles the Fifth himself became embarrassed by his conquest of the Indies, which hindered his levies for European warfare. It was an easy task, however, for Alvarado to find recruits ready and willing to follow him to these new lands; and, accordingly, in the year 1534, when Pizarro was at Cusco, he heard to his dismay that Alvarado, with no fewer than five hundred men-at-arms, had landed on the northern coast of Peru.

Pizarro at once dispatched Almagro in hot haste* to conquer or to gain over this new and formidable rival. The danger, however, to be apprehended from him soon grew less, for the expedition had been unfortunate at its outset. These new invaders, naturally disposed to take a different direction from that of Pizarro, and choosing Quito as their field of conquest, had great hardships to endure on their march to that country. They suffered the utmost extremes of cold and hunger, so much so that in the course of their route they left behind them much of the gold

* "A toda furia."

and emeralds which they had obtained from the Indians;* and the result was, that when Almagro's forces and Alvarado's came into each other's presence, the latter were not disinclined to come to terms. Moreover, there had been desertions on both sides. That discreditable interpreter, Felipillo, had gone over to Alvarado's camp, while Alvarado's own secretary had deserted to Almagro. There was no reason why Spaniards should contend with Spaniards, neither was there any particular enmity on either side toward the other. Negotiations, therefore, were readily entered upon between the two opposing camps, and finally brought to a favorable conclusion by a licentiate named Caldera, who had accompanied Almagro. The substance of the treaty was that Almagro should give to Alvarado one hundred thousand *pesos*, and in return that Alvarado should hand over the armament to the two partners Pizarro and Almagro, and should engage for himself to quit Peru. The articles of the treaty remained secret for a time, and meanwhile the allied forces moved southward together on the road to Cusco. Almagro had not the money wherewith to pay the sum agreed upon, and so they went to meet Pizarro.

This was a most important treaty, and it seemed as if a great danger were thus obviated in the conquest of Peru; but it fell out otherwise, for the principal men in Alvarado's armament, having met first with Almagro, became attached to him, and were among his most zealous partisans, at a time when partisanship was the curse of Peru.

* "Una cosa diré por muy cierta: que en este camino se padeció tanta hambre y cansancio, que muchos dexaron cargas de oro, y muy ricas esmeraldas, por no tener fuerças para las llevar."—CIEÇA DE LEON, *Chrónica del Peru*, parte i[ra], cap. 42.

Pizarro being informed of the result of this negotiation, and not wishing that Alvarado should see more of the riches of the country than could be helped, moved forward to meet his comrade Almagro and the Governor of Guatemala in the valley of Pachacamác. There the three met, and, though "there was not wanting some one who" suggested to Pizarro to seize upon the person of Alvarado, or at least to reduce the amount to be paid for Alvarado's armament, Pizarro loyally and wisely fulfilled the agreement which had been made on his behalf by his partner Almagro. There was then some proposition about a league being formed between the Governor of Guatemala, Pizarro, and Almagro—also about the marriage of the son of Almagro to the daughter of Alvarado; but Almagro would not hear of this league, saying that it would be impossible for three partners to keep the peace.* It was soon to be found how difficult it is for even two partners to agree. The excuse which Alvarado offered for his presence in Peru was "that, being intent on discovering eastward where no other person had been, such news came of the greatness of the treasures of Quito, that, not thinking to find any of Pizarro's captains in that part, he was unable to resist the wishes of his own people to go there." Pizarro listened to this excuse, paid all the money agreed upon, and feasted the allied forces. Then the Governor of Guatemala departed, having made, as far as he himself was concerned, a sordid and sorry end to the enterprise.

Pizarro, relieved from this difficulty, resolved to found a city near the sea-coast, in the valley of Lima, which was at first called Los Reyes, from its being

* "Que seria impossible tener paz tres compañeros."

founded on or about the day of Epiphany, in the year 1535. It afterward received the name of Lima. Before this occurred, however, the compact between the two partners Pizarro and Almagro had been renewed with oaths and other solemn affirmations;* and it was agreed that Almagro should go to reside at Cusco, to govern that part of the country, for which Pizarro gave him powers, as he did also to make farther discoveries southward. The Mariscal (such was the title which had been recently conferred on Almagro) took his leave, accompanied by the greater part of Alvarado's men, whom he had attracted by his amiable nature and profuse liberality.

While these events had been occurring in Peru, Fernando Pizarro had reached the court of Spain. It was in January, 1534, that he arrived at Seville, and as the Emperor was in Spain that year, Fernando Pizarro's business was readily dispatched. The result of his negotiation with the court was, that he obtained for his brother the Marquisate of Atavillos, a valley not far from Xauxa, the habit of Santiago for himself, the Bishopric of Cusco for Vicente de Valverde, and a governorship for Almagro, which was to commence where Pizarro's ended, and was to be called Nueva Toledo. It can not be said that Fernando Pizarro fell into the error formerly committed by his brother of neglecting Almagro's interests at the Spanish court. On the other hand, as some acknowledgment of these honors and dignities, Fernando held out hopes of procuring from Peru a large donation to the Emperor, who was about to commence his expedition to Barbary.

The tenor of the dispatches which were to confer these appointments must have been known to many

* "Con juramento y grandes firmeças."

persons; and while Pizarro was at Truxillo, another town which he founded on the coast, a youth landed there who said that Diego de Almagro was appointed governor of the country from Chincha southward.

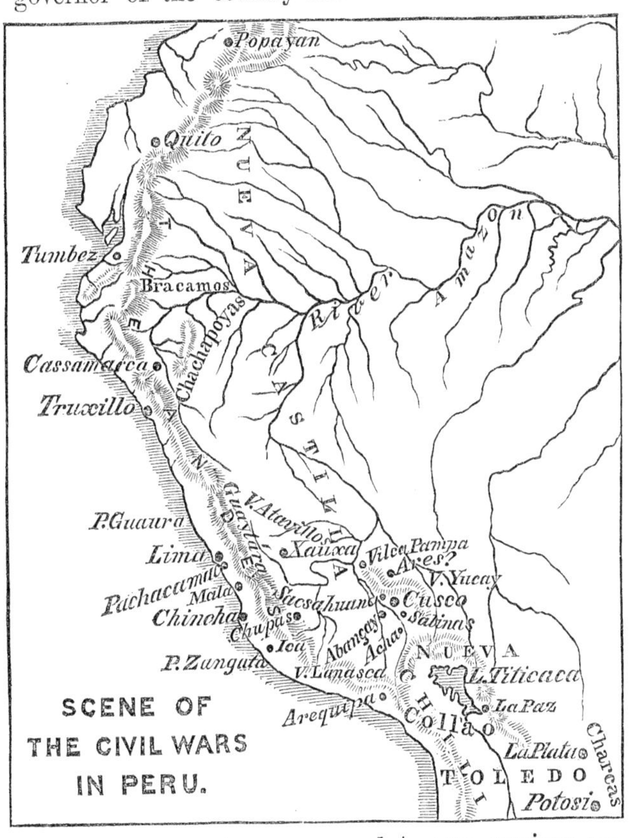

SCENE OF THE CIVIL WARS IN PERU.

Upon this, a certain man named Aguero, anxious, no doubt, to secure the present which it was customary to give on the receipt of great good news, hastened after the mariscal, and found him at the bridge of

Abançay, where he communicated this intelligence to him. It served to exalt Almagro greatly in his own opinion. Some say that he threw up the office which he held under Pizarro, claiming to rule Cusco on his own account; others, that Pizarro recalled the powers with which he had intrusted Almagro for the government of Cusco, appointing his brother Juan Pizarro to be governor. It is certain that dissensions between the younger Pizarros and Almagro arose at this time, which the marquis was obliged to come to Cusco to pacify. Pizarro, on meeting his old friend, after they had embraced with many tears, spoke thus: "You have made me come by these roads without bringing a bed or a tent, or other food than maize. Where was your judgment, that, sharing with me equally in what there is, you have entered into quarrels with my brothers?" Almagro answered that there was no occasion for Pizarro to have come with all this haste, since he had sent him word of all that had passed; and, proceeding to justify himself, he added that Pizarro's brothers had not been able to conceal their jealousy because the king had honored him.

The Licentiate Caldera, a grave and wise man, now intervened, as he had done before, between the mariscal and Pedro de Alvarado; and the result was, that the marquis and the mariscal renewed their amity in the most solemn manner, standing before the altar, and each invoking upon himself perdition of soul, body, fame, honor, and estate if he should break this solemn compact. The oath was taken in the governor's house on the 12th of June, 1535, in the presence of many persons, the priest saying mass, and the two governors having put their right hands above the consecrated hands of the priest which held "the most holy sacrament." This was called "dividing the Host," and was considered a most solemn form of declaring friendship.

The mariscal now resolved to enter his own territory, where he could be free from the Pizarros, and accordingly he prepared to march into Chili, which certainly fell within the confines of his government. In making preparations for his departure he lavished his resources, giving those who would follow him money to buy arms and horses, upon the simple understanding that they would repay him from their gains in the country where they were going. As he was now greatly popular, his service was readily embraced, and some even of those who had *repartimientos* at Cusco resolved to throw them up and follow the mariscal. The Inca placed at his disposal the services of his brother Paullo and of the high-priest Villaoma, who were ordered to accompany Almagro into Chili. These he sent on before; and his lieutenant general Rodrigo Orgoñez was to follow with the rest of the people. It may show how much Almagro's service was sought after that so distinguished a person in Pizarro's camp as Fernando de Soto was greatly disappointed at not being named lieutenant general of the mariscal's forces.

The day before Almagro's departure he is said to have begged Pizarro to send his brothers back to Castile, saying that for that end he would be willing that Pizarro should give them from the joint estate whatever amount of treasure he pleased; that such a course would give general content in the land, for "there was no one whom those gentlemen would not insult, relying upon their relationship to him." To this request Pizarro replied that his brothers respected and loved him as a father, and that they would give no occasion of scandal.*

* OVIEDO describes Fernando Pizarro in the following words: "And of all those (the brothers Pizarro) Fernando Pizarro was the only one of a legitimate bed, and the most imbedded in pride. He was a stout man of lofty stature, with a large tongue and heavy lips, and the end of the nose very fleshy and red; and this man was the disturber of the quiet of all, and especially of the two ancient associates Francisco Pizarro and Diego Almagro." "É de todos ellos el Hernando Piçarro solo era legítimo, é más legitimado en la soberbia: hombre de alta estatura é gruesso; la lengua é labios gordos, é la punta de la nariz con sobrada carne, y encendida; y este fué el desavenidor del sosiego de todos, y en especial de los dos viejos compañeros Francisco Piçarro é Diego de Almagro."—OVIEDO, *Hist. Gen. y Nat.*, lib. xliv., cap. 1.

CHAPTER II.

FERNANDO PIZARRO RETURNS FROM SPAIN.—HE TAKES THE COMMAND AT CUSCO.—FLIGHT AND REBELLION OF THE INCA MANCO.—DESCRIPTION OF CUSCO.

AS the brotherhood of the Pizarros is about to play a very important part in the history of the New World, it is desirable to consider what the advantages and disadvantages would have been of such a course as Almagro counseled. It is true that the promotion of near relatives is, and always has been, a very offensive thing to those who are hoping for advancement from any man in power, or even to those who are merely looking on at his proceedings. But, on the other hand, near relatives, though often more difficult to act with than other men, are nearly sure to be faithful. The certainty of this faithfulness has doubtless weighed much with men like Pizarro, newly and suddenly possessed of power, and it was a difficult question for him to decide whether, in his case, it was not wise to endure the odium* for the sake of the fidelity. Moreover, Pizarro's brothers were all of them good soldiers and brave men. Fernando was a

* The odium, however, is of a kind which no merits can fully counteract. The fickle Athenians were wearied of a single Aristides, but if it had been Aristides and his kinsmen, all equally good, equally just, and equally fit to occupy several of the chief places of the state, even the wisest and gravest nation would have been glad (if not openly, at least in their hearts) of any pretext which should remove so admirable but so absorbing a family from the government of the country.

most skillful captain; Gonzalo was said to be "the best lance" that had come to the Indies; Juan showed his valor at the siege of Cusco; and Martin afterward died fighting by his brother's side.

The marquis, unwilling to deprive himself of the services of such brothers, would not listen to the counsels of the mariscal in this matter, which counsels, however, have been held by commentators to be very sagacious.

The Governor of Nueva Toledo set out to conquer the country that had been assigned to him: the Governor of Nueva Castilla, for that was the name of Pizarro's province, returned to superintend the building of his new town, Los Reyes. Juan Pizarro was left in command at Cusco. Shortly after the reconciliation of the two governors, Fernando Pizarro returned from the court of Spain, bringing dispatches to his brother the marquis which contained the provisions that have already been mentioned. Fernando had undertaken a very odious task when he promised the court of Spain to seek for a "benevolence" from the colonists of Peru. To all his exhortations they replied that they had duly paid their fifths to the king, which had been gained with their blood and labor, at no risk of the royal estate; and they maliciously remarked that Ferdinand Pizarro had brought back nothing for them, though he had obtained a marquisate for his brother, and the Order of Santiago for himself. To these insinuations Fernando Pizarro adroitly and alarmingly made answer, that the ransom of Atahuallpa which they had divided, being the ransom of a royal person, of right belonged to the Emperor. In fine, all the new towns were laid under contribution, and the marquis, partly by persuasion, partly by threat, contrived to raise the royal benevolence from the people around him. In order to obtain the sum required from Cusco, and also to keep the Indians quiet (for an uncle of Manco Inca had been rebelling lately, and endeavoring to persuade his nephew to join in the rebellion), Pizarro resolved to send his brother Fernando to supersede Juan in the government of that city. It is said that the marquis had respect also to any danger there might be from the smothered discontent of the mariscal or his followers, and therefore wished to have a person of Fernando's weight and authority at the city which was nearest to Almagro's province. Fernando accepted the charge, and repaired to Cusco. When he arrived there, he found that his brothers Juan and Gonzalo were absent, being engaged in an expedition to chastise some rebel caciques. Manco Inca was not under any restraint, and Fernando Pizarro did not hesitate to show him much favor, for one of the principal injunctions which had been forced upon his attention at the court of Spain was to look to the good treatment of the Inca. When his brothers had returned from their foray, Ferdinand Pizarro brought the business of the benevolence before the town council of Cusco, saying how much it would become the inhabitants of the town to do his majesty some service, the royal estate being exhausted in the wars with the French and the Grand Turk. His exhortation was received with great disgust, and the part he had undertaken served to make him very unpopular. He seems, however, to have had some success in his mission, for he was engaged in the business of melting gold when news came that the district of Collao was in revolt, that the Indians had killed some Spaniards, and that Villaoma (whom the Peruvians held in the same veneration in which the Spaniards held the

Pope*) had returned from the expedition of the mariscal, with whom he had gone as captain of the Indian forces. Fernando Pizarro asked the Inca if all this intelligence were true. The Inca replied that it was true; that Collao was in revolt, and that Villaoma had returned on account of the ill treatment which he had received from Almagro's people, who had sought to carry him in chains; and the Inca added that his own brother Paullo was in chains. Several of the Spanish historians assert confidently that there was a deep-laid conspiracy between Villaoma and the Inca, concerted before the departure of the mariscal; but nothing appears more probable than that, in the sufferings and difficulties of a long and most arduous journey, the Indian chiefs should have been suspected and ill treated, as Chilicuchima had been in Pizarro's march from Cassamarca to Cusco. The Inca asked leave to go out of the city to receive Villaoma, which request being granted, the two great Indian authorities, the Inca and the high-priest, returned together into Cusco, when they both went straight to the Temple of the Sun, and there, according to Valverde, Villaoma not only complained of his injuries, but counseled revolt. Ferdinand Pizarro, however, had no suspicion of the plot that was being prepared by the Inca and the high-priest. Two days afterward, the Inca, with many of the chiefs, came to Pizarro's quarters to ask leave to go to a valley called Yucay, in order to celebrate certain ceremonies in honor of the Inca's father, Huayna Capac, who was buried there, and to whom it was customary to perform those rites every year. This request was granted.

On the 18th of April, 1536, the Inca, accompanied

* "A quien tienen ellos en la veneracion que nosotros tenemos al papa."—*Carta de* Vicente de Valverde, MS.

by Villaoma, went out of Cusco, leaving behind him some of the principal chiefs who were suspected by the Spaniards. This he did, in order to blind his enemies to the real purpose which he had in view. He

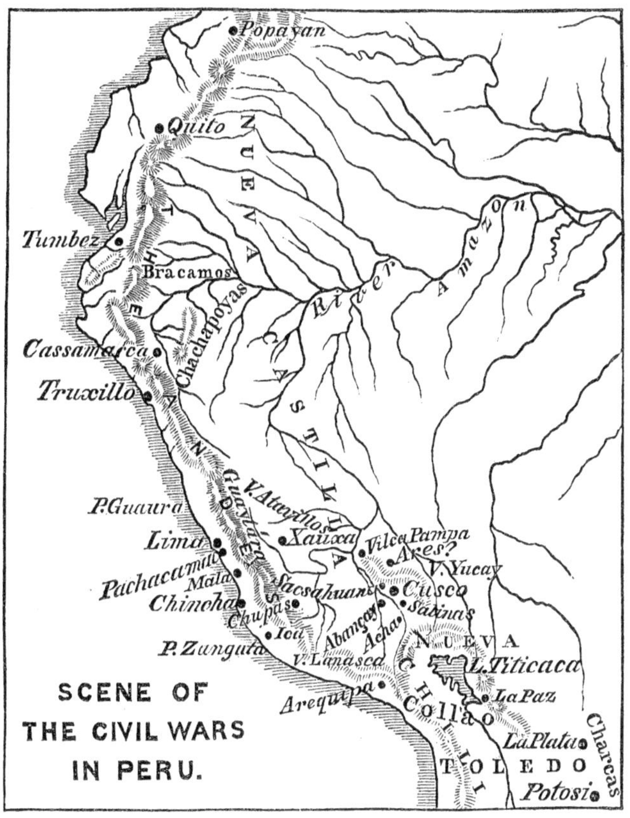

SCENE OF THE CIVIL WARS IN PERU.

had been absent only two days when a Spaniard, one of those probably who had a *repartimiento* in the neighboring country, arrived in the city to inform

Fernando Pizarro that the Inca was going to Ares, a *pueblo* fifteen leagues distant, in a very mountainous district, from which this Spaniard concluded that the Inca was about to revolt. Ferdinand Pizarro gave no credit to this report, but merely sent a message to the Inca, begging him to hasten his return, in order to accompany him in an expedition to chastise the caciques of Collao, who were in rebellion. But the Inca took no heed of this message. On the contrary, being now within the protection of this rugged country, he was enabled to proclaim his designs in all their fullness. A great assembly was held of the caciques and other principal persons of the district; and it may be imagined what orations, full of grief, shame, and lamentation, were uttered on that occasion. Never had an assemblage of men greater reason to complain, greater injuries to redress. Their kings dethroned, their temples profaned, their priests expelled, their sacred virgins scorned and violated, their property seized, themselves, their lands, their wives, and their children given away, in a strange kind of captivity* among this victorious band of strangers—what eloquence that rage or hate could give would be wanting? It is unlikely that any Peruvian chief who spoke on that day was one who had not received some deadly domestic injury, something of the kind which Christians even can hardly pretend to forgive, and which the Spanish Christians of that day would certainly have thought it a sacred duty to revenge. That dusky assemblage might have been seen waving to and fro with emotions of horror and hatred as the chiefs stood upon some level arid spot, with the burning sun pouring down upon them, to whom each fiery

* The system of *encomiendas.*

speaker would appeal as to a god, injured, desecrated, and maddened like themselves.

There can be little doubt that the most ardent and earnest appeals were made on this occasion to the valor, the piety, and the revengefulness of the Peruvian Indians, for a solemn pledge was taken, which the assembly could only have been prepared for by such adjurations. The Inca commanded that two large golden vessels full of wine should be brought before him; and then he said, "I am determined not to leave a Christian alive in all this land, wherefore I intend in the first place to besiege Cusco. Whoever among you resolves to serve me in this design has to stake his life upon it. Let him drink."* In this manner, and with no other condition, many captains and principal persons rose and drank; nor could it be said that they did not afterward fulfill their part in all the dangers and the toils which this fatal draught imposed upon them.

The city of Cusco was worthy of being the spot which elicited the last great effort of the Peruvians to rid themselves of their invaders. It was constructed with great regularity. The streets were at right angles to one another, and thus the city was formed into those blocks of building which the Romans called *insulæ*. The pavement was made of small stones; and a large stone conduit of water passed through the middle of each street. There was a great square, in which stood the palace of the late Inca, Huayna Capac, the most beautiful building in Cusco, its gateway being made of marble of different colors. This

* "Yo estoi determinado de no dexar Cristiano á vida en toda la tierra, y para esto quiero primero poner cerco en el Cusco. Quien de vosotros pensare servirme en esto, ha de poner sobre tal caso la vida. Beva."—*Carta de* VICENTE DE VALVERDE, MS.

palace was so extensive that it was afterward divided into many shares for the chief conquerors. Adjacent to it were three other palaces, painted on the outside, and richly decorated with sculpture. On three sides of the great square there were three covered buildings, resembling the *loggie* in Florence. These buildings stood upon terraces, and were for the purpose of celebrating great festivals in bad weather. Their size may be conjectured from the fact that a fourth *loggia* in another quarter of the town afterward formed a large church. There is no capital in Europe that has been constructed on so grand a plan. Cusco was, as it were, a microcosm of the whole empire. As the men of different tribes came up from Antisuyo, Condesuyo, Collasuyo, and Chinchasuyo, they ranged themselves in the outskirts adjacent to the four quarters of the town corresponding with these four divisions of the empire, and each tribe took up its position as nearly as possible in the same geographical order which it held in its own country. The tribe that was to the north of it in its own country was to the north of it also in Cusco. Each tribe had an especial head-dress, and was discernible from all the rest either by a difference in the color of the sash wound round the head, or by a difference in the color of the feathers. The Inca, in traversing his city, was thus enabled to review every section of his empire, and to recognize the inhabitants of each district at a glance.

The greater part of the houses in the city were constructed either wholly or partly of stone, though some were built of bricks burnt in the sun. The Peruvians had not arrived at the art of making tiles; and their houses were covered with pieces of wood in the shape of tiles, or with straw.* Some of the prin-

* The Spaniards called it straw, but it was probably a kind of rush.

cipal quarters were named "The Place of the Great Snakes," "The Place of Proclamations," "The Street of Gillyflowers," "The Ward of the Post of Lions," "The Ward of the Lion's Tail."

Two streams entered Cusco and traversed the city. They entered under bridges with flood-gates, to prevent inundation. These streams, in their passage through the city, had beds of masonry to run in, so that the water might always be clear and clean. One of the streams passed through the great square.

A huge fortress overawed the city. It was built on the summit of a high hill called Sacsahuaman, lying to the northeast. On the side toward the city this hill was precipitous, and needed little defense from art. On the other side, however, it descended gently toward a plain; and here it was defended by three walls rising one above another, in the shape of demilunes, each about twelve hundred feet in length, with salient and retiring angles.*

On the top of the walls were terraces forming ramparts. These ramparts had breastworks, so that the Peruvians could fight almost under cover. The narrowest of the ramparts was wide enough to be traversed by three carriages abreast. In the centre of each demilune was a narrow gateway with a stone portcullis.

The main body of the fortress consisted of three towers placed in a triangle, the apex of the triangle being occupied by the great tower, which was circular. The other two were rectangular. The great

work made with great care, which was very durable.—See HUMBOLDT'S *Researches*, vol. i., p. 244.

* "The walls are built with salient and retiring angles, twenty-one in number, and corresponding with each other in each wall, so that no one point could be attacked without being commanded by others."—MARKHAM'S *Cuzco and Lima*, chap. iv., p. 114.

tower consisted of four or five stories, each story being more lofty than the one below it. This tower had large windows or openings (*finestre grandi*) that looked toward the town. The towers were connected by subterraneous passages; and the ground beneath them was hollowed out to such an extent that there was almost as much space laid out in rooms and galleries below the towers as there was above ground.* In the great tower was a plentiful fountain of excellent water brought from a distance. The knowledge of the sources by which this fountain was supplied was a state secret, known only to the Inca and his principal counselors. After the conquest there was room in the citadel for five thousand Spanish soldiers.

The stones, or rather rocks, of which the demilunes and other parts of the fortress were constructed, seemed of Cyclopean work. The Spaniards said that not even "the bridge of Sègovia, or the other buildings which Hercules and the Romans had made, were worthy to be compared to the citadel of Cusco."† An eye-witness says, "I measured a stone at Tiaguanaco twenty-eight feet long, eighteen feet broad, and about six feet thick; but in the wall of the fortress of Cusco, which is constructed of masonry, there are many stones of much greater size."‡ It appears from mod-

* See Garcilaso de la Vega, *Comentarios Reales de los Incas*, lib. vii., cap. 29.

† "Gli Spagnuoli, che la veddono, dicono che nè il ponte da Secovia, nè d' altri edifici che fece Hercole, nè i Romani, non sono cosi degni da vedere come questo."—*Relatione di* Pero Sanco. Ramusio, *Viaggi.*

‡ "En Tiaguanaco medí yo una de treynta y ocho piés de largo, y de diez y ocho en ancho, y el gruesso seria de seys piés, y en la muralla de la fortaleza del Cuzco, que esta de mamposteria, ay muchas piedras de mucha mayor grandeza."—Acosta, *Hist. Moral. de Indias*, lib. vi., cap. 14.

ern research that some of these stones were fifty feet long,* twenty-two feet broad, and six feet thick.† How they were conveyed thither is a problem which has exercised ingenious men ever since the conquest. But the works of despotic monarchs of the olden time, who could employ an army to fetch a single stone, have always astonished more civilized nations, accustomed to a reasonable economy in the use of human labor.‡

It seems that cement was used by the Peruvians; but the work at Cusco was so exquisitely finished that none of this cement was visible, for the masonry appeared "as smooth as a table."§ This, however, was only at the junction of the stones: the rest of the stonework was left in the same state as it had been when taken from the quarry. Part of the fortress was an immense arsenal, which, under the rule of the Incas, had contained large stores of arms and accou-

* A Spanish foot is an inch less than the English measure of the same name.

† "Habia entre ellas algunas que tenian cincuenta piés de largo, veinte y dos de alto, y seis de ancho."—*Antiguedades Peruanas, por* Mariano Eduardo de Rivero, y Juan Diego de Tschudi, cap. 9, p. 250.

‡ Moreover, the patience and perseverance of the Indians compensated for the inferiority of their tools. See what Ulloa says of their workmanship in emeralds: "These curious emeralds are found in the tombs of the Indians of Manta and Acatames, and are, in beauty, size, and hardness, superior to those found in the jurisdiction of Santa Fé; but what chiefly raises the admiration of the connoisseur is to find them worked, some in spherical, some cylindrical, some conical, and of various other figures, and all with a perfect accuracy. But the unsurmountable difficulty here is to explain how they could work a stone of such hardness, it being evident that steel and iron were utterly unknown to them. They pierced emeralds and other gems with all the delicacy of the present times furnished with so many tools."—Ulloa's *Voyages*, vol. i., p. 466.

§ "Le pietre sono cosi liscie che paiono tavole spianate."—*Relatione di* Pero Sanco. Ramusio, *Viaggi*.

trements of all kinds—also of metals, such as tin, lead, silver, and gold.

On a hill which overlooked the city there were certain small towers that served as gnomons, and were used for solar observations.*

In Cusco and its environs, including the whole valley which could be seen from the top of the tower, it is said that there were "a hundred thousand" houses. Among these were shops, and store-houses, and places for the reception of tribute. A strange practice of the Peruvians may account in some measure for this enormous extent of building. It appears that when the great lords died, their houses were not occupied by their successors, but were, nevertheless, not suffered to fall into decay, and an establishment was kept up in them, in honor of the deceased master.

There was a large vacant space left in the town for the erection of future palaces, it being the custom for every reigning Inca to build a new palace.

The great Temple of the Sun had, before the Spaniards rifled Cusco, been a building of singular gorgeousness. The interior was plated with gold; and on each side of the central image of the Sun were ranged the embalmed bodies of the Incas, sitting upon their golden thrones raised upon pedestals of gold. All round the outside of the building, at the top of the walls, ran a coronal of gold† about three feet in depth. Adjacent to the Temple of the Sun

* "Por otra estava el cerro de Carmenga, de donde salen á trecho ciertas torrezillas pequeñas, que sirvian para tener quenta con el movimiento del sol, de que ellos mucho se preciaron."—PEDRO DE CIEÇA, *Chronica del Peru*, parte i., cap. 92.

† "Por lo alto de las paredes del Templo, corria una azanefa de oro de un tablon de mas de una vara en ancho, en forma de corona, que abraçava todo el Templo."—GARCILASO, *Comentarios Reales de los Incas*, lib. iii., cap. 20.

were other buildings, also beautifully adorned, which had been dedicated to the moon, the stars, to thunder, lightning, and the rainbow. Each of these minor buildings had its appropriate paintings and adornments. Then there were the schools of the learned Amautas and the Haravecs, or poets, which might be entered by a private way from the palace of the Inca Roca, who had delighted to listen to the discourses of the wise men of his dominions.

Cusco, independently of its temples, and its palaces, and its court, was in itself an object of fond admiration to the Peruvians; and, as Garcilaso declares, it was to them what Rome was to the rest of the world.*

Such was the city, not less dear because dishonored and disfigured, that Manco Inca and his brave companions in arms had pledged themselves to regain.

* PEDRO DE CIEÇA, one of the persons who saw Cusco within the first twenty years after the Spanish conquest, says, "Cusco was grand and stately: it must have been founded by a people of great intelligence." "El Cusco tuvo gran manera y calidad: devió ser fundada por gente de gran ser."—PEDRO DE CIEÇA, *Chronica del Peru*, parte i., cap. 92.

CHAPTER III.

THE SIEGE OF CÚSCO BY THE REVOLTED PERUVIANS.

FERNANDO PIZARRO, having been soon informed that Manco Inca really had revolted, far from awaiting the attack, lost no time in making an endeavor to seize upon the Inca's person. The friendly heights, however, protected the Indian sovereign, and Pizarro could not come near him. There were now many skirmishes near Ares between the Spaniards and the Peruvians, in which the slaughter of the Inca's forces was immense. Still the Indians from all their four provinces, Chinchasuyo, Collasuyo, Condesuyo, and Antisuyo, came pouring in upon the scene of action. On the heights the Indians began to prevail, though in the plains, where the Spanish cavalry could act, it was like a company of butchers amid innumerable flocks of sheep. In one of these skirmishes, the Indians, who were beginning to learn the craft of war, retreated until they led their enemies into an ambuscade where no less than twenty thousand Indians poured down upon the Spaniards. The ground was so rough that the horses were disabled from acting, and though Juan and Gonzalo Pizarro did all they could to retrieve the day, they were obliged to withdraw their forces into the city. Their Indian followers, who had been stationed in the fortress commanding Cusco, were driven out of it, and it was occupied by the enemy. But Fernando Pizarro, one of the most valiant men, not only of the captains in America, but of any in that age, beat back the pursuers and regained the fortress. Juan Pizarro was wounded in this battle.

The whole aspect of affairs now began to look very threatening for the Spaniards. A question arose whether it would be better to occupy the fortress or to abandon it to the enemy. Juan Pizarro contended that it should be abandoned, arguing that if the Indians were to occupy the fortress, the Spaniards could retake it whenever they pleased, and that it would be unwise to divide their small force. This advice seemed to be judicious, and was adopted.

Fernando Pizarro now resolved to form his horsemen into "three companies," placing each company under a captain. He had but ninety horsemen, and he gave thirty to each of the three commanders, committing to his guard a third part of the town. To the foot-soldiers he did not assign any especial part of the town to defend, because they were very few, and the enemy made little account of them. The next day, being Saturday, the Feast of "St. John before the Latin Gate," when the garrison awoke, they found the fortress occupied by the hostile Indians, and then the siege of Cusco may be said to have commenced. The disproportion of numbers was immense. There may have been one or two thousand Indian auxiliaries attached to the Spanish cause; but the besiegers, as was afterward ascertained, amounted to a hundred thousand warriors and eighty thousand attendants for camp-service. They immediately set fire to those houses which lay between the fortress and the town; and, under cover of this fire, they continued to gain ground, making barricades in the streets, and digging holes, so that the cavalry could not act against them.

It is impossible not to sympathize in some measure

with the Peruvians, and to rejoice whenever they obtain any success on their side, so that, if only for a moment, the tide of war is turned against those remorseless missionaries, the Spaniards. On this day, which was probably the last on which the natives in all that vast continent had any real chance of disembarrassing themselves of their invaders, not only fire, but air, came to the weaker side. There was, fortunately for them, a high wind, and the roofs being of straw or rushes, the fire spread so rapidly that at one moment it appeared as if the whole city were one sheet of flame. The war-cries of the assailants were appalling. The smoke was so dense that sight and hearing were alike confused. But the Spaniards were not men to be easily daunted. Each captain held his ground in his own quarter, where, however, the Indians pressed in upon them in such a manner that they could do no more than hold their ground, having scarcely room to fight. Fernando Pizarro was to be seen, now in one quarter, now in another, wherever the distress was greatest. The Indians, who supposed that the day was really theirs, threw themselves with the greatest bravery into the streets, fighting hand to hand with the Spaniards; displaying that desperate valor which takes no heed of the inequality of weapons, and giving blows which they must have been aware would be returned on the instant with a hundred fold the vigor and effect that there could be in their own.

Fernando Pizarro saw that, without some change in the mode of resistance, all was lost for the Spaniards. Drawing, therefore, from each company a few men, amounting altogether to only twenty, he made a sally on the road to Condesuyo; and, coming round upon the Indians from that quarter, charged them vigorously and drove them back with great slaughter to the rough part of the sierra, where they again re-formed their ranks and renewed the battle. Still, however, the ardor of the fight did not abate in the central part of the city, to which Fernando Pizarro returned to resume his command-in-chief. There was still no rest for the Spaniards. The city continued to burn. The Indian high-priest, Villaoma, who was likewise the general, occupied and maintained the fortress. In the city, as the houses were burnt, the Indians mounted upon the blackened walls, and, moving along them, were enabled, in that favorable position, to press on the attack. Thence they could deride all the efforts of horsemen to dislodge them. So the contest continued for days. Neither by day nor by night did they give any rest to the Spaniards, who were obliged to make perpetual sallies in order to throw down walls, destroy barricades, fill up great holes, and break up channels by which the Indians were letting water in upon them, so as to produce an artificial inundation. Thus for six days the warfare continued, until the Indians gained nearly the whole of the city, the Spaniards being able to hold only the great square, and some houses which surrounded it.

Many of the Spaniards now began to look upon their cause as hopeless. Flight by means of their horses was comparatively easy; and there were not wanting those who counseled the abandonment of the city, and the attempt to save their own lives, if it could be accomplished by this sacrifice. Fernando Pizarro, who was as great in council as in war, with a smile replied, "I do not know, señores, why you wish to do this, for in my mind there is not, and there has not been, any fear." From shame they did not dare to declare their thoughts in his presence, and so the matter passed off until the evening, when he summoned the chief Spaniards together, and, with a serene countenance, he thus addressed them: "I have called you together, señores, because it appears to me that the Indians each day disgrace us more and more, and I believe that the cause of this is the weakness that there is in some of us, which is no little, since you openly maintain that we should give up the city. Wherefore, if you, Juan Pizarro, give such an opinion, how is it that you had courage to defend the city against Almagro, when he sought to rebel; and as for you," turning to the treasurer, "it would appear a very ugly thing for you to talk in this fashion, since you have charge of the royal fifths, and are obliged to give account of them with the same obligation that he is to give account of the fortress. For you other señores, who are alcaldes and regidors, to whom the execution of the laws is committed in this city, it is not for you to commit such a great folly that you should deliver it into the hands of these tyrants."

Words have been often misused in speeches, but never more, perhaps, than in calling the Peruvians who came to take possession of their own "these tyrants."

Then he spoke of his own duties. "It would be a sad tale to tell of me," he exclaimed, "were it to be said that Fernando Pizarro, from any motive of fear, had abandoned the territory which his brother, Don Francisco Pizarro, had conquered and colonized. Wherefore, gentlemen, in the service of God and of the king, sustaining your houses and your estates, die rather than desert them. If I am left alone, I will pay with my life the obligation which lies upon me, rather than have it said that another gained the city, and that I lost it." He then reminded them of the commonplace remark, "that with vigor, that which appears impossible is gained, and without vigor even that which is easy appears difficult."

The courage of the assembled Spaniards answered to this bold appeal; and as it was now agreed upon to defend the city to the utmost, Fernando did not hesitate in putting the worst before them. He said, "The men are worn out, the horses are exhausted, and in the state in which we are, it is impossible to hold the city two days longer, wherefore it is necessary to lose all our lives or to gain the fortress. That being gained, the city is secure. To-morrow morning I must go, with all the horsemen that can be mustered, and take that fortress." They answered that the horsemen were ready to a man to die with him, or to succeed in that enterprise. Upon this, Juan Pizarro, wounded as he was, claimed the principal part in the next day's action, saying, "It was my fault that the fortress was not occupied, and I said that I would take it whenever it should be necessary to do so. Ill would it therefore appear if, while I am alive, any other person should undertake the duty for me."

Fernando Pizarro consented. This question of leadership being settled, and two subordinates having been chosen, Juan Pizarro lost no time in selecting a company of fifty men for the work of the morrow, the three captains being himself, his brother Gonzalo, and a cavalier named Fernando Ponce.

Very early in the morning, the fifty men, with their leaders, were drawn up in the great square. Fernando Pizarro addressed some parting advice to his brother Juan, namely, that when out of the town he should take the royal road from Cusco to Los Reyes, and should not turn until he had gone about a league, for, although the fortress was very near, so many holes had been dug, and barricades thrown up by the Indians, that there was no hope of taking the fortress except by coming round on the far side of it.

Fernando Pizarro had hardly finished giving this advice, when a body of Indians came down with the intent of taking a fort which had been made as a place of refuge from the great square, and which overlooked the whole of it. The two sentinels on guard at this fort were asleep — a thing not to be wondered at, considering the fatigues of the last few days—and before any succor could be given, the Indians had mastered the fort. The day, therefore, began with an ill omen for the Spaniards.

Fernando Pizarro ordered in great haste some active foot-soldiers to retake this fort, which they soon succeeded in doing. When this had been accomplished, Fernando united all his forces, horse and foot, to gain possession of a very strong barricade which the Indians had thrown up, in order to prevent the Spaniards from going out of the city in the direction of the plain. A body of twenty thousand Indians from the district of Chinchasuyo kept this barricade. It was fortunate for the Spaniards that the Indians had not delayed their attack upon the fort until a little later in the day, for by this movement toward the barricade Fernando Pizarro was obliged to leave the great square nearly undefended. But the main body of the Indians had not yet come down from their quarters to commence their usual attacks upon the city.

When the Chinchasuyans who had the charge of the barricade saw the Spaniards advancing upon them in full force, some of them shouted out to one another, "Those Christians who have the good horses are flying, and the others which remain are the sick.* Let us allow these to draw off, and then we shall be able to kill them all." This plan of suffering the Spaniards to divide their forces may have had some effect in weakening the resistance of the Indians at the barricade; still they fought on with great bravery, but they could not prevent the fifty horsemen making their way out of the city. The rest of the Spaniards returned with all haste to the grand square; for a column of the enemy—from the same division, I conjecture, which had once captured the fort in the morning—came down again to make another attack on it, having seen or heard the skirmish at the Chinchasuyan barricade. Fernando Pizarro, whose part in the conflict it was to make decisive charges on critical occasions, rushed out with his men, and soon put the Indians to flight; for, as the main body of the enemy was still asleep in their quarters, this one watchful division could not alone resist Pizarro's charge.

Meanwhile Juan Pizarro had conducted his men along the royal road to Los Reyes; and, after proceeding as far as had been previously agreed upon, had turned to the right, had fought his way along the ridges wherever he had encountered any enemy, had come down upon the open ground before the fortress, and so established a communication between himself and his brother in the city. The Indians posted between the fortress and the city decamped, some throwing themselves into the fortress and others into other strong positions.

The communication was now so complete that Fernando Pizarro was able to re-enforce his brother with

* "Aquellos cristianos que tienen los cavallos buenos se van huyendo, y estos que quedan son los dolientes."—*Carta de* VICENTE DE VALVERDE, MS.

all the Spanish foot-soldiers and the friendly Indians. At the same time he sent Juan word on no account to make the attack upon the fortress until nightfall, for the enemy were so many, and the position so strong, that the Spaniards could gain no honor in the attack. Fernando also begged his brother not to adventure his own person in the fight; for, on account of the wound which Juan had already received, he could not put on his morion, and Fernando said it would be absolute madness to go into battle without that. Juan Pizarro did not adopt his brother's advice; for, though he made a show of preparation as if he were going to bivouac upon the plain for the night, it was only a feint, and when he saw that the Indians were less on their guard, he gave orders for a sudden attack upon some strong positions in front of the fortress. Gonzalo Pizarro was intrusted with a troop to make this attack. When the Indians saw the Spaniards moving upward, they came down upon them in such a multitude* that Gonzalo Pizarro and his men could not even succeed in approaching these fortified outposts. Indeed, the Spaniards began to give way before the weight of numbers, when Juan Pizarro, "not being able to endure" this check, hurried onward to support his brother. The men, animated by this sight, for Juan and Gonzalo fought in the front rank, rushed forward, and succeeded in taking these strong positions, so that they found themselves now under the walls of the principal building. Juan Pizarro, not satisfied with this partial success, made a bold dash at the entrance into the fortress. This entrance was an outwork projecting from the body of the fortress, inclosed on each side by two low walls, but open at the top, so that it might be thor-

* "Grandissima infinidad de ellos."

oughly commanded from the battlements, having an outer gate corresponding with the principal gate of the fortress.* The walls which formed this outwork had roofs to them, doubtless in order that those of the besieged who had to defend the post might be under cover while their assailants were exposed to missiles from the higher parts of the building. Beneath this outwork the crafty Indians had recently dug a deep pitfall. But, unfortunately for them, as they came flying in from the pursuit of the Spaniards, they fell one upon another, heaped together in such a manner that "they filled up with their own bodies that which their own hands had made." Juan Pizarro, still fighting in front, advanced upon this road made for him by the bodies of his enemies; but just as he entered, a stone, hurled from the heights of the fortress, descended upon his unprotected head, and laid him senseless on the spot. His men recovered, and bore off the body of their commander, in which life was not extinct, though the wound was of a fatal nature, for Juan Pizarro never rose from his couch again.

After this great check, Gonzalo Pizarro, on whom the command had now devolved, did what he could to reanimate his men; but his efforts were of no avail. The numbers of the enemy brought to bear upon the points of attack continued to increase, and the Spaniards were obliged to draw off from the fortress. The following morning, however, the indomitable Fernando made a circuit of the strong-hold of the Indians, and, seeing that it was surrounded by a very high wall, came to the conclusion that, without

* "La qual era de esta manera. Desde la puerta del muro salian de una parte y de otra unos paredones hasta hacer otra puerta adelante, y estos cubiertos por cima, y alli hicieron cava, ahondando todo lo cubierto."—*Carta de* VICENTE DE VALVERDE, MS.

scaling-ladders, there was no hope of taking the place. The whole of the day, therefore, was spent in making scaling-ladders by all who could be spared for that service. They were not many who could be spared, for the enemy gave Gonzalo Pizarro and Fernando Ponce no rest all day, endeavoring to force the strong position which these commanders occupied. The Indians in the fortress did all they could by words and signs to animate their friends, even calling by name upon particular chiefs to come to the rescue; but the Spaniards maintained their positions.

That day Fernando Pizarro was to be seen every where throughout the Spanish quarters. He knew that not only the existence of all the Spaniards who were there, but that the security* of the Spanish empire in that part of the world was in peril. Here, he hurried with his small party of reserve, and left them; there, alone, he threw himself into some post where the effect of his personal presence was wanted. The contest grew so furious and the shouts so loud (the Indians, like all partially civilized people, were great shouters in war), that it seemed "as if the whole world was there in fiercest conflict."

The Inca, whose position was at a spot about three leagues' distance from Cusco, was not inactive. Knowing that the fortress was besieged, and being as well aware as Pizarro how important the possession of that strong-hold was, he sent a re-enforcement of five thousand of his best soldiers.† These fresh troops pressed the Spaniards very hard. They not only fought with the animation of untired men, but all the energy that fanaticism could give them was called

* "Conociendo que la vida de todos y el seguro destos reinos estavan en que se tomase la fortaleza."—*Carta de* VICENTE DE VALVERDE, MS.

† "Gente muy lucida."

forth to succor Villaoma, their chief priest, who was within the fortress.

In the city itself the battle languished; for, though some encounters took place there in the course of the day, the best part of the troops were fighting round the fortress. This was an oversight on the part of the Indian generals. More pressure on the Spanish posts in the grand square would have compelled the withdrawal of some of the Spaniards engaged in investing the fortress; and when the contending parties are greatly unequal in point of numbers, to multiply the points of attack is a mode of warfare which must tell disastrously against the less numerous party.

The day went on without either side having gained or lost much. But the Spaniards had maintained their positions while the scaling-ladders were being made. These being finished, Fernando Pizarro and the foot-soldiers commenced their attack at the hour of vespers. This was an excellent disposition of the troops. The horsemen could fight, as they had been fighting all day, to clear the ground about the place, while the hardy foot-soldiers, fitter for the work of scaling the fortress, must have seemed almost a new enemy to the beleaguered Indians. Fernando and his men pressed up to the walls with the utmost fury and determination. The conflict had now lasted about thirty hours, and the re-enforcements of Indians had not succeeded in making their way into the fortress. The succor most wanted there was fresh ammunition. Stones and darts began to grow scarce among the besieged; and Villaoma, seeing the fury of his new enemies, resolved to fly. Communicating his intentions to some of his friends, with them he made his way out of the fortress at the part which looked toward the river. The ground there was very precipitous, but there were some winding passages in the rocks, so constructed that they were invisible to the Spaniards below, but which were known to the Peruvians. Taking this secret route, Villaoma and his friends made good their flight, without being perceived by the Spaniards; and when beyond the walls of the fortress, Villaoma collected and drew off the division of his army which consisted of the Chinchasuyan Indians. From thence the recreant high-priest went to his master the Inca, who, when he heard the ill news, was ready to die of grief.

At the time Villaoma fled, the fortress was not altogether lost. In it there remained an Indian chief of great estimation among his people, one of those who had drunk out of the golden vases, and with whom were all the rest of the gallant men who had pledged themselves in the like simple but solemn manner. The whole night through these devoted men maintained their position. Fernando Pizarro's efforts throughout those eventful hours were such as desperation only could inspire; and as the day dawned, he had the satisfaction of perceiving that the defense of the Indians began to slacken; not that their brave hearts were daunted, but that the magazine of stones and arrows was fairly exhausted.

The fate of the beleaguered Indians was now clear to all beholders, to none clearer than to themselves; still this nameless captain gave no signs of surrender. "There is not written of any Roman such a deed as he did." These are the honest words of the Spanish narrator. Traversing all parts of the fortress with a club in his hand, wherever he saw one of his warriors who was giving way, he struck him down, and hurled his body upon the besiegers. He himself had two arrows in him, of which he took no more account than if they were not there. Seeing at last that it was not an Indian here and there who was giving way, but that the whole of his men were exhausted, and that the Spaniards were pressing up on the scaling-ladders at all points, he perceived that the combat was hopeless. One weapon alone remained to him, his club. That he dashed down upon the besiegers; and then, as a last expression of despair, taking earth in his hands, he bit it, and rubbed his face with it,* "with such signs of anguish and heartsickness as can not be described."† Having thus expressed his rage and his despair, resolving not to behold the enemy's entrance, he hurled himself, the last thing he had to hurl, from the height down upon the invaders, that they might not triumph over him, and that he might fulfill the pledge he had given when he drank from the golden vases. The hero of the Indians having thus perished, no pretense of farther resistance could be made. Fernando Pizarro and his men made good their entrance, and disgraced their victory by putting the besieged to the sword, who were in number above fifteen hundred.‡

* "And they rent every one his mantle, and sprinkled dust upon their heads toward heaven."—*Job*, ch. ii., v. 12.

† "Tomando pedaços de tierra la mordia fregandose con ella la cara con tanta congoja y vascas que no se puede dezir."—*Carta de* VICENTE DE VALVERDE, MS.

‡ "Pasando á cuchillo los que estavan dentro, que serian pasados de mil y quinientos ombres."—*Carta de* VICENTE DE VALVERDE, MS.

CHAPTER IV.

CUSCO AND LOS REYES ARE RELIEVED FROM A STATE OF SIEGE.—ALMAGRO RETURNS FROM CHILI AND THREATENS CUSCO.

SUCH was the dismay occasioned among the Peruvians by the capture of the fortress that they deserted their positions near the city, and retired to their encampments, which were well fortified. Fernando Pizarro sallied forth the next morning, and attacked and routed the Indians from the Chinchasuyo district. The day after he made an onslaught with equal success upon those of Collasuyo. The succeeding day this iron man marched out against the Indians of Condesuyo. On each occasion the Spaniards, having open ground for their cavalry to act upon, were entirely triumphant, and the slaughter of the Peruvians must have been immense. These transactions took place at the end of May, 1536.

It might now be imagined that the Spaniards in Cusco would be allowed to have some repose after the unwearied exertions they had made in the defense of the place, and the chastisement, as they would have called it, of the Indians. But the provident mind of Ferdinand Pizarro thought otherwise. Calling all his men together, he thus addressed them: "Since God has been pleased to give us this glorious victory by which we have gained the fortress, and saved the city from a state of siege, it seems to me, noble and valorous gentlemen, that in order that we may enjoy henceforward some rest and peace, and that we may secure the city better, it is necessary that we should store up, in time, provisions, bringing them from the valley of Sacsahuana. For if we do not seize upon the maize that is there, the Indians may anticipate us, and we shall then have to obtain our supplies from afar."

The conclusion of this speech greatly disconcerted the Spanish garrison, who had set their minds upon having now some repose. Pizarro, however, wisely persevered in his determination, telling his men that, as for expecting succor from Los Reyes, they must not reckon upon that; on the contrary, it was possible that they themselves were the only Spaniards left in Peru in whom they could place confidence. He meant, perhaps, darkly to insinuate that Los Reyes might have been invested at the same time as Cusco; that his brother the marquis might not have been able to drive back the besiegers; and that from Almagro and his men in Chili no friendly interference could be expected. Wherefore, he said, they must make up their minds to be prepared for the worst. To use his own words, "they must make their hearts broad enough for every thing that might occur to them."* Accordingly, Gonzalo Pizarro was sent to obtain these supplies, and in five days he returned, accompanied by a number of Indian men and women laden with maize.

Gonzalo Pizarro had hardly returned to Cusco when the Indians recommenced their siege. It seems that these unwise warriors had desisted from their attack, not from ill success only, but from being called away by certain religious ceremonies. These cere-

* "Y que pues esto era ansi, se determinasen de hacer el coraçon ancho á todo lo que les viniese."—*Carta de* VICENTE DE VALVERDE, MS.

monies were sacrifices made to the new moon;* and so rigidly kept was this observance, that the Peruvians, in all their battles and sieges, ceased to fight at the time of the new moon.† It is easy to see what a great relief this truce of the new moon must have afforded to the Spaniards.

The Indians, having completed their sacrificial ceremonies, recommenced the siege of Cusco, but under very different auspices to those of their former enterprise. The Spaniards now not only occupied the fortress, but had extended their works beyond the city, and the Indians were not able to gain an entrance into any part of it. This second and futile siege lasted twenty days, when it was time again for the Indians to withdraw in order to make their imperative sacrifices.

No sooner was the siege raised than Fernando Pizarro resolved to act upon the offensive and to attack the Indians in their encampments, in which he was, as usual, successful, and great slaughter of the enemy again took place. Still they were not daunted in their main purpose of investing Cusco; and when the Spaniards withdrew into their quarters, the Indians recommenced the siege. Fernando Pizarro now took a terrible resolve. He was not a cruel man, and, indeed, was noted for his kindness to the Indians. He had received instructions from the Spanish court, always mindful of humanity toward its new subjects, to look to the welfare of these Indians; but, like Cæsar and many other great captains, Fernando Pizarro hesitated at nothing which was likely to insure the suc-

* "And in the beginnings of your months ye shall offer a burnt-offering unto the Lord."—*Numbers*, ch. xxvii., v. 11.

† "En todos los cercos ó guerras que hazen tienen por costumbre de todas las lunas nuevas dexar á pelear y entender en hacer sacrificios." —*Carta de* VICENTE DE VALVERDE, MS., p. 36.

cess of his operations. Accordingly, he gave orders —orders how unbecoming a cavalier of Santiago, the cross of which he wore embroidered on his breast—to all his men that in their pursuit of the enemy they should slay every Indian woman they came up with, in order that the survivors might not dare to come and serve their husbands and their children.* This cruel scheme, in which, however, the bishop only recognizes the sagacity, was so successful that the Indians abandoned the siege, fearing to lose their wives, and the wives fearing death.†

The Spanish general was now quite at liberty to become the assailant, which he did with his usual vigor and success, though occasionally with the utmost peril to himself and his troops. In one of these skirmishes, at no great distance from Cusco, he put to flight some Indians, who left on the ground two bundles, which were secured and carried back to the city, and which, when opened, caused the greatest distress and grief throughout the garrison, for in one of them were found six heads of Spaniards, and in the other a great number of torn letters. Among these letters there was one, nearly uninjured, from the Empress, in which she informed the colony of the victory which the Emperor had obtained over the galleys of Tunis, fighting against Barbarossa and the Turks who were with him. This good news from Spain did not console the men of Cusco for their own loss and peril,

* "Viendo Hernando Piçarro la perseverança que tenian en cercarle la ciudad, mando á todos los Españoles que en los alcances no dexasen muger á vida porque cobrando miedo las que quedasen libres, no vendrian á servir á sus maridos y hijos."—*Carta de* VICENTE DE VALVERDE, MS.

† "Fue tan bueno este ardid, que cobraron tanto temor assi los Indios de perder á sus mugeres como ellas de morir, que alçaron el cerco."—*Carta de* VICENTE DE VALVERDE, MS.

more especially as they found from private letters that the governor had sent succor from Los Reyes to Cusco, which they naturally concluded had been cut off. Fernando Pizarro, seeking truth in a way but too familiar in that age, put some of his captives to the torture, and extracted from them the information that large succor had been sent from Los Reyes, but that the various parties of Spaniards who had thus been sent to their assistance had all been intercepted and slain on their way to Cusco, and that the Inca had as trophies two hundred heads of Christians, and one hundred and fifty skins of horses. These tortured Indians also said that the governor, with all his people, had embarked from Los Reyes and deserted the country. This last information was not true, but it was very possible that the Indians believed it to be so, for Los Reyes, as well as Cusco, had been invested, and in great peril.

On hearing this bad news, a deep despondency fell upon the Spanish garrison at Cusco. Fernando Pizarro, whom nothing daunted, thus sought to reanimate his men. Calling them together, he said, "Noble and very valorous gentlemen, I am exceedingly astonished, and with great reason, that where there are persons who so much esteem honor, they should in any way show weakness at a time when they have need for the greatest hardihood." Now was the occasion, he urged upon them, now that Indian affairs, to use his own phrase, "were not quite so certain," when they might show the desire that they had to distinguish themselves in the service of their prince. If the bad news were true to its fullest extent, their companions had died in the service of God and in the defense of these kingdoms. Then, in the spirit of an exalted chivalry, he added that they ought to be glad that the governor had departed, as it left more glory for them. Much, he said, as he was indebted to his brother, he was not sorry that he should not participate in the victory which he himself still intended to achieve in keeping these provinces. They had provisions for a year and a half; they must take care to sow more grain; "and then," he said, "I think we can hold this city for six years, and I shall be glad if in all that time we receive no succor." His words found an echo in some noble breasts, but in others there was no response.

Considering what had taken place at Los Reyes, which has now to be narrated, the report among the Indians of the flight of the marquis was not an unreasonable one. Fernando Pizarro, at the beginning of the Indian revolt, had taken care to inform his brother at Los Reyes of the peril which threatened him at Cusco. The marquis had sent a body of men under Gonzalo de Tapia, who had been cut off; and the loss sustained by the Spaniards, in this and other attempts of the same kind, amounted to four principal captains, two hundred men, and a great number of horses. When the bad news of these troops having been cut off reached Pizarro at Los Reyes, and when he received no news whatever from his brothers at Cusco, he concluded that they were in great straits. The marquis felt his position to be most critical. He summoned back one of his principal captains, Alonzo de Alvarado, whom he had sent to conquer the province of Chachapoyas. He also wrote to Panamá, Nicaragua, Guatemala, New Spain, and to the *Audiencia* in Hispaniola, informing the Spanish authorities of the state in which he was placed, and praying for instant succor. In the letter which he wrote to Alvarado at Guatemala he said that if that governor would come to his rescue, he would leave him the land of Peru, and would return himself to Panamá or Spain.

Meanwhile the Indians in great numbers began to invest Los Reyes. Pedro de Lerma, another of Pizarro's principal captains, being sent out with twenty horsemen to reconnoitre, found that fifty thousand Indians were coming down upon the town. These Indians, who were under the command of a great chief named Teyyupangui, took up their position on some heights near the town. Here they remained for five or six days; and it may serve to show the wonderful temerity of the Spaniards, that it was seriously debated among them whether they should not become the besiegers and invest the Indians in their rocky citadel. They resolved to prepare shields of a peculiar construction, to protect themselves from the stones that would be thrown by the Indians; but these shields, when made, were found to be too heavy for the purpose, and so the Indians were suffered to commence the attack.

Their general, Teyyupangui, resolved to take the city, or to perish in the attempt. Calling together his men, he said, "I intend to force my way into that town to-day, and to kill all the Spaniards who are in it. Then we will take their wives, with whom we will marry and have children fitted for war. Those who go with me are to go upon this condition, that if I die they shall all die, and if I fly they shall all fly." All the principal Indians agreed to this, and their army moved forward, bearing a great number of banners, from which the Spaniards inferred that the attack was to be a serious one. Pizarro made his preparations. The Indians advanced toward the town, and forced their way over the walls and into the streets, their general, with a lance in his hand, advancing in front of his men. But, as the ground was level, the Spanish cavaliers were enabled to act with all the tremendous superiority which their arms, their horses, and their armor gave them. Their success was instantaneous. Unfortunately for the Indians, Teyyupangui, and the principal men who surrounded him, were slain in this first encounter. The loss of their general entirely dispirited the Indian forces. The Spaniards, following up their advantage, drove the enemy back to the foot of the sierra from whence they came; and when the governor, on the succeeding night, would have pursued his original plan of storming the heights where the Indians had taken refuge, he received intelligence that they had broken up their camp and fled. This was the end of the siege of Los Reyes.

That town being now free from its besiegers, and Alonzo de Alvarado having obeyed the summons which had been sent to him, and having arrived at Los Reyes, the governor began to take immediate steps for the relief of his brother at Cusco. The forces, however, which he had at his command were very inadequate for that purpose. The number that he could spare amounted only to a hundred horsemen and one hundred and fifty foot-soldiers. With these, however, Alonzo de Alvarado was ordered to march to the province of Xauxa, and there to chastise the Indians who had cut off the forces that had been previously sent to Cusco; but the Spanish commander was not to move on to Cusco until he should receive re-enforcements. This captain left Los Reyes about the month of October, 1536. He had soon a hostile body of Indians to encounter, whom he put to flight, and made his way without farther opposition to the town of Xauxa. He sought, by submitting his prisoners to torture, to discover from them what was the condition of Fernando Pizarro and the Spaniards at Cusco. Some of the captives said that the Christians were alive, but were in a state of siege; others, that the Christians had made their way into the open country, and were maintaining themselves there; but the reports were so variable that Alonzo de Alvarado did not know what to believe, and he remained at Xauxa for four months, awaiting farther orders from the governor.

Meanwhile Fernando Pizarro, supposing himself to be alone in the country, and becoming, if possible, more resolute and daring on that account, did not cease to send out expeditions for the purpose of attacking the Indians and of obtaining provisions. Occasionally he was in greater peril than ever, but his bravery and his address always preserved him. In one of these expeditions, the Spaniards having captured some Indians and brought them within the town, they resorted to the cruel expedient of cutting off the right hands of no less than four hundred of them, and sending these poor maimed creatures to the Inca.* This so terrified the enemy that they broke up their garrisons in those parts, and the Spaniards had more rest, though each month, after their festivals in honor of the new moon, the Peruvians recommenced their attacks; and, as it was Fernando Pizarro's plan always to send out a body of his men in pursuit when the Indians raised these monthly sieges, it so happened that for the year during which the war

* "Se vinieron aquel mismo dia á esta ciudad; y, en la plaça della, cortaron las manos derechas á quatro-cientos que se trujeron presos, embiando los al Inga. Fue tanto el temor que desto los demas cobraron que todas las guarniciones que estavan en esta Comarca se deshicieron."—*Carta de* VICENTE DE VALVERDE, MS.

lasted there was no instance of the whole Spanish garrison having a day's rest, as, when one company came within the walls from a foray, another company sallied out to make a fresh attack.*

This unprofitable and murderous warfare between Fernando Pizarro and the Indians was now coming to an end. A more formidable enemy was soon to enter on the scene. Rumors began to arise about this time that Almagro was returning from Chili. This was first communicated by the Indian captives, and some credit was given to their intelligence, because, whenever the revolted Indians fell in with the Spaniards, they threatened them, saying that the Adelantado was coming; that he was their friend, and intended to kill all the Spaniards of Cusco. These sayings and reports were current for two months, and at last there arrived certain intelligence of the fact that the Adelantado, with five hundred Spaniards, was within seven leagues' distance of the city of Cusco.

The reason of his coming, the mode of his coming, his intention with regard to the Pizarros, and the consequences of his return, form a narrative that was of the utmost significance for the whole of Spanish America.

The foregoing account of the sieges by the Indians of Cusco and Los Reyes has been given in much detail, because it shows that the Spanish Conquest was not such an easy task as some historians have supposed; also because it manifests great valor on the part of the Peruvian Indians, and, moreover, gives an

* "Como la gente de guerra alçava el cerco, iva él luego y sus capitanes en busca dellos, de manera que en todo un año que la guerra duró no se halló que todos juntos tuviesen un dia de descanso, porque viniendo una compañia salia otra."—*Carta de* VICENTE DE VALVERDE, MS.

instance, of the many to be met with, that the second great resistance of a conquered people is often the most difficult to overcome. In the history of England, the battle of Hastings was by no means conclusive as regards the Norman Conquest; and the conquered Anglo-Saxons, under the gallant Hereward, maintained a most obstinate and dangerous resistance to the Norman troops. The internal dissensions of the Peruvians, which were at their height when Pizarro first arrived in the country, must be considered as having furnished no slight aid to the Spaniards; and, in the absence of such dissensions, the conquest might have been deferred for many years. Each year the Peruvians would have attained more skill in resisting horsemen; and, as it has been observed before, horses were the chief means of conquest which the Spaniards possessed. The transport of these animals in the small vessels of those days must always have been difficult and expensive, and many years might have elapsed before a body of two thousand Spanish horse could have entered Peru, especially if the invasion had not at first been brilliantly successful. How completely the Peruvians were dismayed by horses may be inferred from the fact that, when they had these animals in their power, they put them to death instead of attempting to make use of them. There is no good evidence to show that a single horse* was spared when the Inca's troops succeeded

* The passage subjoined from HERRERA may seem to contradict the assertion in the text; but Herrera's account of the proceedings connected with the siege of Cusco is very brief and incomplete, and little reliance can be placed in any account of that siege, except the one given by the Bishop of Cusco, Vicente de Valverde, who says that he was an eye-witness (*testigo de vista*), and whose letter was addressed to the Emperor himself. Herrera's words are: "Vieronse en aquella ocasion muchos Indios con Espadas, í Rodelas, í Alabardas, í

in overpowering the cavalry that was sent by Pizarro to re-enforce his brothers at Cusco.

algunos à caballo con sus Lanças, haciendo grandes demonstraciones, í braveças; í algunos, embistiendo con los Castellanos, hicieron hechos, en que mostraron animo, mas que de Barbaros, í la industria aprendida de los nuestros."—*Hist. de las Indias*, Dec. v., lib. vii., cap. 6.

CHAPTER V.

ALMAGRO'S ENTRANCE BY NIGHT INTO CUSCO. — HE IMPRISONS THE BROTHERS PIZARRO, AND DEFEATS ALONZO DE ALVARADO AT THE BRIDGE OF ABANÇAY.

THE career of Almagro was so singular and so disastrous that it needs all the explanation that can be given to it. Almagro himself was in a position not above his ambition, but far above his capacity. In such a case it is always well to look to the counselors by whom a man is surrounded. The two counselors who had most influence over Almagro's mind were men whose dispositions presented a strange and violent contrast. One was Diego de Alvarado, a person of the utmost nobility of nature, and, at the same time, delicacy of character. GARCILASO describes him as "a knight, very knightly in all respects."* The other adviser was Rodrigo de Orgoñez, a hard, fierce, fanatic soldier, who had served in the wars of Italy. The conduct of the governor varied according to the advice which he listened to from one or other of these widely-different counselors. They seem also, which makes the career more strangely fluctuating, to have prevailed with the governor at very short intervals of time. The mild counsels of Alvarado were listened to in the morning; and some unscrupulous deed, prompted probably by Orgoñez, was transacted in the evening. To illustrate this by characters that are better known to the world, it was as if a man were

* "Caballero muy caballero en todas sus cosas."

equally impressed by the writings of Machiavelli and Montaigne, so that he now formed himself upon one model, now upon the other; or as if he chose for his agents two such different characters as Cæsar Borgia and Cardinal Borromeo, combining their services in the same transaction, so that what was begun by the good cardinal was left to be completed by the prince, or what was devised by the subtle brain of the Borgia, dissevered from all thoughts of justice or of charity, was left to be carried into action by the piety and high honor of the gracious cardinal.

The return of Almagro from Chili was not much to be wondered at. From the first landing of Pizarro to the taking of Cusco, the advance of the Spaniards had been little other than a triumphant march. Conquerors had been borne along in hammocks on the shoulders of obsequious Indians to rifle temples plated with gold; but the advance into Chili was an enterprise of a different kind. Almagro and his men went by the sierras and returned by the plains. In both journeys they had great hardships to suffer. In the "snowy passes" men and horses had been frozen to death, and on their return by the plain they had been obliged to traverse a horrible region, called the desert of Atacáma, which could only be passed with the greatest difficulty.

On what pretext did they return, as there were no new circumstances to justify such a course? The dispatches from Spain, appointing Almagro governor of New Toledo, only reached him after he had commenced his journey into Chili; but he had been informed of their contents before, and he had taken that solemn oath, when the Host was broken by the two governors, in perfect cognizance of his rights. The revolt of the Indians was made known to him, but it can not be for a moment assumed that this was the real cause of his return.

It is very likely that the question of the limits of his government was often renewed and discussed by his men and his officers in the course of their march and over their watch-fires, and, being discussed with all the passion and prejudice of eager partisans, it is very probable that there was not a man in Almagro's little army who did not think that Cusco fell within the limits of his commander's government. Their misery doubtless sharpened their prejudices, and Almagro's weary, frostbitten men must have sighed for the palatial splendors and luxuries of Cusco, which they had foolishly given up, as they would have said, to these Pizarros. Even the mines of Potosi, had they been aware of their existence, would hardly have proved a sufficient inducement to detain Almagro's men in Chili. But Potosi was as yet undiscovered, and Cusco was well known to every individual in the army. Under such circumstances the mariscal's return may be set down as faithless, treacherous, or unwise, but it can not be considered otherwise than as most natural. A greater man than Almagro might have carried his companions onward, but Almagro was chiefly great in bestowing largesses, and Chili afforded no scope for such a commander.

It must not be supposed that the question of the limits to Pizarro's government was an easy one, and that it was merely passion and prejudice which decided in the minds of Almagro's followers that Cusco fell within the province of New Toledo. There were several ways of reckoning the two hundred and seventy-five leagues which had been assigned to Pizarro. They might be measured along the royal road. This would not have suited Pizarro's followers, who contended that the leagues were to be reckoned as the crow flies. "Even if so," replied Almagro's partisans, "the line is not to be drawn from north to south, but from east to west." They also contended that these leagues might be measured on the sea-coast, in which case the sinuosities of the coast line would have to be taken into account. In short, it was a question quite sufficiently dubious in itself to admit of prejudice coming in on both sides with all the appearance of judicial impartiality.

However that may be, Almagro and his men took the fatal step of returning to maintain their supposed rights, which step a nicer sense of honor would have told them that they had, whether wisely or not, abandoned when they quitted Cusco.

What effect their approach must have had upon Fernando Pizarro and his immediate adherents may be easily imagined. For many months he and his men had scarcely known what it was to have two days of rest. The efforts of the Indians were now slackening; and just at this moment there arrived an enemy who was to replace the softly-clad and poorly-armed Indians by men with arms, spirit, and accoutrements equal to those of the Spaniards of Cusco, and in numbers greatly superior.

The first movement, however, of the mariscal was not directed against the Spaniards in Cusco. Previously to attacking them he strove to come to terms with their enemy, the Inca Manco. Had he succeeded in this politic design, he would then have been able to combine the Inca's forces with his own, and would also have had the appearance of having intervened to settle the war between the Indians and the Spaniards. This plan, however, failed. Meanwhile Fernando Pizarro had made several attempts to negotiate with Almagro, or at least to penetrate his designs. He endeavored, by messengers, to lay before the mariscal some of the motives which should regulate his conduct at this crisis, saying how much it would be for the service of God that peace should be maintained between them: if it were not, they would all be lost, and the Inca would remain lord of the whole country. He offered Almagro to receive him in the city with all honor, saying that Almagro's own quarters were prepared for him; but, before all things, Fernando Pizarro urged that a messenger might be sent to the marquis in order that he might come and settle matters amicably, and that meanwhile the mariscal should enter the town with all his attendants. To this message an evasive reply was sent by Almagro, who, on a Monday, the 18th of April, 1537, made his appearance, with all his people, and pitched his camp at a league's distance from Cusco.

Fernando Pizarro invited him again to enter the city as a friend. To this Almagro haughtily replied, "Tell Fernando Pizarro that I am not going to enter the city except as mine, or to lodge in any lodgings but those where he is," meaning that he would occupy the governor's apartments. Fernando Pizarro sent another message, pointing out to Almagro the danger to be apprehended from the revolted Indians, and begging that there might be amity between them until the marquis should arrive. To this Almagro replied that he had authority from the king as governor, and that he was determined to enter Cusco. Having said this, Almagro advanced nearer, encamping within a crossbow shot of the city. Both sides now prepared for battle; but Fernando Pizarro, whose prudence throughout these transactions is very remarkable, called a council, and it was agreed by them that an alcalde with two regidors should go to Almagro's camp to demand of him, on the part of the Emperor, that he should not disturb the city, but that, if he had powers from his majesty, he should present them before the council, in order that they might see whether his majesty had conferred upon him the governorship of that city. As Fernando Pizarro had procured the powers and brought them from Spain, he knew very well what they contained; but it was a reasonable request that the grounds upon which Almagro sought to enter the town should be laid before the governing body.

Almagro, especially if he listened at all to Diego de Alvarado, could not well refuse his assent to this proposition. Accordingly a truce was made for that day, and until the next at noon. Early on the ensuing morning Almagro sent his powers to be laid before the Town Council, but he demanded that before they should be produced, Fernando Pizarro, as an interested party, should absent himself from the council. Fernando Pizarro conceded this point. The powers were formally laid before the alcaldes and the regidors, who, taking into council a graduate,* perhaps Valverde himself, gave the following answer. They said that they were ready to obey the orders of his majesty; and, in obedience thereto, as his majesty had given Almagro for territory two hundred leagues to be reckoned from the spot where the territory governed by Don Francisco Pizarro ended, and as the said government was not set out nor defined, and as Don Francisco Pizarro had occupied this city of Cusco and held it as part of his government, that the division-line of the respective governments should be made, and that, until this should be settled by "pilots,"

* "Con consejo de letrado."

Almagro should not give room for such a great scandal as forcing an entrance into the city, which they declared would be the ruin of all parties. "If," they said, "when the division has been settled, this city should fall within the limits of Almagro's government, they would be ready to receive him as governor, but upon any other footing they would not receive him."

Almagro, having received this spirited and sensible decision of the council, gave orders to his men, it being now midday, to prepare themselves for making an attack upon Cusco. Fernando Pizarro gave similar orders for the defense of the city. At this last moment, however, the royal treasurer and a licentiate named Prado went out of the town to Almagro's camp to endeavor to bring the disputants to terms, and they succeeded in prevailing upon Almagro to extend the time of truce to the hour of vespers on the Wednesday in that same week, Almagro saying that he wished to prove how Cusco fell within his limits.

That evening, Almagro, to his great dishonor, must have listened favorably to his less scrupulous counselor; and, indeed, there were not wanting arguments which such a counselor could urge. He would say that at this point of time Almagro was the strongest; that there was no use in waiting for any negotiation with the marquis; that nothing would come from him but men and ammunition to assist his brother; that this was an affair which arms or stratagem must decide; that many men in Cusco were adverse to Fernando Pizarro; and that much good Spanish blood might be saved if an attack were to be made this very night upon the city. Moreover, their camp was deep in snow and mud, and altogether their position was very perilous.

Diego de Alvarado could not have boen consulted on this occasion, certainly could not have been listened to. The evil counsel prevailed, and it was resolved by Almagro to surprise the city.

Fernando Pizarro, who was a perfect cavalier, was completely at his ease that night, expecting now that he and Almagro would be able to come to terms until he should have time to let the marquis know what was passing. As a man of honor, he made up his mind that he could not deliver up the fortress without his brother's permission. At midnight there was a disturbance in Almagro's camp, it being given out that the bridges which led to the city were broken down. Immediately the soldiers shouted "Almagro, Almagro! Let the traitors die!" and they rushed over all the four bridges (not one of which was broken down) into the great square. Thence they spread themselves into the streets, Orgoñez, with a large body of troops, making his way to the governor's apartments, still shouting "Almagro, Almagro!" Fernando Pizarro was in bed when the alarm was given. He had time, however, to put on his armor. The greater part of his men fled, but fifteen remained with him and his brother Gonzalo. Fernando placed himself at one door, Gonzalo at another. The palace was "as large as a church," and the doorways were proportionately large, without doors to them. Still the brothers defended themselves with the utmost valor. The building was set on fire. Of their fifteen comrades, several were cut down fighting by their side, and it was not until the roof began to fall in upon these brave Pizarros, and until they were quite overpowered by numbers, that they were overcome and made prisoners. The brothers were taken to the Temple of the Sun, where they were confined, and heavy chains were placed upon them. Almagro took formal possession of Cusco as its governor, and began to persecute those who held with the Pizarros.

Meanwhile Alonzo de Alvarado was waiting at Xauxa for orders to proceed to the relief of Cusco. The Marquis Pizarro had now received men and arms from all parts of Spanish America,* succors which he lost no time in sending on to Alonzo de Alvarado, and, indeed, would have gone himself, but that the citizens of Los Reyes had insisted that, on account of his age, he should not undertake this expedition. The forces under Alonzo de Alvarado were considerable, namely, two hundred horsemen and five hundred foot, all well armed; but, unfortunately, he carried with him a very discontented man high in command. This was Pedro de Lerma, who had expected to have the conduct of this expedition himself. On their way to Cusco, Alonzo de Alvarado learned what had happened there, and how the mariscal was now in possession of the city. Almagro, on his side, learned from Alvarado's letters to Fernando Pizarro that he was coming, and, not supposing that Alvarado knew of what had happened, he sent a forged letter in Fernando Pizarro's name, in which Fernando was made to say that he had been able to maintain his position against Almagro, and suggested that Alvarado should take a certain route which he mentioned. This route Almagro knew would lead into a defile, where the horsemen could only go one or two abreast, and where Almagro hoped to place his men in such a position that they could disarm the others easily. Alonzo de Al-

* Cortez assisted Pizarro on this occasion. "Fernando Cortèz embiò con Rodrigo de Grijalva en un propio navio suio, desde la Nueva España, muchas armas, tiros, jaeces, adereços, vestidos de seda, i una ropa de martas."—GOMARA, cap. 136.

varado, having by some means learned the true state of the facts, was only amused at such an attempt to deceive him. Almagro, finding that his artifices had failed, now sent an embassage, consisting of Diego de Alvarado, Gomez de Alvarado, and other persons, to treat with Alonzo de Alvarado. After the gross treachery practiced in the surprise of Cusco, Almagro could hardly expect the usual terms of courtesy and good faith to be kept with him. It was represented by the friends of the Pizarros to Alonzo de Alvarado that, being a relation of those Alvarados who had come to the camp, if he did not seize them, it would appear like a confederation on his part with the enemies of the marquis. This seemed a just view of the case to Alonzo, and accordingly, though he showed much courtesy to these friends of Almagro, and begged them to excuse him, he took away their arms and placed them in confinement.

Almagro, receiving no answer to his embassage, moved out from Cusco to the bridge of Abançay, where Alonzo de Alvarado had taken up his position.

Almagro had not omitted, since his occupation of Cusco, to attempt to come to terms with the Peruvians. He had failed, however, in negotiating with Manco Inca, and had, in consequence, given the *borla* to Manco's brother Paullo, who now proved very serviceable to him; for Paullo's Indians were able to communicate with Alvarado's camp, and, being less observed than Spaniards would have been, to convey letters to the discontented there.

At this juncture, Alonzo de Alvarado sent fourteen horsemen to inform the marquis of all that had happened; and had these messengers waited, they would soon have had to convey worse intelligence. Pedro de Lerma wrote to Almagro or Orgoñez, telling them that they had more friends than enemies in Pizarro's camp. This treachery of Pedro de Lerma was not long in coming to the ears of Alonzo de Alvarado, who ordered them to be apprehended; but the traitor,

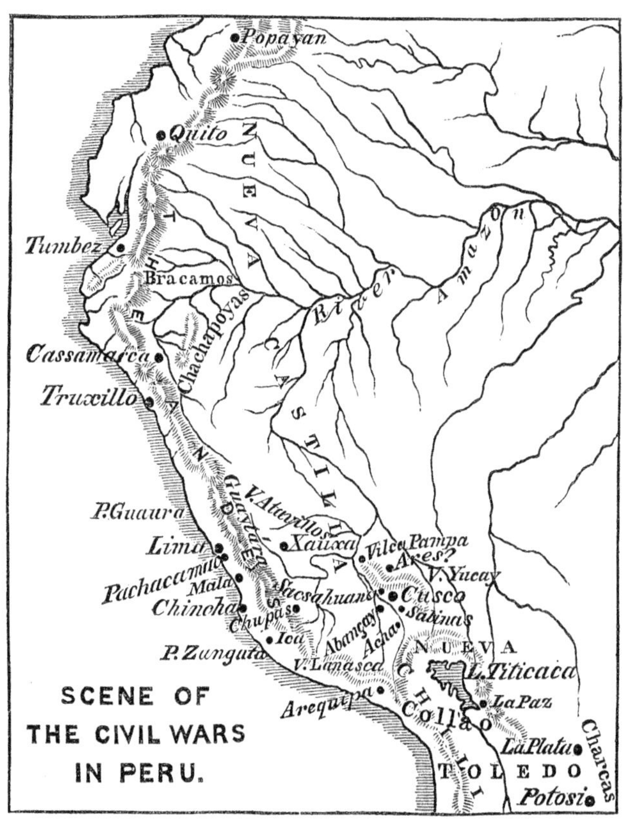

SCENE OF THE CIVIL WARS IN PERU.

seducing from their allegiance some of the very men who captured him, made his way to the camp of Almagro. That governor's forces, independently of the Indians, were more in number than those of his opponent, and the Indians under Paullo amounted to ten thousand. The military position, however, of Alvarado was strong. He occupied the bridge of Abançay, and he had constructed a large bulwark on the edge of the river, made of stones, behind which he placed crossbow-men, arquebusiers, and pikemen.

There was much negotiation between the hostile parties, but as it proved fruitless it need not be recounted here. Alonzo de Alvarado, in the first instance, had demanded that the brothers Pizarro should be set at liberty. This was a demand not likely to be listened to by the Almagristas; and, in fact, the state of affairs was such that there was nothing left but an appeal to arms. Accordingly, an attack on Alvarado's position was made at nightfall, when Almagro's artillery began to play upon it. The Indians under Paullo also did good service on that side, for they made such use of their slings that Alvarado's men could not act except when protected by the bulwark. Moreover, the shouting of the Indians lasted all night, so that they kept Alvarado's men in constant alarm. Half an hour before daybreak the real attack commenced on the part of the Almagristas, when three hundred horsemen threw themselves into the river and began to attempt the passage. They had no difficulty in passing, for the treachery on the other side was flagrant. An historian, whose father was one of Alvarado's principal captains, and who was, therefore, likely to have heard a true account of this battle, says, "And because those men of Almagro, by reason of its being night, and their not knowing the ford, did not dare to enter into the river, those on the other side entered to guide them."* These traitors

* "Y porque los de Almagro, por ser de noche, y no saber el vado, no osavan entrar en el Rio; los de la otra vanda entravan á guiarles."

also did what they could to prevent the alarm being given; and when the Almagristas reached the bulwark, they only found two or three men to resist them, who fled toward the bridge, crying out "Arm, arm!" Almagro's men dismounted, as the ground was rough, and they could fight better on foot. Alonzo de Alvarado, having learned that the bulwark was taken, found himself with about fifty men in a narrow pathway which lay between the river and the sierra, where he defended himself with vigor, and drove the enemy back. Almagro's men shouted to one another, "Up, up, let us gain the heights." Alvarado, who heard these shouts, instantly perceived that all was lost if the heights were gained, and he, with his few followers, made also for the heights. But the enemy reached this position as soon as he did, and as he found himself entirely outnumbered, the enemy being at least ten to one, he was obliged to surrender, and was carried by his captors down to the river, which Almagro had already passed by the bridge, over which he had forced his way. The victory was complete. Diego and Gomez de Alvarado were instantly set at liberty, Alvarado's camp was sacked, and his relations, Diego and Gomez, so lately his prisoners, were now suppliants for his life. It was not without difficulty that they obtained what they asked, for the fierce Orgoñez, whose maxim was "that the dead dog neither barks nor bites," was desirous to put Alonzo de Alvarado to death, and was very much dissatisfied at being prevented from ordering his instant execution.

Almagro's troops, flushed with success, declared that they would not leave one "*Pizarra*" (a slate) to stumble over.* The counsel given by Orgoñez, al-

—Garcilaso de la Vega, *Comentarios Reales del Perú*, parte ii., lib. ii., cap. 34.

* "Ni una pizarra en que tropezar."

ways the most uncompromising that could be thought of, was to kill the Pizarros, and march at once to Los Reyes. The plan of marching upon Los Reyes was so far adopted that it was proclaimed by sound of trumpet that all should prepare themselves for the march. There were, however, persons in Almagro's camp who had wives and families at Los Reyes, and they did not approve of this proposal. After the matter had remained two days in doubt, it was resolved to return to Cusco. When they arrived there, Almagro issued a proclamation that no inhabitants of that city should make use of his Indians; for he, the governor, suspended the *repartimientos*, as the Bishop of Cusco remarks, not wishing that any one should have any thing for certain until he himself should make the general *repartimiento*.* This led to the greatest disorder, as no one had any certain interest in the welfare of any of the Indians, and consequently the Spaniards behaved to them with careless insolence and cruelty.† The next thing that was resolved upon at Cusco was for Orgoñez to make an attack upon the rebel Inca, which he did with great success, coming so close upon him that he made himself master of a golden ornament, called "the sun," which was greatly venerated among the Indians, and which Orgoñez brought home for Paullo. Thus, in every way, Almagro's faction was triumphant.

* "Mandó pregonar que ningun vecino se sirviese de sus Indios, porque él suspendia los repartimientos no queriendo que ninguno tuviese cossa conoscida hasta que él hiciese el repartimiento general."—*Carta de* VICENTE DE VALVERDE, MS.

† *Á rienda suelta*, "with loose bridle," as the bishop says.

CHAPTER VI.

NEGOTIATIONS BETWEEN THE MARQUIS AND THE MARISCAL RESPECTING THE BOUNDARIES OF THEIR GOVERNMENTS.—THE RENEWAL OF HOSTILITIES.—FERNANDO PIZARRO TAKES THE COMMAND OF HIS BROTHER'S ARMY.

MEANWHILE the whole family of Pizarro were in great sadness and affliction. Fernando and Gonzalo must have heard in their prison the joyous return of those who had conquered their friends; and the marquis, who did not even yet know the worst, when he received the news brought him by Alvarado's fourteen horsemen, broke out into loud complaints of his ill fortune. He sent orders at once to Alvarado not to move on to Cusco; but, before his messengers had left Los Reyes, the fatal battle of Abançay had taken place. When Pizarro heard of this, he resolved to send an embassage to treat with Almagro. The persons he chose were the Factor Illan Suarez de Carvajal, the Licentiate Gaspar de Espinosa, Diego de Fuenmayor, a brother of the President of the Audiencia at San Domingo, and the Licentiate de la Gama.

When these important personages had arrived at Cusco, they found that they could make no way in their mission. Almagro said that he would not give up a hand-breadth of the land which his majesty had conferred upon him, and that he was determined to go to Los Reyes and take possession of that city. Diego de Fuenmayor produced an ordinance from the *Audiencia* of San Domingo which had been prepared in contemplation of the probability of these feuds. But Almagro made light of this authority. The exhortations of Gaspar de Espinosa met with no better fate; and yet, if there were any one to whom Almagro might be expected to listen, it was this licentiate. He had been a partner in the original enterprise of Pizarro and Almagro. He was a man of great experience in colonial affairs. He had been judge in Vasco Nuñez's case, and was not likely to underrate the evils arising from the infraction of authority. "Are not, in truth," he said, "these regions wide enough to extend your authority in, without, for the sake of a few leagues more or less, doing that which will irritate Heaven, offend the king, and fill the world with scandals and disasters?"

But Almagro held firm to his resolve of maintaining what he considered to be his rights; whereupon Espinosa exclaimed, "Well, then, Señor Adelantado, that will come to pass here which the old Castilian proverb speaks of, 'The conquered conquered, and the conqueror ruined.'"*

Espinosa fell ill and died at Cusco; and the embassage proved entirely abortive. There is this to be said in defense of Almagro's conduct, that it was impossible for him now to do any thing which was not full of danger and difficulty. Finally, he resolved to move forward to Los Reyes, carrying Fernando Pizarro with him, and leaving Gonzalo Pizarro and Alonzo de Alvarado, with many other prisoners, at Cusco, in the charge of a numerous body of guards. Fernando Pizarro was watched by twenty horsemen on the march, whose sole duty it was to have charge of his person; and he was not allowed to wear spurs.

* "El vencido vencido, y el Vencedor perdido."

When Almagro and his men entered the valley of Lanasca, news reached him that Gonzalo Pizarro and the other prisoners had bribed their guards, and had escaped. Never was the life of Fernando Pizarro in greater danger. Orgoñez might now add to his proverb "that the dead need no guards;" but Diego de Alvarado's milder council prevailed, and Fernando Pizarro was borne in the cavalcade of Almagro to Chincha. There Almagro halted, and founded a new town, which was called after his own name.

Meanwhile a favorable turn had taken place in the fortunes of the Marquis Pizarro, who was at Los Reyes, surrounded by auxiliaries, who had come to him from the different quarters to which he had appealed for assistance. The fugitives from Cusco had also arrived; and when he reviewed his forces, he found that he had one thousand men-at-arms, and among them one hundred and fifty arquebusiers. These last obtained a special mention at this time, because, from recent improvements in their arms and in the mode of handling them, they had become a more formidable kind of force than they had hitherto been.

Almagro, having been informed of the nature and the number of Pizarro's forces, abandoned at once his plan of attacking Los Reyes. Indeed, he sought to strengthen his own position in the valley of Chincha by digging pitfalls and raising bulwarks; and, in order to prevent any surprise, he stationed parties of the friendly Indians under Paullo at the several entrances to the valley, in order that no Spaniards might come into or go out of that district without his knowledge.

Pizarro's moderation and prudence were not abated by his growing strength in men and arms. Resisting the vehement counsels of those captains who were smarting from their recent defeat at the bridge of Abançay, he sought to bring the question at issue between himself and Almagro to an end by means of

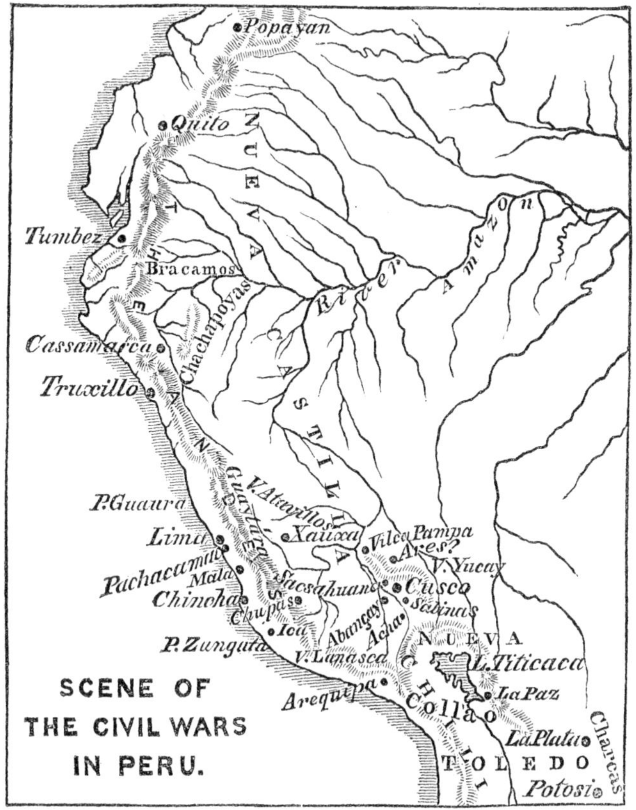

SCENE OF THE CIVIL WARS IN PERU.

arbitration. Almagro, notwithstanding his recent successes, was in a humbler mood than when he refused the prudent mediation of the Licentiate Espinosa. Finally, therefore, it was agreed on both sides that the

Provincial Bobadilla, of the Order of Mercy, should be appointed as judge in the case, who, with the assistance of "pilots," should fix the limits of the respective governments of New Castile and New Toledo. The fiery Orgoñez did not at all approve of this arbitration, and his reason for disapproving of the person to whom the arbitration was intrusted is very singular. He said, "In case the matter were submitted to any one to decide, it ought to be, not to a man 'exempt,'* as that *religioso* was, but to persons who feared God, and also feared men; and, he added, that their real security did not consist in frivolous negotiations, but in being prepared to meet their enemies."† The Provincial Bobadilla, however, was accepted by both sides as a fitting arbiter, and he took up his station with his "pilots" at an Indian town called Mala, midway on the high road from Los Reyes to Chincha. Thither he summoned both governors to appear before him, each to be attended by twelve horsemen only. Both governors prepared to come; but, as might be expected, the gravest suspicions occupied the minds of their respective partisans. After the marquis had set out, his brother Gonzalo was induced by Pizarro's followers to advance with the army in the direction of Mala. The treachery of Almagro, by which he had gained an entrance into Cusco, and his sending forged letters to Alonzo de Alvarado, had put him, as it were, beyond the pale of confidence.

When, however, the old companions Pizarro and

* He meant, who could not be condemned by the civil authorities.

† "Í que tampoco era su parecer, que se sometiese á juicio arbitrario de un hombre esento, sino de personas, que por el temor de Dios, í de los hombres, mirasen bien lo que hacian."—HERRERA, *Hist. de las Indias*, dec. vi., lib. iii., cap. 2.

Almagro met, it was with such tears and loving words as if nothing hitherto had happened to disturb their amity; and there was even some hope of their coming to terms before the sentence of arbitration should be pronounced, which was to be delivered on the next day. Meanwhile, however, Almagro's troops had become aware of the movement of Gonzalo Pizarro toward Mala; and one of Almagro's captains, named Juan de Guzman, brought a horse to the door of the house where the governors were conferring, entered the apartment where they were, and contrived to give notice to Almagro of the supposed stratagem, upon which the mariscal went down stairs without taking leave, got upon his horse, and went off with his friends at full gallop. It was said that Francisco de Godoy, one of Pizarro's captains, had given notice to Almagro of some intended treachery by singing the first words of a *romancillo*, which ran thus—

> "Tiempo es, caballero,
> Tiempo es ya de andar de aqui,"

and that the mariscal was therefore ready to leave the room when Juan de Guzman entered to give him information. The minds of both factions were in a morbid state of suspiciousness. It was, therefore, of no avail for the marquis to send, as he did next day, to tell the mariscal that the army had moved without his leave, and that Almagro should return to complete the agreement which they had commenced on the previous day, for the mariscal would not resume the interview. The arbiter, however, ordered certain persons who had been appointed by Almagro to appear before him; and he gave sentence entirely in Pizarro's favor, declaring that Cusco was within the two hundred and seventy-five leagues which the Emperor had assigned as the extent of Pizarro's government, and consequently that the mariscal should quit that territory, and go and conquer the land of his own government, since that was in a state of war.

When this sentence was communicated to the mariscal, he declared that he would not abide by it, and his men maintained that it was a most unrighteous judgment.

It was so much, however, for the interest of both parties that some amicable conclusion should be arrived at, that negotiations were again commenced. The good Diego de Alvarado was consulted, and his voice was, as it always had been, for measures of peace. Finally, a treaty was concluded, of which the principal stipulations were, that Fernando Pizarro should be liberated, and that Chincha should be evacuated; that Cusco should be put in deposit until the king should decide upon the disputed question, that city remaining in the same state in which it was when Almagro entered it, having the same alcaldes and regidors, and the *repartimientos* which had then been in existence continuing to belong to their owners; also, that Almagro and his people should conquer the country in one direction, Pizarro and his in the other. Lastly, that Pizarro should give Almagro a ship, which ship, notwithstanding the above, should be allowed to enter the port of Zangala or Chincha, wherever the vessel might happen to touch. Almagro's messengers, having settled these terms on behalf of their master, returned to his camp. There the mariscal, and those of his friends who were for peace, having met and determined to ratify these conditions, they sent for Rodrigo Orgoñez, whom the mariscal begged not to disturb himself because a thing had been agreed upon which he had always opposed, for if they attempted to carry matters by rigor, it would be the cause of ruin to all of them; and men would come from Castile who had never seen a lance, and knew not what suffering was, to enjoy those conquests which they had gained with their blood. To prevent this, he had determined to set Ferdinand Pizarro at liberty, that he might go to Spain to present himself before the Emperor.

Rodrigo Orgoñez was furious on hearing this intelligence. He declared that he had no faith whatever in the contract being kept. "Never," he said, "were excuses wanting to the perfidious to prevent their fulfilling what they had promised." Then, taking his beard in his left hand, he made a movement with his right as if he were cutting off his own head, exclaiming, "Orgoñez, Orgoñez, for the friendship which you bear to Don Diego de Almagro, this will have to be cut off." Many of the soldiers fully entered into the apprehension of Orgoñez; and the camp abounded with anonymous verses and witty sayings, all tending to the same point, and intimating the danger of setting Fernando Pizarro free. But Almagro and the friends of peace were not to be deterred from their resolve. Accordingly the mariscal, proceeding to the place of Fernando Pizarro's confinement, ordered him to be released. Immediately they embraced; and, after an interchange of courtesies, the mariscal said that, forgetting the past, he should hold it for good that henceforward there should be peace and quietness among them all. Fernando Pizarro replied very graciously, declaring that it would not be his fault if it were not so, for it was what he most desired, and immediately he took a solemn oath pledging himself to fulfill what had been agreed upon. When he had given these securities, the mariscal carried him to his house, and regaled him splendidly. All the chief men of the army then visited him. Afterward they accompanied him about half a league from the camp, and then, with great demonstrations of amity, took their leave. There must now have been thorough trust for the time on the part of Almagro, for he sent, in company with Fernando Pizarro, his son Dion de Almagro, commonly called *el moço*, "the youth," together with the Alvarados, and other cavaliers of his party. These were all very well received by the marquis, who lavished courtesies and gifts upon them, paying particular attention to Almagro's son. After these principal persons had returned to the camp of Almagro, it was broken up, and his army marched to the valley of Zangala, where he began to found a town, instead of the one which he had founded at Chincha, and which he was bound by the treaty to evacuate.

At this point of time, when, to all appearances, there was some hope of peace, at least for the Spanish colonists in Peru, if not for the Indians, there suddenly arrived a messenger from the court of Spain. The messenger's name was Pedro de Ançurez, and the day on which he arrived was the very day on which Fernando Pizarro had been set at liberty. The main provision of his dispatches was, that each of the governors should retain whatever they had conquered and peopled until any other arrangement should be made by his majesty.*

* "Paresciendole á el adelantado que le estava bien esta capitulaçion, porque alli él no era parte, con parecer de sus capitanes y letrados soltó á Hernando Piçarro debajo de este concierto. Este dia llegó el capitan Pedro Anzures con una provision de V.M. en la qual mandava que cada uno de los governadores tuviesen y poseisen lo por ellos conquistado y poblado hasta que otra cosa se proveiese por V.M." —*Carta de* VICENTE DE VALVERDE, MS.

This royal order was in the highest degree satisfactory to the Pizarros, as it seemed to settle the question in the marquis's favor with regard to the occupation of Cusco. Fernando Pizarro sought leave at

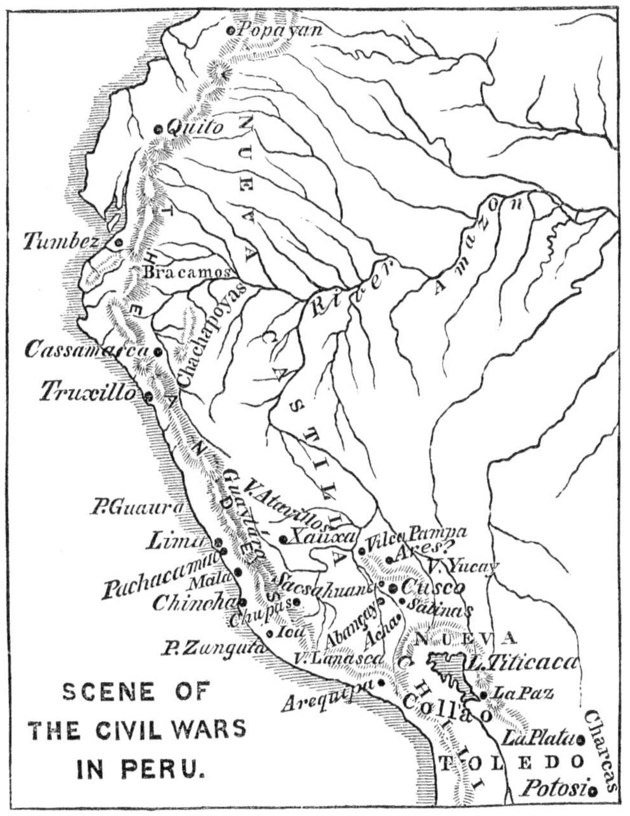

SCENE OF THE CIVIL WARS IN PERU.

this time to return to Spain and give an account to the Emperor of what had taken place in Peru; but his brother would not consent, saying that the Emperor would be better served by Fernando's staying to help him, the marquis, to maintain his government.

Meanwhile the mariscal had, according to agreement, retired from Chincha, and the marquis went there to seek provisions and to recommence the arrangements with Almagro which would be necessary in consequence of the new ordinance from the court of Spain. On the road to Chincha the marquis's troops found the wells filled up, which they attributed to the mariscal's men. When Pizarro had arrived at Chincha, he sent to Almagro to notify the royal orders to him, to which the mariscal replied that these orders were in his favor, for from where he was to Chincha he had conquered and peopled the country, and, accordingly, he it was who was within the limits of his own government, and he begged that Pizarro would move out of it.

There is no doubt that both sides now believed themselves to be wronged and affronted. Orgoñez and his party, no doubt, clamored loudly about the perfidy of the Pizarros. No sooner had a treaty been settled than these Pizarros hastened to recommence hostilities. This came of injudicious clemency.

On the other side, the conduct of the Almagristas was stigmatized by Pizarro's partisans in the harshest terms. The word they used was "tyranny," taken in the old Greek sense of the unlawful seizure of sovereignty; and, to punish such tyranny, the whole of Pizarro's army moved forward. The mariscal, being made aware of this by his spies, withdrew to Guaytára, a pass in the sierra so difficult that to surmount it was considered equivalent to passing a great river three times. Pizarro's troops followed the Almagristas. In the course of their march, at one of the places where they halted, Fernando Pizarro made the following speech to the troops: "Already is known to all of you the bounty which his majesty has shown to the governor, my brother; and although, before this royal order arrived, the justice on our side was very clear, the confirmation of it, which his majesty now makes, gives us more certainty. On our side, then, we have justice; on that of Almagro is covetousness." He then intimated that for their services to the crown in placing this province under its authority, they would be repaid from the lands of the province. Then, in a grand, chivalrous way, for Fernando Pizarro's words are always full of dignity, he continued, "I know well that it is a great error on my part, where there are so many cavaliers and men zealous in the service of their prince, to put before them the obligation which they have to serve him, since I can not magnify it so much as I know that, in the breasts of all, there is the wish to show it by deeds; so, with that confidence, I wish to leave to the coming time the demonstration of your loyalty and your sense of the justice of our cause. If any of you has need of arms or horses, let him tell me, and I will cause him to be provided with them according to his needs; for," as he delicately added, "as you come from afar, señores, you may be wanting in some things." This speech gave great satisfaction. Its inspiriting influence, the pressure from want of subsistence (for the camp of Pizarro was almost without provisions), and the fear that Almagro might move by the coast upon Los Reyes and take it suddenly, combined to make Pizarro's army resolve to take the pass of Guaytára, which was admirably defended by nature, by Almagro's Indian auxiliaries, and by a strong body of Almagro's own troops, occupying the heights. At Guaytára itself the main body of Almagro's army was posted in a fortified camp. When the spies gave notice to the Almagristas that Pizarro's army was coming, it was but a subject of jesting for them, as they looked upon their own position as impregnable.

Fernando Pizarro, however (probably the greatest captain of his time in this kind of warfare), looked only to where the difficulty was greatest, and where, therefore, the care of the enemy would be least, and this was where the body of Spanish troops was posted on the height. Early one evening, Fernando Pizarro, taking with him three hundred of his most active men, made for this part of the sierra. At the foot of it they dismounted, and they had now a league of mountain to ascend—all of it sheer ascent. Moreover, Almagro's captain was informed of their enterprise (the Almagristas were much better served by spies than the other party), and he and his men waited for Fernando Pizarro, considering him to be a lost man. The marquis staid at the foot of the sierra, intending to follow if Fernando Pizarro should gain the pass. And the pass was gained. With darkness alone to aid them, heavily encumbered with arms and armor, being obliged sometimes to climb the more precipitous parts on their hands and knees, the Indians hurling down great stones upon them, sometimes sinking in the sand in such a way that instead of moving forward they slid down again, they still contrived to reach the summit. It was an arduous task for Fernando Pizarro, a heavy man with ponderous armor, totally unaccustomed to go on foot; but his exertions were so strenuous as to astonish all beholders. It happened that five or six of Pizarro's soldiers gained the height at the same moment. They shouted "Viva el Rey!" with such vigor that the enemy, supposing the whole of the army was upon them, were panic-stricken, and fled at once. To show the difficult nature of this pass, it may be mentioned that it was midday before the whole three hundred reached the summit. Fernando Pizarro was greatly delighted with the success of his enterprise, and held it to be a happy omen for the future. The marquis, with the rest of the troops, were now able at their ease to surmount the pass. Almagro and his troops retreated, and Pizarro's forces moved onward in an irregular and disjointed manner, being informed that Almagro was making his way to Cusco. After a few days' march they arrived at the highest point of a barren waste, where it rained and snowed much, and the forces were so scattered that on that night they had only two hundred men together.

Now it happened that on that very night the Almagristas were much nearer to Pizarro's men than these imagined. Indeed, Almagro's camp was not more than a league off, and he was very much bent upon making an attack upon Pizarro's forces. His reason for this was that a large part of the marquis's men were new-comers, and it was well known that in the snowy wastes of Peru all strangers were apt to suffer from snow-sickness, experiencing the same sensations as if they were at sea;* but Orgoñez, for once in his life cautious, and (as mostly happens when a man acts or advises against the bent of his own disposition) acting wrongly, dissuaded Almagro from an enterprise which would probably have been fatal to the enemy.

As day broke, Pizarro's army saw the situation in which they were, and Fernando Pizarro, whose valor never left his wisdom far behind, counseled instant retreat. Their march had hitherto been but a disor-

* "Se marean como en un golfo de mar."

derly pursuit, whereas the enemy's forces were in a state of good preparation for immediate action. The marquis listened to his brother's advice, and the army retreated to the valley of Ica to recruit themselves. Then the principal captains besought Pizarro to return to Los Reyes, as, on account of his age, they said he was unfit to endure the labors of such a campaign. The governor consented; and, leaving Fernando Pizarro as his representative, returned to Los Reyes.

CHAPTER VII.

FERNANDO PIZARRO'S MARCH TO CUSCO.—THE BATTLE OF SALINAS.—THE EXECUTION OF THE MARISCAL ALMAGRO.—RETURN OF FERNANDO PIZARRO TO SPAIN.

FERNANDO PIZARRO, now placed in full command, resolved that, with those who would follow him, whether they were many or whether they were few, he would go and take possession of that city Cusco which he had lost. Marching to the valley of Lanasca, he halted there, and reviewed his men. He found that they amounted to six hundred and fifty, two hundred and eighty of them being horsemen, and the rest pikemen, arquebusiers, and cross-bow-men. Of the horsemen he formed six companies, assigning them to captains whom he felt sure would give a good account of the charge intrusted to them. He himself addressed the infantry in a speech of much policy, in which he told them that he was informed it was said among them that those soldiers who had no horses were held in little esteem when the time for giving *repartimientos* came; but he gave them his word and honor that such a thought never entered into his mind. Good soldiers were not to be judged by whether they had horses or not, but by their own valor. Each man should be rewarded according to his services: if he had not a horse, that was an accident of fortune, and not a personal defect.

They were all much pleased at this speech, and the words appeared to them the words of a good captain. Fernando Pizarro was personally not much loved.

He was haughty, imperious, a stern disciplinarian, and a resolute protector of the Indians; but men in different circumstances soon discern what there is in a man, and Ferdinand Pizarro's army well knew what a leader they had with them.

Almagro retired to Cusco, where he made the most vigorous preparations to withstand the coming attack of Fernando Pizarro. In Cusco nothing was heard but the sound of trumpets summoning to reviews, and the hammering of silver on the anvil, for of that metal it was that they made their corslets, morions, and arm-pieces, which, using double the quantity of silver that they would have used of iron, they rendered as strong "as if they had come from Milan." They resolved to await the attack of Fernando Pizarro within the city, fortifying it toward that part of the river where the defenses were weak.

Meanwhile Fernando Pizarro was advancing slowly to Cusco, being so watchful against any surprise of the enemy that his men marched in their armor. He, too, went armed, and with his lance in his hand. They had to make long circuits, for it was winter, and the rivers being swollen, they were obliged to ford them high up in the course of their streams. Fernando Pizarro strictly forbade his men to rob or distress the natives, and having chastised some of those who had offended in this way, many of his followers were much displeased, and remained behind, hidden in the Indian villages which the army passed through. When informed of this, Pizarro merely replied that he could not consent to the Indians being robbed; that whoever wished to follow him must do it upon that condition, and not for the sake of one hundred or two hundred defaulters would he desist from his enterprise. Having arrived at a place called Acha, he rested there five days for his men to recover from their fatigue. Afterward he proceeded to a spot where there were three roads, and, to deceive the enemy's scouts, he pretended to pitch his tent there. Then, when information had been carried to Orgoñez, who hastened to occupy a certain pass, Fernando Pizarro suddenly ordered the tents to be struck, marched the whole night, and occupied the pass at which the enemy had thought to stop him. Almagro's captains now changed their plan of remaining in the city. Their men were better armed than Pizarro's, their horses were fresh, and they knew of the numerous desertions from Pizarro's camp which had taken place during his march. After a review, in which the men were found to be in the highest order, Almagro's forces marched out of the city to battle, in number about six hundred and eighty, three hundred of them being horsemen. It appears, however, that some of the foot-soldiers went with an ill will, for the city was not altogether of Almagro's faction, and eighty of these men returned that very night.

Before Orgoñez left Cusco to take the command, he went on his knees in Almagro's presence, and spoke thus: "May it please our Lord, that if this thing which I am going to do is not for His service, and is not thoroughly just, He may permit that I should not come alive out of the battle; but if the contrary is true, may it please Him that you should gain the victory, as we all desire." It is evident that the generous nature of Almagro had won true friends for him. He embraced, with many tears, his bold champion Orgoñez, who then quitted the city. All that day Fernando Pizarro expected to meet his enemies in a great plain which there is three leagues from Cusco, and as he did not find them, he left the royal road, with the intent of placing himself in an elevated spot of those plains, which are called the Salt Pits (*Salinas*).

Orgoñez was instantly made aware by his scouts that Fernando Pizarro had pitched his camp near the salt-pits, and he moved his own camp to a spot three quarters of a league from the city, between a sierra and the river. His infantry he put under the shelter of some ruined houses which were there, flanking their position by some artillery which he had in very serviceable order.

The Indians, commanded by the Inca Paullo, to the number of fifteen thousand, were placed on a declivity close to the royal road. Orgoñez himself occupied the plain with all his cavalry, who wore white vests over their armor. The disposition was very skillful. The royal road was between the infantry and the cavalry, and Orgoñez reckoned that if Pizarro's army came by that road, it being very narrow by reason of the salt-pits which were on one side and on the other, he could easily destroy them.

Fernando Pizarro also made his preparation for battle. Over his armor he put on a surcoat or vest (*ropeta*) of orange damask, and in his morion a tall white feather, which floated over the heads of all. He did this not only that he might be known by his own men, but by those of the opposite side, to whom, it is said, he sent notice of his dress. He had received indignities when in prison, and was anxious to meet his personal enemies in the field. Then, having heard mass with all his army, they descended into the plain, where he placed his men in order, choosing in the first place twenty of his most dexterous arquebusiers for an advanced guard. Of the remainder, with the rest of the infantry, he formed one division, consisting of three "companies." Gonzalo Pizarro was to command the infantry. Of all the horsemen he formed another division, consisting of two companies

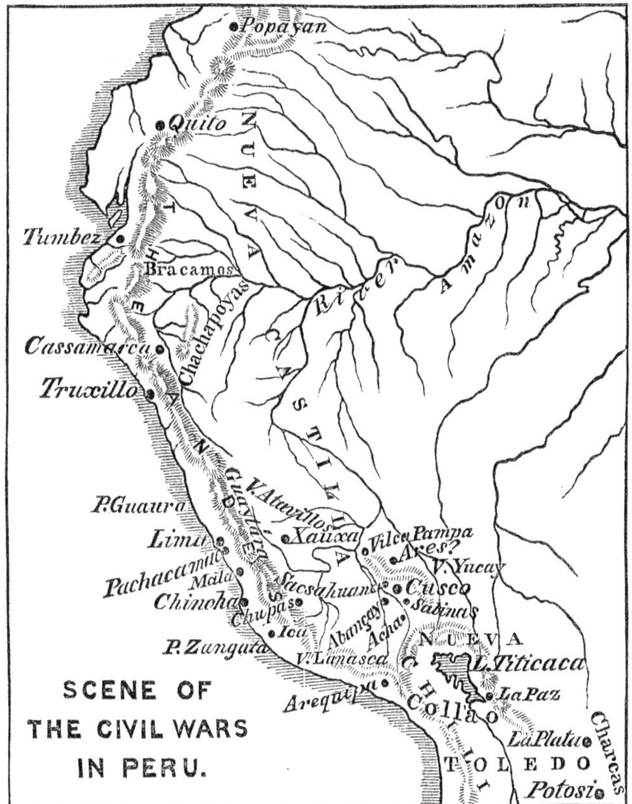

SCENE OF THE CIVIL WARS IN PERU.

commanded by Alonzo de Alvarado and Pedro Ançurez. Lastly, a company, under the command of a captain named Mercadillo, was formed into a reserve.

The scouts on both sides gave notice of the disposition of the respective armies. Pizarro, knowing that Orgoñez was waiting for him, sent on a notary to make a formal requisition that the city of Cusco should be delivered up to him. Meanwhile he made a speech to his men, telling them that he knew it was not necessary to give them the usual words of encouragement, but rather to impress upon them the necessity for restraint. "I pray you," he said, "moderate, with the patience that on these occasions is necessary, the desire for victory." Knowing the bitter feelings of many of the men who had been beaten at the battle of Abançay, he particularly addressed his words of caution to them. Having made his speech, and having received fresh intelligence from his scouts of the position of the enemy which induced him to change his plan of moving along the royal road (it appears he had returned to it), Fernando Pizarro left the road again, and, advancing through some plains, approached the spot where the enemy had pitched their camp. When there, however, he began to regret this movement, for he had now the river between him and the enemy. Moreover, there was rising ground on the opposite bank of the river, and there was a swamp to be passed before reaching the river. There was nothing, however, to be done but to make the best of a bad position. Orgoñez on his part also was probably much disconcerted by Pizarro's change of plan, and his deviation from the royal road.

Both sides were now ready for battle. We should judge but poorly of these combats in Spanish America if we estimated them according to the smallness of the number of men engaged on each side, and not according to the depth and amount of human emotion which they elicited.* There was more passion in the two little armies now set over against each other than is to be found in vast hosts of hireling soldiers combating for objects which they scarcely understand. I have no doubt the hatred in these bands of Almagristas and Pizarristas greatly exceeded any thing that was to be found in the ranks of the French and Spaniards that fought at Pavia. Even in religious wars there has hardly existed greater fierceness than among these Spanish conquerors, where each man in the army was an aristocrat, fighting for lands, houses, slaves, and whose angry soul was often largely occupied by the remembrance of slights and injuries received from men in the opposite ranks, well known to him. It appears at first a slur upon the good sense of Fernando Pizarro, and a sad inconsistency, that he, being a commander, should give way to such feelings in his own case, while he strove to restrain the fury of others, and his orange damask surcoat and floating white feather seem but childish emblems in a general. But the spirit of the times must not be forgotten. It was only in the preceding year that the outwardly sedate and almost always cautious Charles the Fifth, in the presence of the Pope and the College of Cardinals, had, after a passionate speech, publicly challenged the King of France to personal combat, staking Burgundy or Milan on the issue of the encounter. It is hardly to be wondered at, therefore, that Fernando Pizarro should give his personal enemies the means of knowing where he was to be found in the battle.

* "Estas batallas de América, que en Europa apenas pasarian por medianas escaramuzas, llevan consigo el interés de los grandes resultados que tenian, y el del espectáculo de las pasiones, manifestadas en ellas frecuentemente con mas energía que en nuestras sábias maniobras y grandes operaciones."—QUINTANA, *Vida de Francisco Pizarro.*

On the heights the Indians under Paullo were clustered by thousands, looking down upon the Spanish armies; and, whichever way the battle might go, they must have thought that the result could only be for their advantage. There were some skirmishes between them and Fernando Pizarro's Indians; but, as these latter were comparatively few in numbers, the conflicts were not of much importance. The Spanish writers have asserted that the Indians on this occasion had some great plot, and that they would have destroyed the victors if the victory had been obtained with much destruction of life on both sides. There is no evidence of this, but it was a natural conclusion to be arrived at by those Spaniards, if any such there were, who had aught in their minds at that moment but raging hostility against their Spanish enemies.

No answer was vouchsafed by Orgoñez to the formal demand made by Pizarro's notary for the cession of Cusco, and the battle commenced by Almagro's artillery beginning to play upon the advancing Pizarristas. At the first discharge it took off two of Fernando Pizarro's foot-soldiers, but the whole body of infantry pressed on. The picket of arquebusiers threw themselves forward, passed the swamp, which was found to be not so deep as had been expected, and, taking up a position in the river, discharged their weapons at the enemy.

Their fire was very fatal. Orgoñez drew his men back behind a little hill on the skirt of the sierra, not, however, from a motive of fear, but with the design of letting some of the cavalry and of the infantry on the other side pass the river. Almagro, who was too ill to enter into the battle himself, but who watched it from a distance in a litter, construed this movement most unfavorably for his own fortunes. Descending from his litter, he got on horseback and rode off to Cusco, where he retreated into the fortress.

Meanwhile Fernando Pizarro passed the swamp, and fifty horsemen had passed with him, when Orgoñez came out of his position and prepared to charge. Pizarro's arquebusiers had now a good mark to fire at in the large body of Almagro's troops advancing, and they were able to protect the Pizarristas until they had all passed the swamp and the river.

The first movement of Orgoñez, who came down with both horse and foot, seemed to be directed against the infantry of Pizarro; but suddenly he turned and charged their cavalry in a furious manner, "as a most valiant man, but not as a wise man," says one who was probably a spectator, "for these turns that he made were like the work of a madman."* It is said that Orgoñez exclaimed "O divine Word, let those follow me who please, but I go to die."†

Pizarro's squadron stood the shock: indeed, they had advanced to meet it. The cavalry on both sides were now mingled in a hand-to-hand encounter, and Fernando Pizarro, well known by his enemies, was conspicuous in the mêlée. Pedro de Lerma, with all the fury of a traitor and a renegade, was the first to make his way to where that white plume towered above the rest, and to bear down upon its owner. His lance, however, only struck Pizarro's horse in the neck, and drove it down upon its knees, but the more skillful Fernando pierced his adversary with his lance. Pedro de Lerma, however, was but one of many who

* "Como valentissimo ombre aunque no como sabio, porque estas bueltas que dió fueron de ombre desatinado."—*Carta de* VICENTE DE VALVERDE, MS.

† "O Verbo Divino, siganme los que quisieren, que yo á morir voy."—ZARATE, *Hist. del Peru*, lib. iii., cap. 11.

had resolved on that day to chastise the insolence, as they would have said, of Fernando Pizarro. Though dismounted, Fernando was not injured, and, drawing his sword, he fought with his usual valor. It was not the first time in his life that he had had great odds to encounter. His followers soon rescued him from his perilous position.

In the mean time, the movement of Orgoñez had laid open his infantry to a charge from the infantry of the Pizarristas under Gonzalo Pizarro, which proved most effective. In truth, Almagro's infantry had never charged, being checked midway by the sudden change in the movements of Orgoñez. The consequence was that they were soon broken, and took refuge behind the walls of the ruined houses that have been spoken of before.

The battle, as far as the cavalry on both sides was concerned, was well contested. The lances of most of the combatants had been shivered, and they fought hand to hand with swords, the confusion being so great that sometimes the Almagristas hewed down Almagristas, and Pizarro's men the Pizarristas. Fernando Pizarro rushed from one spot to another, wherever his aid was necessary; nor was the bravery of the opposite chief, Orgoñez, less manifest. But Gonzalo Pizarro's charge had been the turning-point of the engagement. He carried such slaughter into the infantry on the opposite side, that, abandoning their shelter amid the ruins, they fairly turned and fled up the sierra, eagerly pursued by Gonzalo, who feared lest the fugitives should make themselves strong in Cusco.

Some horsemen on the side of Almagro still continued to maintain the contest, though they were gradually being worsted, their comrades having fallen thickly around them. At last, however, these survivors were dismounted, and were obliged to yield. Being protected by persons on the opposite side who knew them, they were brought before Fernando Pizarro, who, thinking "that the second victory which remained for him to gain was to conquer himself, not listening to private vengeance," in his clemency spared them all.

Gonzalo Pizarro headed the pursuit. There was little danger, however, of the enemy being able to form again. Orgoñez lay dead upon the field, with fifty others of the Almagristas. Almagro himself, who, before he reached the citadel, was informed of the flight of his men, in his sickly state could do nothing to restore order or courage in his army. Fernando Pizarro sent Alonzo de Alvarado to take the mariscal prisoner. It is said that one of Pizarro's captains, seeing the mariscal for the first time, and being disgusted with his ugly countenance and mean presence, raised his arquebus to kill him, exclaiming, "Look at the man for whom so many cavaliers have died." He was not, however, killed, but was conducted to the same apartment in which he had formerly confined Fernando Pizarro. While this was passing in the town, Fernando Pizarro was doing all he could to restrain the vengeful feelings of his men toward their now vanquished enemies, and also to prevent the lower class of his soldiers from acts of robbery and pillage, for which interference they were furious with him.

It was noticed that almost all the wounds received this day were in the face, for so completely were the Spaniards armed that it was difficult to get at any man except in the face. What fearful odds, then, must the Indians have had to encounter, when they exposed their soft bodies to Spaniards cased in steel or silver, whom it was a labor even for skilled opponents, with fit weapons, to destroy!

The Indians under Paullo, who had taken no part in the battle, when they saw the Spaniards of their own side routed, partook the flight. Fernando Pizarro sent for Paullo, who came to the conqueror, not without some shame, it is said, for the part which he had acted.

Fernando Pizarro, having done his duty in the field, entered Cusco, and, at Almagro's request, came to see him in the citadel. Almagro, overcome by sickness and disaster, burst into tears and uttered ignoble lamentations. Fernando Pizarro consoled him, saying "that such reverses were wont to happen to valiant persons; that he should not grieve in this way, but should show the valor which became his greatness; that he would be kindly treated, and justice well considered in his case." Access was not denied to him until it was found that he was endeavoring to gain over Pizarro's captains. A formal process on the part of the king's officers was instituted against Almagro, and the preparation of this process occupied nearly four months.

The battle of Salinas was fought on the 6th of April, 1538. Some instances of ferocity to the vanquished on the part of individual conquerors are recorded, but their general showed singular moderation in the use he made of his victory. There is no mention of any executions having taken place. Indeed, Fernando Pizarro went to the extreme of graciousness in his conduct to the vanquished. He ordered that every thing which had been plundered on the day of battle should be returned to the owners, and he appointed two persons whose sole duty it was to see that this was done. Then, considering that all the neighborhood round Cusco was much exhausted, and that he had a large number of soldiers, his own and Almagro's, to maintain and to employ, he resolved to

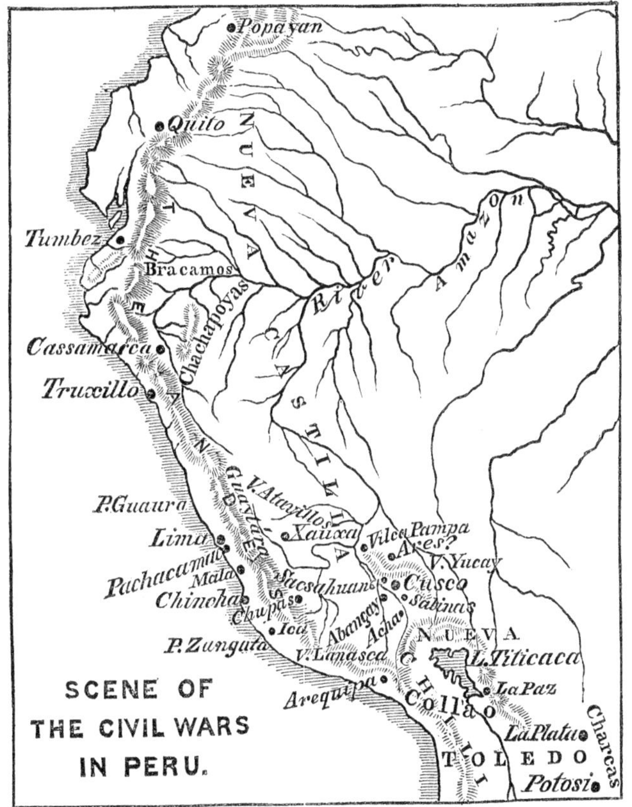

SCENE OF THE CIVIL WARS IN PERU.

disperse them in the following manner. To a commander named Mercadillo was appointed the discovery of the district of Xauxa; to Pedro de Vergara, that of the country of the Bracamoros; to Alonzo de

Alvarado (for the second time), the conquest of the Chachapoyas; while Pedro de Candia was sent on an expedition to the Andes. A large number of Almagro's men joined themselves to this captain with no good intentions; for when he had gone out of the city about twenty leagues, they halted there as if for the purpose of reorganizing their ranks, but in reality to keep up a correspondence with Almagro's friends in the city. They even went so far as to offer the captain of the arquebusiers, who had charge of Almagro's person, fifteen thousand *castellanos*, together with one thousand *castellanos* for each of his men, if he would fall into their plans and set Almagro free. But this captain, being a faithful man, informed Fernando Pizarro of these offers, who immediately seized upon those persons who were concerned in the negotiation, and also gave orders that Pedro de Candia should pass on to his conquest. The expedition accordingly entered the country for about sixty leagues, when, finding the journey to be very difficult, and it being given out among them that there was a much easier route by Collao, they made that a pretext for retracing their steps. As a large body of them were Almagristas, they did not care to make a secret of their plans. They said they did not know who Fernando Pizarro was. They raised their standard in the name of the King of Spain, and in this rebellious manner they moved back to Cusco with the intention of liberating Almagro.

Within the city as well as without there was treachery. A certain man, named Alonzo Enriquez, informed Pizarro that there were two hundred persons banded together to release Almagro, and that they had asked him to take the command of them. Moreover, they had informed him that they had posted friends of theirs at the difficult passes on the road between Cusco and Los Reyes, in order that they might set Almagro at liberty, if Fernando Pizarro should send him to be shipped to Spain, there to be judged by the Emperor. Fernando Pizarro, upon this intelligence, doubled the guards and waited patiently until the process in Almagro's case was completed, about which time there came a letter from a certain man named Villacastin, an alcalde of Cusco, who had gone out to visit the Indians which had been given in *encomienda* to him. This man had met with Pedro de Candia's people, had been ill treated by them, and had heard of their intention to resist Gonzalo Pizarro, who had been sent out to compel them to proceed with their enterprise.

Upon the receipt of Villacastin's letter, Fernando Pizarro summoned a council of the regidors, the alcaldes, with some of the captains of best repute for judgment, and who appeared to him most dispassionate, and thus addressed them: "Already you know the revolt which there is among this people of Don Diego de Almagro, and also that many of my people, because I took away from them the booty which they had made in battle, and by reason of the offers which have been made them on the part of the mariscal, have joined themselves to Almagro's men. I have received this letter, which says that Pedro de Candia is nine leagues from here, with three hundred and fifty men; and, according to the words they utter, they come in a very rebellious mood. You, señores, are in charge of this city, as I am, and you have to look to that which concerns his majesty's service and the peace of the city, and as it may be that extreme anger, or some dislike, may make me do something different from that which would appear to you reasonable, I pray you look to the state in which every thing is, and the damage which may occur, and the punishment which there may be for it, and, as men of honor and good judgment, counsel me as to what ought to be done, that his majesty may be served and this city maintained in peace. And as it may be that some of you might not give their opinions in my presence with perfect freedom, I shall prefer to go out of the council. I pray you look well to what you advise, for I will not act otherwise than as you counsel, since I would rather err upon the opinion of all than succeed upon my own."

Having said these words he went out; and when they had talked and consulted about the matter, they sent to call him back, and told him that they saw no other remedy for pacifying the land but passing sentence upon Almagro, who, for his notorious crimes, deserved to die, and whose death would prevent many other deaths. Fernando Pizarro replied that they should look to this, that, before God, he had discharged his conscience by having submitted the matter to them for decision. Although he had said that he was well aware that if this thing were not done, the land would be lost, and the lives of all placed in the greatest danger, he had expressed at the same time his trust in them that they would not go beyond their own opinions in the matter. The council replied that, deserving death as Almagro did, the lesser evil would be to pass sentence upon him, and to execute the sentence, since, if this were not done, a great mischief was impending over them.

All that night Fernando Pizarro kept two hundred men in his quarters, to be ready for any attack which Pedro de Candia's people might make upon the city. Early in the morning he went to the mariscal and told him that it was necessary for completing the process that he should make his confession, who thereupon, it is said, admitted the greater part of the accusations laid to his charge, and with regard to the rest, though he gave some color of excuse for them, he did not substantially deny them.

The confession being taken, sentence was passed upon Almagro, and was notified to him. Great was the anguish of the aged and decrepit mariscal on receiving this notification. He at once appealed from Fernando Pizarro to the Emperor, but Fernando would not allow this appeal to be received. Then the mariscal besought his captor in the most piteous manner to spare his life, urging as a plea for mercy the great part which he had taken in the early fortunes of Fernando's brother, the marquis; also reminding him of his own (*i. e.*, Fernando's) release, and that no blood of his family had been shed by him. Lastly, he bade him consider how old, weak, and infirm he was, and begged that he would allow the appeal to go on to the Emperor, so that he might spend in prison the few and sorrowful days which remained for him to mourn over his sins. Fernando Pizarro was moved with compassion, but his stern purpose was not changed. He went out of the apartment, and ordered that the priest should enter and receive Almagro's confession. The mariscal, however, would not confess until Fernando Pizarro should again return to see him. Fernando Pizarro did return. He said that, though Almagro's crimes had been very great, he would not have sentenced him, but would have sent him to the Emperor, had not the conspiracies of his partisans been such as to prevent that course. Then he told him that he wondered that a man of such valor should show this fear of death; to which the other replied that, since our Lord Jesus Christ feared death, it was not much that he, a man and a sinner, should fear it. But Fernando Pizarro would not recede from his purpose, though, it is said, he felt the greatest pity for Almagro. Pizarro having quitted the apartment, Almagro made his confession; and being counseled, as his estate was forfeited for treason, to leave it by will to the Emperor, he did so. His worldly and his spiritual affairs being thus settled, he was strangled in prison, in order to avoid any outbreak which a public execution might have caused in Cusco. That there might be no doubt, however, of his death, the body was shown in the great square, with the head cut off. This was on the 8th of July, 1538.

Thus died Almagro at the age of sixty-five years. Like his partner, the marquis, he was a natural son, brought up in ignorance, for he could not read. He had all the gifts of a first-rate common soldier, but seems to have had no especial ability as a commander. Profusely and splendidly generous, he had the art of attaching men to him who were far greater than himself in most things, and these attachments did not die out at his death. As men are seldom really attracted to other men but by some great quality, Almagro's generosity must have been of that deep nature which goes far beyond gifts, and where the recipient perceives that his benefactor loves as well as benefits him. In watching the career of Almagro it is necessary to account in some such way for the singular affection which he uniformly inspired.

As for Fernando Pizarro, it is most probable that, in this matter, which has darkened his name with posterity, he had no other intention at first but that of sending Almagro to Spain for judgment.* But the

* "Á los principios no tuvo Hernando Piçarro intencion de ma-

unwise endeavors of Almagro's own people made it seem a duty to the stern Fernando to put the mariscal to death; and Fernando Pizarro was a man of that mould upon which the speeches of other men, past, present, and to come, would have but little influence. He probably foresaw that he would be severely condemned for this transaction, and, far from being deterred on that account, would resolutely beware of giving way to any feeling for his own reputation which might be detrimental to the public service. His conduct, however, on this occasion, is one of those things which can never be made clear, and where a man, let him have acted from what good motive he may, must go down to posterity with a grievous stain upon his reputation.

This execution, like most cruelties, did not insure the desired object: it did not prove final, but, on the contrary, formed a fresh starting-point for calamities of still deeper dye.

As on Atahuallpa's death, so on that of the mariscal, the funeral rites due to his dignity were not forgotten. Pizarro's captains were the supporters of Almagro's bier. He was interred very honorably in the Church of "Our Lady of Mercy;" and the brothers Fernando and Gonzalo Pizarro put on mourning in honor of the Mariscal of Peru.

As if to show how little the shedding of blood avails, the funeral rites were no sooner ended than the king's officers who had served under Almagro, namely, the treasurer, the contador, and the veedor, made a formal intimation to Fernando Pizarro that the government now belonged to them, and they required him to quit that country. To this audacious

tarle, sino de embiarle á Hispaña con la Informacion."—GARCILASO DE LA VEGA, *Comentarios Reales del Perú*, parte ii., lib. ii., cap. 39.

requisition, which was merely reopening a question which had been settled, as Fernando Pizarro thought, he replied by seizing upon their persons, and then went out immediately to quell the mutineers under Pedro de Candia. For this purpose he took with him eighty horsemen. Many of the mutineers, when they heard the news of Almagro's death and of Fernando's approach, fled; and the captains came out of the camp to receive Fernando Pizarro. With his usual dignified bravery, when he was within half a league of them, he left his guard behind and approached the opposite party, attended only by an alguazil and a notary. He then took the necessary informations, and, ascertaining that a captain of his own, named De Mesa, had been the ringleader of the revolt, he caused him to be immediately executed, while he sent Pedro de Candia, with some others of the principal captains, to the marquis, his brother.

On that same day Fernando Pizarro busied himself in giving liberty to many Indian men and women whom Pedro de Candia's people had brought as prisoners in chains, and he also provided for their return to their own lands, for which the poor Indians were very grateful, giving thanks to their gods, and praising Fernando Pizarro. He appointed Pedro de Ançurez as captain in Pedro de Candia's room; and, still fearing for the welfare of the Indians, Fernando himself accompanied the expedition, "For," as it is said, "as he went with them, they did not dare to do any mischief to the peaceable natives, nor to seize them, nor to put them in bonds. It is impossible not to give Fernando Pizarro credit for a stern sense of duty when we find him ready to offend friends and enemies alike by acts which could only have been dictated by natural goodness of heart, or by his regard for the orders he had received from the home government, on behalf of the Indians, when he was in Spain.

Fernando Pizarro had sent the young Almagro, commonly called "*Almagro el moço*," to the marquis, who did not fail to give the young man comforting assurances respecting his father's life. After a time, the marquis, thinking that it would be necessary for him to set affairs in order at Cusco, as Fernando Pizarro was going to Spain, proceeded from Los Reyes to that city. It was not until he reached the Bridge of Abançay that he heard of the condemnation and execution of Almagro. Casting down his eyes, he remained for a long time looking on the ground, and weeping. There have been writers who supposed that the marquis had sanctioned Almagro's death; but there is no ground whatever for such a supposition, and there is no doubt that the tears shed by him for his old comrade were tears of genuine sorrow. Had he left Los Reyes earlier the mischief would have been averted. When he reached Cusco the marquis found both his brothers absent, as they were engaged in an important expedition among the Indians in the vicinity of the great lake of Titicaca. After his return from this enterprise Fernando Pizarro quitted Peru for Spain, in order to give his majesty an account of what had taken place; but several friends of Almagro, among them Diego de Alvarado, to whom Almagro had communicated the execution of his last wishes, had reached Spain before Fernando Pizarro. A suit was instituted against Fernando; and Diego de Alvarado challenged him to mortal combat, which was prevented by the sudden death of the challenger. Fernando Pizarro, however, was not freed from the suit. One of the principal charges against him was his having given liberty to Manco Inca, which was alleged to have been the cause of the Indian revolt.* In this matter, however, he was only so far to blame that he had been indulgent to the Inca, and had permitted him to go out of the city of Cusco to make certain sacrifices to his father. For the death of Almagro, which was the next great charge against Fernando Pizarro, his motives have already been given. Fernando Pizarro failed, however, to exculpate himself, and being deprived of the habit of Santiago, he was detained in prison at Medina del Campo for twenty-three years. Being at last freed, he retired to his estate in the country, where he died, having attained the great age of one hundred years. It was a melancholy ending for so renowned a man, and one who, to the best of his ability and understanding, had labored largely for the crown. Still it must be admitted that the events which followed in Peru formed a standing condemnation of the harshness of his conduct in prohibiting the appeal of Almagro to the Emperor, a harshness which in his long years of durance (how wearisome to so impatient a spirit!) he must have had ample time to understand and to regret.

Thus closes another act of the drama of the Conquest of Peru, which is one long tragedy, involving in a common ruin nearly all the personages concerned in it, the insignificant characters as well as the great actors in the scene.

* "*El mas principal* (y en que insistia el oficio Fiscal) era de aver dado libertad á Mango Inga, quitandole las prisiones; que dezian fue causa de todos los levantamientos de los Indios, y de aver sucedido tantas muertes, y grandes gastos de los Quintos de su Magestad, y de los particulares." — *Varones Ilustres del Nuevo Mundo*, por DON FERNANDO PIZARRO Y ORELLANA, p. 338. Madrid, 1639.

CHAPTER VIII.

THE MARQUIS AND THE MEN OF CHILI. — GONZALO PIZARRO DISCOVERS THE AMAZON.

THE marquis now remained the sole possessor of supreme authority throughout the empire of Peru. His brother Fernando, fearing lest Almagro's son should prove a centre of faction, had before his departure urged the marquis to send the young man to Spain; but Pizarro did not listen to this prudent advice. Neither was his treatment of the conquered party judicious in other respects. Not knowing the maxim of Machiavelli, that in such cases it is better to destroy than to impoverish, Pizarro left the men of Chili in poverty and idleness, but scorned to persecute them. Finding, however, that they resorted to the house of the young Almagro, the marquis was persuaded by his counselors to deprive him of his Indians. The men of Chili fell into the most abject poverty; and there is a story that seven of them who messed together had only one cloak among the seven. And these were men who had been accustomed to command, who had known many vicissitudes of prosperity and adversity, and were not likely to accept any misfortune as if it were final. One attempt Pizarro made to aid and favor these dangerous persons, but his overtures were coldly rejected by them. They were waiting, with a patient desire for vengeance, the arrival of a judge from Spain, named Vaca de Castro, from whom they expected the condemnation of those who had been concerned in the death of Almagro.

Meanwhile the marquis pursued his course of conquering new territories and founding new cities. He dispatched Pedro de Valdivia, his master of the camp, to Chili; and Valdivia, succeeding where Almagro

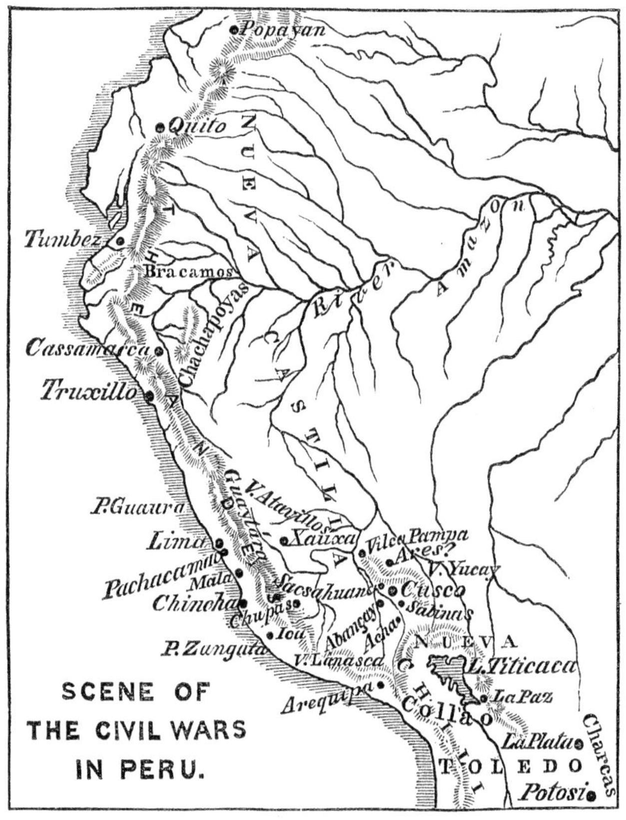

SCENE OF THE CIVIL WARS IN PERU.

had failed, has always been considered the conqueror of that country. The marquis sent his brother Gonzalo to the southern district of Collao, conquered that territory in which lay the mines of Potosi, and gave rich *repartimientos* (whose riches, however, were not then known) to his brothers Gonzalo and Martin, and their followers.

After all his conquests, it was but a strip of seaboard which Pizarro occupied and governed when compared with the boundless regions of South America, even to this day but sparsely occupied or ruled over by civilized man. The marquis, however, now originated an enterprise, which, leading men to the eastern side of the Andes, was to make them acquainted with regions of the New World far more extensive than had ever yet been discovered in any single enterprise by land. It does not seem to have been gold that on this occasion tempted the explorers. There was a region where cinnamon-trees were known to abound, and it was into this cinnamon country, neighboring to Quito, that the marquis sent his brother Gonzalo at the end of the year 1539.

In order to facilitate the enterprise, the marquis bestowed on his brother the government of Quito. Gonzalo commenced his march from Quito in January, 1540, with three hundred Spaniards and four thousand Indians. From the first the march was very difficult. Gonzalo and his men underwent great sufferings in passing the Cordillera Nevada, and many Indians were frozen to death in the journey over the mountains. The country the expedition then arrived at was uninhabited. They hastened through that, and entered a province named Sumaco, in or near which is the cinnamon country. Here it was that a great atrocity is stated to have been committed by Pizarro. He is said to have asked the natives whether in any other country there were any of these cinnamon-trees. They replied No, and that they knew nothing of any other country. The answer, though

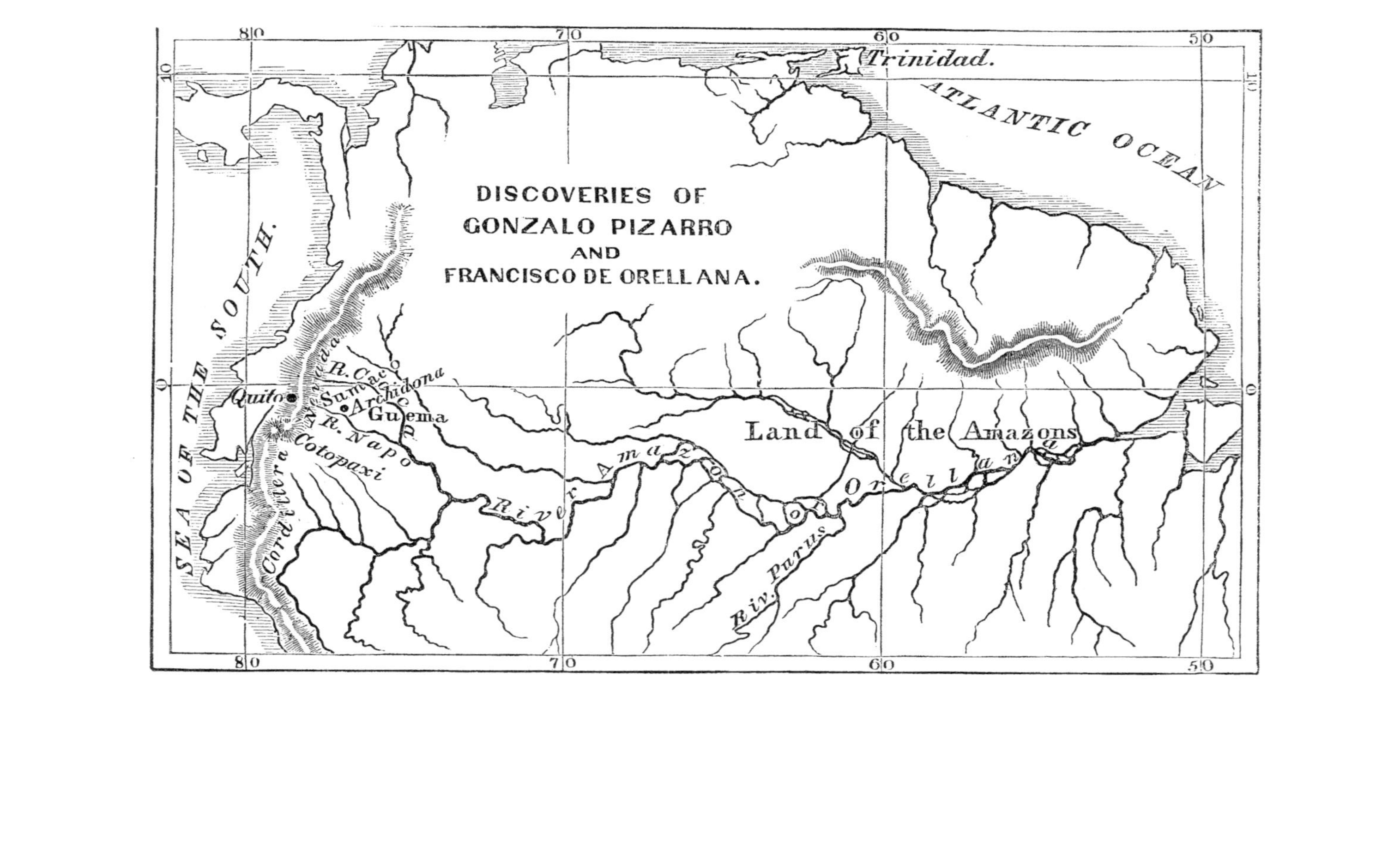

DISCOVERIES OF
GONZALO PIZARRO
AND
FRANCISCO DE ORELLANA.
SEA OF THE SOUTH.
ATLANTIC OCEAN
Trinidad.
Quito
Cordillera
Nevada
Cotopaxi
R. Napo
R. Coca
Sumaco
Archidona
Guema
River Amazon or Orellana
Riv. Purus
Land of the Amazons
80
70
60
50
10
0

it appears contradictory, was substantially true. As other tribes came to obtain cinnamon from them, they naturally inferred that there were no cinnamon-trees elsewhere, but they abided in their own forests, and knew nothing for certain of any other district. They added, that if Pizarro were to journey onward he would perhaps find those who could inform him. Being asked again the same question, they made the same answer; and it is alleged that then Gonzalo Pizarro, angry at not being able to obtain the information he required, tortured these poor Indians, burning some, and throwing others to his dogs to be torn in pieces.* Such accusations are to be received with much caution, because the Pizarros were afterward defeated rebels, and nothing is too bad to be alleged against such persons by those who write history for the conquering party. I do not find that the Pizarros were more cruel than other conquerors, whether Spanish, German, or English. Gonzalo Pizarro, to the end of his career, was much reverenced by the Indians; and Fernando Pizarro, according to the testimony of the Bishop of Cusco, was the most strenuous defender of the Indians of any conqueror that had appeared in those regions.†

* "Y porque siempre estaban en el mismo proposito, los mandó atar, í que con fuego los atormentasen; í no solo mataron algunos de aquellos tristes con fuego, pero despedaçados de los Perros."—HERRERA, *Hist. de las Indias*, dec. vi., lib. viii., cap. 6.

† Even such a careful writer as SOUTHEY has spoken of the Pizarros in a manner which is thoroughly unjustifiable, and which a larger acquaintance with Spanish conquerors would have prevented. The following are his words: "But when he asked what countries lay beyond them, and they could give no intelligence of El Dorado, the golden kingdom which he coveted, with the true spirit of a Pizarro, a name never to be uttered without abhorrence, he tortured them to extort a confession of what they did not know, and could have no motive to conceal; burnt some alive, and threw others alive to his dogs—blood-

At Sumaco Gonzalo left behind a great number of his men, while with those who were more active or less sickly he pushed on through a miserable region where his men had to endure great hardships, and to feed on herbs and roots. At last he entered a province and town called Coca, which was more civilized, and where he obtained food from the Indians. There he halted for nearly two months until his men had joined him from Sumaco. Near to this town of Coca there runs a great river, which is one of the branches of the Amazon.

Having somewhat recovered from their fatigue, the Spaniards resumed their march, keeping close to the banks of this river. Their route is traceable to this day by means of the natural wonders which marked the course of their journey. After proceeding for fifty leagues by the side of this river Coca, finding neither shallows which they could wade, nor any bridge by which to pass, they heard an awful noise, such as had never greeted the ears of men of the Old World before. Continuing their course for six leagues, the noise becoming more awful and bewildering as they advanced, they came upon a fall of the river which leapt from a rock more than two hundred fathoms in height. Their astonishment was great, but not greater than that with which, after marching forty leagues farther, they perceived all "this immensity of waters" passing through a narrow canal not more than twenty feet broad, hollowed out of the solid rock, the height of the chasm above the surface of the canal being not less than two hundred fathoms.*

hounds, which were trained in this manner to feed upon human flesh!" —*History of Brazil*, vol. i., chap. 4.

* "Y vieron con nueva admiracion, que toda aquella inmensidad de

Here was an opportunity for passing the river. They threw beams across the narrow chasm; put to flight, by means of their fire-arms, the Indians who defended the passage; and, forming a bridge, succeeded in bringing over safely all the army, the horses, and the baggage.

Thence they made their way into a land called Guema, utterly poor, sterile, and with few inhabitants. The food of the army consisted of herbs, roots, and the young buds of trees. The moist hot climate made terrible havoc among the expedition by sickness. Still they proceeded onward until they came into a region, not named, where the Indians were more civilized, possessing maize, being clothed in cotton garments, and having huts to shelter themselves from the rain.

Here Gonzalo Pizarro made a halt, and sent out scouts to examine the country. Their report was most unfavorable. They all returned with the same news that the land was full of forests, marshes, lakes, and ponds.

Pizarro had mistaken the nature of the country he was to traverse. All the horses in the world, in such a region, were not equal as a means of transport to one vessel. Pizarro resolved to build a brigantine, and to launch it upon the river, which, at the spot the camp then occupied, was not less than two leagues in breadth.

The difficulties were immense. To make the iron work for the vessel they had to construct a forge. The rain was incessant, and all their labor had to be

aguas se recogia, y passava por una canál de otra peña grandissima, tan estrecha, que de la una ribera á la otra no ay mas que veinte pies de ancho, y tan alta la peña tajada, que abria otras docientas braças, hasta el agua que corria en su profundidad."—RODRIGUEZ, *El Marañon y Amazonas*, lib. i., cap. 2.

executed under cover. The iron work was partly made out of the shoes of their horses; the pitch out of the resin from the trees; the tow out of their own linen, already half-rotted by the continual dampness. Their commander, Gonzalo Pizarro, a worthy brother of the great marquis, at least as regards perseverance, was always foremost in the work, whether it was cutting down timber, making charcoal, or laboring at the forge. Neither was any occupation too mean or too laborious for him; and men must follow when their chief is the first to do and to suffer.

The brigantine was at last completed, and, to the great joy of all, launched upon the river. Their chief difficulties were now, they thought, surmounted.

Though many had already perished from want of proper sustenance and by disease, the expedition probably still numbered more than two thousand men, and one brigantine was but a poor means of transport for such a company. The plan of Pizarro, therefore, was to convey in this vessel the sick and the baggage, while the rest pursued their way by the banks of the river. When they launched their brigantine, the distance they had advanced from Quito was about two hundred leagues. Their journey was still most difficult. Those who went on foot had often to cut their way with hatchets through the dense forests. Those who guided the brigantine had to be constantly watchful lest the force of the current should carry them beyond the ken of their companions. When the land march was impossible on one side of the river, the army passed over to the other in the brigantine, and also in four canoes they had made. These passages sometimes occupied two or three days. Hunger dogged their footsteps. Still they maintained this painful and laborious mode of journeying for two months, at the end of which time they learned from some Indians whom they met with that, at a distance of ten days' journey, there was a rich land abounding in provisions, where this great river they were upon joined another great river. The intelligence was true as regarded the junction of the rivers. They learned this fact partly by signs, and partly by some words which Pizarro's Indians could interpret, thus showing some community of language between these tribes bordering on the Amazon and the Indians of Peru.

Again a halt was proclaimed. Pizarro resolved to send the brigantine down the river until it should reach the spot where these two great rivers joined. There the sick and the baggage were to be left, and then the brigantine was to return with provisions to the main body of the expedition.

Gonzalo Pizarro, though in other respects a skillful leader, does not seem to have been a good calculator, else, seeing the strong current of the river, he might have computed the time that it would take for the brigantine to get back, and have appreciated the danger of his plan. Besides, on general grounds, it is seldom wise to part company from comrades in a perilous expedition of this kind. Pizarro, however, persevered in his resolve. He manned the brigantine with fifty soldiers, placing at their head a captain of good repute, named Francisco de Orellana. The voyage was commenced; and, without using oars or sails, they sped down the river, making eighty leagues in three days, at the end of which time they found themselves at the junction of the rivers. There is scarcely a doubt that this is the spot where the streams of the Napo and the Coca unite.*

* "This river of Napo flows from its source, between great masses of rock, and is not navigable until it reaches the port where the citi-

A distant land is always rich—in report at least; but this report is often found to be false, and so it was in the present instance. At the junction of the rivers there were neither people nor provisions. Orellana maintained, and probably was sincere in what he said, that it would take them a year to force their way up the river that distance which they had come down in three days, and that to make the attempt was useless both for themselves and for those they had left behind them. The thought of making himself independent of Pizarro, and of prosecuting the enterprise on his own account, may have entered at once into his mind; but, if so, he kept it for a time concealed, and the position he and his men were in was such as to excuse in some measure, though not by any means to justify, their not attempting to retrace their steps and succor their companions in arms. Nearly all of Orellana's company at first resisted his suggestions. At the head of the malcontents were a priest named Gaspar de Carvajal, and a young gentleman named Hernan Sanchez de Vargas. But Orellana's self-favoring views were sure to gain by each day's delay, as the difficulty of acting generously became more and more apparent. Ultimately he gained over the main body of his men, left Hernan Sanchez de Vargas in that desert spot, renounced his commission from Gonzalo Pizarro, caused himself to be elected captain by his soldiers, and stole away to fame.

zens of Archidona have established the hamlet for their Indians. Here it becomes more humane and less warlike, and consents to bear a few ordinary canoes on its shoulders, conveying provisions; but from this point, four or five leagues, it does not forget its former fury until it unites with the River Coca. The united stream has great depth, and becomes tranquil, offering a good passage for larger vessels. This is the junction of rivers where Francisco de Orellana, with his party, built the barque with which he navigated this River of the Amazons."—*Translation of* ACUÑA'S *Discovery of the Great River of the Amazons*, by CLEMENTS R. MARKHAM; Hakluyt Society, 1859.

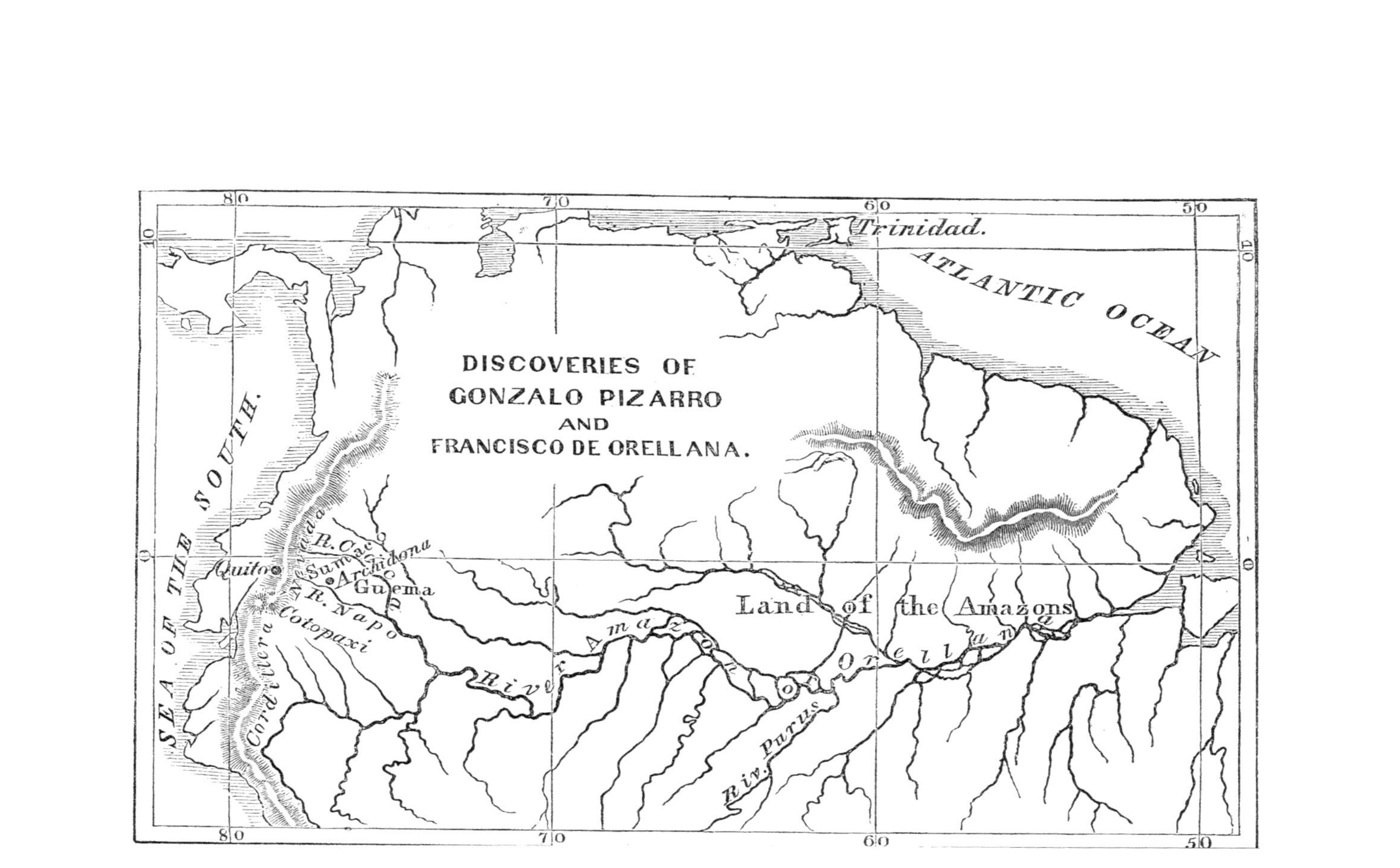
DISCOVERIES OF
GONZALO PIZARRO
AND
FRANCISCO DE ORELLANA.
SEA OF THE SOUTH.
ATLANTIC OCEAN
Trinidad.
Quito
Cordillera
Nevada
Cotopaxi
R. Napo
R. Coca
Sumaco
Archidona
Guema
River Amazon or Orellana
Land of the Amazons
Riv. Purus
80
70
60
50
10
0

In the course of his voyage he came upon some tribes where the women fought by the side of their husbands, and hence he called that country the Land of the Amazons. Swiftly the brigantine bore its crew onward. They were the first men to traverse that vast continent; and at the end of their voyage of two thousand five hundred miles, they found themselves in the Atlantic, nearly in the same degree of latitude at which they had started. Thence they made their way to Trinidad, where Orellana, enriched with the gold and emeralds that had been placed on board the brigantine, purchased a vessel, and sailed for Spain. He went to court, procured a royal license for securing the territories he had discovered, and fitted out an expedition for that purpose. The great river, now known by the name of the Amazon, was then called, after its discoverer, the Orellana. That traitor, however, did not live to profit by his discovery, but died on his voyage outward.

Meanwhile Gonzalo Pizarro, finding that Orellana did not return, constructed some canoes and rafts, and, partly journeying by land and partly by water, contrived in two months' time to reach the junction of the rivers. He had conjectured that the strength of the current was the cause of Orellana's not returning, but he hoped to find him established with abundance of provisions at the appointed spot. There was, however, but one man who came to greet Pizarro, a wasted figure, which proved to be that of the loyal young hidalgo, Hernan Sanchez de Vargas, whom Orellana had cruelly left to perish. From him Pizarro learned the full details of Orellana's treachery, and that he would never see again the brigantine which had cost them all so much labor to construct, and which, throughout their misfortunes, had been their chief source of solace and of hope.

CHAPTER IX.

THE CONSPIRACY OF ALMAGRO'S FRIENDS. — THE MARQUIS PIZARRO IS MURDERED BY THE MEN OF CHILI.

LEAVING Gonzalo Pizarro at this sad juncture of his affairs, the history returns to his brother, the marquis, at Los Reyes, who was in still greater peril. All this time the governor had done nothing to soothe or to destroy his untiring enemies, "the men of Chili." The head of the defeated faction was a resolute and clever soldier, named Juan de Rada, who had been major-domo in the household of the mariscal. This man took the young Almagro, a youth of eighteen or nineteen, under his guardianship, and entirely managed the affairs of the men of Chili. They lived together in Los Reyes; and what little each man could get was brought to Juan de Rada to provide for the sustenance of the whole body. They had taken care to dispatch to the judge who was coming from Spain an important hidalgo of their own body, Don Alonzo de Montemayor. He left Los Reyes to meet Vaca de Castro at the beginning of April, 1541.

A great disappointment came upon the men of Chili in hearing, not from their own embassador, but probably from the friends of the marquis, that this judge was not intrusted with powers to condemn, but only with a commission to inquire, and to transmit the result of his inquiries to Spain. They had hoped to find an avenger in him.

The men of Chili were no longer few in number. There had gradually come into Los Reyes about two hundred of them—needy, disfavored, discontented men. Insults began to be interchanged between the rival factions — insults, as mostly happened in these colonies, of a grotesque and dramatic nature. One day, early in the morning, the populace of Los Reyes were amused by seeing three ropes suspended in the public pillory in the great square. The upper end of one rope was so placed as to point to the marquis's palace, while the house of his secretary, Juan Picado, and that of his alcalde mayor, Doctor Velasquez, were pointed at in a similar manner by the ends of the other two ropes. The marquis's friends saw in this insult the handiwork of the men of Chili, and begged the marquis to punish them. The good-natured Pizarro said that they were already sufficiently punished in being poor, and conquered, and ridden over. The Spanish blood of his followers, however, could not brook the insult they had received, or desist from attempting to reply to it. Accordingly, the populace of Los Reyes were again amused by seeing Antonio Picado ride through the street where the young Almagro lived, wearing a cap adorned with a gold medal that had a silver fig embossed upon it, and a motto in these words, "For the men of Chili." Great was the wrath of the followers of Almagro at this absurd insult.

The rumor that the men of Chili meditated something desperate was rife even among the Indians, and the marquis's friends warned him of his danger. Besides, it was noticed that Juan de Rada was buying a coat of mail. On the other hand, it was observed by the men of Chili that Pizarro had been purchasing lances.

Juan de Rada was sent for by Pizarro. The governor was in his garden, looking at some orange-trees, when the leader of the men of Chili called upon him. "What is this, Juan de Rada," said the marquis, "that they tell me of your buying arms to kill me?" "It is true, my lord, that I have bought two cuirasses and a coat of mail to defend myself." "Well," replied the marquis, "but what moves you to buy armor now more than at any other time?" "Because they tell us, and it is notorious, that your lordship is buying lances to slay us all. Let your lordship finish with us; for, having commenced by destroying the head, I do not know why you should have any respect for the feet. It is also said that your lordship intends to slay the judge who is coming from Spain; but, if your intention is such, and you are determined to put to death the party of Almagro, at least spare Don Diego, for he is innocent. Banish him, and I will go with him wherever fortune may please to carry us."

The marquis was enraged at these words. "Who has made you believe such great villainy and treachery of me?" he exclaimed; "I never thought of such a thing, and I am more desirous than you that this judge should come, who already would be here if he had embarked in the galleon which I sent for him. As to the story of the spears, the other day I went hunting, and among the whole party there was not one who had a spear. I ordered my servants to buy one, and they have bought four. Would to God, Juan de Rada, the judge were here, so that these things might have an end, and that God may make the truth manifest."

"By heaven, my lord," replied Juan de Rada, somewhat softened by the governor's response, "but they have made me get into debt for more than five hundred *pesos*, which I have spent in buying armor, and so I have a coat of mail to defend myself against whoever may wish to slay me." "Please God, Juan de Rada, I shall do nothing of the kind," responded the marquis. The conference ended thus, and Juan de Rada was going, when Pizarro's jester, who was standing by, said, "Why don't you give him some of these oranges?" As they were the first that were grown in that country, they were much esteemed. "You say well," replied the marquis; and he gathered six of them, and gave them to Juan de Rada, adding that he should tell him if he wanted any thing. They then separated amicably, Juan de Rada kissing the governor's hands as he took leave.

This interview reassured Pizarro, and did not divert the conspirators from their designs. Again and again Pizarro was warned. Twice he received intelligence from a certain clerigo in whom one of the conspirators had confided. The second time the marquis told the clerigo that the report had no truth in it, that it was "an Indian saying,"* and that the man who had made the pretended revelation did so to get a horse, or some other present. So saying, he went back to dinner; but it was observed that he could not eat a mouthful. That same evening, just as he was going to bed, one of his pages told him that, through the whole city, the rumor ran that on the following day the men of Chili were going to murder him. "These things are not for you to talk about, you little rascal," was all that the marquis replied.

On the following morning some persons conveyed the same information as the page had done. Pizarro, seemingly wrapped in an imperturbable security, contented himself with giving orders, in a lukewarm

* "Dicho de Indios."

manner, to his alcalde mayor to arrest the principal men of Chili. It was on this occasion, or, perhaps, upon some previous one, that the alcalde mayor replied that his lordship need have no fear as long as he had the rod of office in his hand. This officer seems to have been as blindly confident as his superior.

The next day was Sunday. Pizarro did not go to mass, probably from some fear of being attacked. When mass had ended, the principal inhabitants called upon the marquis, but, after paying their respects, went away, leaving him with his brother Martin, his alcalde mayor, and Francisco de Chaves, an intimate friend.

Meanwhile the conspirators were collected together in the house of Don Diego Almagro. Nothing was resolved upon as to the day on which they were to make the attack, and Juan de Rada was sleeping, when a certain Pedro de San Millan entered, and exclaimed, "What are you about? In two hours time they are coming to cut us to pieces, for so the Treasurer Riquelme has just said." This was probably a version of the fact that Pizarro had ordered the arrest of the principal conspirators.

There is a strong family likeness in conspiracies. For a time there is much indecision, until some imminent peril to the conspirators hastens the result, and determines the hour of the deed. Juan de Rada sprang from his bed, armed himself, and addressed a short speech to his followers, urging them to avenge the death of Almagro, to aspire to dominion in Peru, and, if these motives weighed not with them, at least to strike a blow in order to protect themselves against a pressing danger. This speech was received with acclamations, and immediate action was resolved upon. The first thing the conspirators did was to hang out a white flag from the window as a signal to their accomplices that they must arm and come to their assistance. They then sallied forth. It is probable, as it was at midday, that there were not many persons in the streets or in the great square. The conspirators shouted "Down with the tyrant traitor who has caused the judge to be killed whom the king has sent." The few persons who noticed the march of this furious band merely observed to one another, "They are going to kill Picado or the marquis." As they entered the great square, one of them, named Gomez Perez, made a slight detour in order to avoid a little pool of water which by chance had been spilled there from some conduit. Juan de Rada splashed through the pool, went straight to the dainty person, and said to him, "We are going to bathe ourselves in human blood, and you hesitate to dip your feet in water. You are not a man for this business: go back;" nor did he suffer him to proceed farther.

The conspirators gained the house of Pizarro without opposition. It was strong, having two courts and a great gate. The marquis was not entirely surprised. His brother Martin, the Alcalde Doctor Velasquez, and Francisco de Chaves, had dined with him. The dinner was just over, when some of his Indians rushed in to give him notice of the approach of the men of Chili. He ordered Francisco de Chaves to shut to the door of the hall, and of the apartment in which they were. That officer, supposing that it was some riot among the soldiers, which his authority would quell, went out to meet them, and found the conspirators coming up the staircase. They fell upon him at once, slew him, and threw the body down the stairs. Those who were in the dining hall, chiefly servants, rushed out to ascertain what was the matter; but, seeing Francisco de Chaves lying dead, fled back, and threw themselves out of the window, which opened upon the garden. Among them was Doctor Velasquez, who, as he leaped from the window, held his wand of office in his mouth, so that it was afterward jestingly said that he was right in telling his master, the marquis, that he was safe as long as he, Doctor Velasquez, held the rod of office in his hands.

The conspirators pressed through the hall to the room where the marquis himself was. He had found time to throw off his purple robe, to put on a cuirass, and to seize a spear. In this extremity there were by his side his half-brother, Francis Martin de Alcantara, a gentleman named Don Gomez de Luna (not hitherto mentioned), and two pages. Pizarro was then about seventy years old. He had commanded small companies of Spaniards, making head on the field against innumerable Indians, and had felt no doubt about the result. But now, with two men and two lads, he had to contend for his life against nineteen practiced soldiers. The heroic courage of the marquis did not desert him at this last moment. He fought valiantly, while he denounced, in the boldest words, the treachery and the villainy of his assailants. They only exclaimed, "Kill him! kill him! let us not waste our time." Thus the mortal contest raged for a short period. At length Juan de Rada thrust one of his companions forward upon Pizarro's spear, and gained an entrance into the room. The combat was now soon closed. Martin de Alcantara, Don Gomez de Luna, and the two pages, fell slain by the side of Pizarro, who still continued to defend himself. At last a wound in the throat brought him to the ground. While lying there, he made the sign of a cross upon the ground, and kissed it. He was still alive, and was asking for a confessor, when some base fellow dashed a jug upon his prostrate face; and, on receiving that contemptible blow, the patient endurer of wearisome calamities, the resolute discoverer of long-hidden lands, the stern conqueror of a powerful nation, breathed his last.

CHAPTER X.

ARRIVAL OF VACA DE CASTRO.—HE DEFEATS THE ALMAGRISTAS AT CHUPAS.—RETURN OF GONZALO PIZARRO FROM THE AMAZON.

THE conspirators, with their swords in their hands, rushed out into the great square, shouting "Live the king; the tyrant is dead; let the land be placed in the hands of justice." The rest of the men of Chili gathered round their comrades. Diego de Almagro was set on horseback, and proclaimed governor. The houses of the marquis, of his brother, and of the secretary were plundered. The inhabitants were ordered to keep within doors. The public treasure was seized upon, and the wands of office were taken away from the alcaldes who had been appointed by the late governor.

The bishop, and the monks of the Order of Mercy, did what they could to allay the tumult, and to render the proceedings of the conspirators less dangerous to their fellow-townsmen. The monks brought out "the Host," and went in procession with it through the streets.

Finally, a meeting of the Town Council was called. Almagro was received as Governor of Peru, and dispatches were sent off to the principal cities announcing the fact.

This revolution in favor of the Almagristas did not take place without considerable opposition in Los Reyes, in Cusco, and in other places; but this opposition was greatly borne down by the vigor of the principal conspirator, Juan de Rada.

Meanwhile the long-expected judge, Vaca de Castro, arrived in Popayan, in the northern parts of Peru. His detention, upon which so much misfortune depended, had been caused by the loss of an anchor in his voyage from Panamá to Peru. Then commenced a series of miserable transactions throughout the kingdom, such as mostly happens when the supreme power is handed from faction to faction, each faction having attained its momentary superiority by some signal deed of violence. "I could wish," says the historian HERRERA, "that this part of my history could tell of battles well fought out, of warlike stratagems, of sieges, and of all those military events which take place in just wars, instead of disloyalties, homicides, robberies, and other crimes."

The king's authority, however, in the person of his judge, Vaca de Castro, ultimately prevailed. This was likely to be the case, as Vaca de Castro had not only the advantage of the king's name, but also the good wishes of the Pizarro faction, some of whom were to be found in every town and district. Vaca de Castro moved down the country to the south, his army increasing as he went along, until he entered the valley of Chupas, where he found himself in close proximity to the rebel army. Vaca de Castro sent a message to the young Almagro, requiring him to disband his army and join the royal standard, promising a full pardon if he should obey this summons. At the same time, however, he sent a common soldier, disguised as an Indian, with letters for some of the principal persons in Almagro's camp. The ground was covered with snow, and the tracks of this spy were observed.

He was seized and put to death. Almagro complained bitterly of this treasonable practice on the part of Vaca de Castro: that, while he was treating openly with him, he should endeavor secretly to seduce his

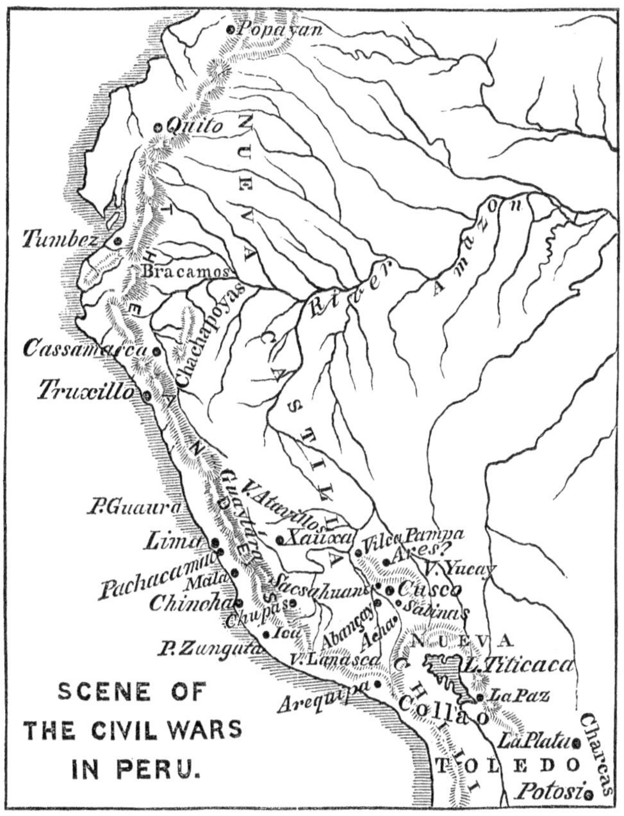

SCENE OF THE CIVIL WARS IN PERU.

officers. To the message of Vaca de Castro he replied that, as long as that officer was surrounded by his enemies, the Pizarristas, he could not obey him, and that he would not disband his army until he should receive a pardon from his majesty, signed by his own hand.

Vaca de Castro saw that there was no use for farther negotiation, and that the question at issue must be decided by a battle. There was, however, some reluctance on the part of his own captains to come to an engagement. Not that they feared the young Almagro; but they doubted whether, if they gained the battle, it would be reckoned as good service by his majesty, seeing that Fernando Pizarro, who had gained the battle of Salinas, was now lying in prison in Spain.

To remove their doubts, Vaca de Castro pronounced sentence against Diego de Almagro, condemning him as a traitor and a rebel; and, having signed this sentence in the presence of all his principal commanders, they were satisfied.

The next day the battle, which is called the battle of Chupas, commenced. The forces were very skillfully arranged on both sides. Pedro de Suarez, a soldier practiced in the wars of Italy, ordered the battle on the young Almagro's side, and he placed the artillery, in which arm the rebels were very strong, in an excellent position. Pedro de Candia, one of the early conquerors and companions of the Marquis Pizarro, was appointed captain of the artillery.

On Vaca de Castro's side, Francisco de Carvajal, an officer also versed in European warfare, and of whom much more will be heard hereafter, was the sargento mayor, and marshaled the royal army.

The fight then began, but the artillery on the rebel side did no execution, as the balls went over the heads of the enemy. Pedro de Candia was suspected of treachery. It is said that he had assured Vaca de Castro that the artillery should do the royal forces no harm. The young Almagro rushed toward the traitor, slew him with his lance, and, dismounting from his horse, sprung upon one of the cannon, ordering at the same time that it should be discharged. By the weight of his body it was depressed, and the shot was so successful that it made a long line in the advancing forces of Vaca de Castro, from the vanguard to the rear-guard. The ranks, however, of Vaca de Castro's men closed up, Francisco de Carvajal placing himself in front of the opening which the cannon ball had made. Being a very corpulent person, he was enabled to encourage his men by saying that he offered twice as broad a mark as any one of them for a cannon ball, and that he was not afraid of the enemy's artillery, saying which he took off and threw upon the ground his coat of mail and his morion.

Meanwhile the young Almagro and some of his captains resolved, instead of awaiting the enemy's attack, to advance upon them. Now was the occasion when the prudent sagacity of Juan de Rada was most needed. But he had died some time before at Xauxa, and there was no one to restrain the fervent ardor of Almagro and his captains. They even got in front of their own artillery. This movement so disgusted and infuriated the old soldier, Pedro de Suarez, that he set spurs to his horse, and went over to Vaca de Castro's camp. It is said that he shouted in a loud voice to the young Almagro, "If your lordship had followed my advice, you would have had the victory to-day, whereas now you must lose it. I do not intend to be conquered; and, since your lordship does not wish that I should be a conqueror in your camp, I choose to be one in the other camp."

Pedro de Suarez was right in his anticipations. The

armies met; and, though the victory was for some time well contested, the Royalist forces at last prevailed. It was late in the day when the battle commenced, and it was not ended until nine o'clock in the evening. Almagro's men had worn white scarfs over their armor: Vaca de Castro's were in red. Favored by the obscurity of evening, several of the vanquished party changed scarfs with the Royalists, who lay dead or dying on the field; and, thus disguised, contrived to escape. The young Almagro was among these fugitives; but he was afterward captured by Vaca de Castro, who, by the advice of a council which he summoned for the purpose, condemned the young man to death. Vaca de Castro was then universally acknowledged as Governor of Peru.

The new governor's great difficulty was how to deal with a very powerful personage who had recently appeared upon the scene. This was Gonzalo Pizarro. When last spoken of, he was in the desert region where the rivers Napo and Coca unite, astounded but not utterly disheartened by the cruel desertion of Orellana. After undergoing almost incredible sufferings and privations, Gonzalo Pizarro made his way back to the vicinity of Quito. Some of the inhabitants of that town, hearing of his arrival, came out to meet him; and with a strange kind of delicacy, truly Spanish, seeing the half-naked, miserable figures that Gonzalo and his band presented, these good friends threw off their own clothes, strove to make themselves look as miserable as the men they came to welcome, and re-entered the town in company with them.

Gonzalo's claim to power as the brother of the late marquis was considerable; and, having some of the same nobility of nature, he was justly looked up to as the head of the Pizarro faction. The governor, Vaca de Castro, naturally did not wish to have any thing to do with either faction. He sent for Pizarro; and partly by a show of force, partly by a noble open way of dealing with him, persuaded him to retire to his estate near La Plata, where he resided with considerable magnificence, having, as HERRERA remarks, revenues larger than those of the Archbishop of Toledo.

This difficulty being thus surmounted, Vaca de Castro could give his attention to the affairs of government. He made several wise regulations about the *repartimientos* of the Indians; he strove to bring the population into communication by means of the royal roads; and, in a word, the land had some short breathing time of peace. Events, however, were occurring at this time in Spain which were to bring about a state of anarchy in Peru such as it had not yet known, and were in great measure to change the destinies of the human race throughout the vast continent of South America.

BOOK XVIII.

THE NEW LAWS.

CHAPTER I.

THE NEW LAWS.—BLASCO NUÑEZ VELA IS SENT AS VICEROY TO PERU TO ENFORCE THESE LAWS.

CHAPTER II.

DISMAY OF THE SPANISH COLONISTS IN PERU.—VIOLENCE OF THE VICEROY.—THE MURDER OF THE FACTOR ILLAN SUAREZ DE CARVAJAL.

CHAPTER III.

THE AUDITORS SEIZE UPON THE PERSON OF THE VICEROY, AND EMBARK HIM FOR SPAIN.—GONZALO PIZARRO IS APPOINTED GOVERNOR OF PERU.—DEFEAT AND DEATH OF THE VICEROY.

CHAPTER I.

THE NEW LAWS. — BLASCO NUÑEZ VELA IS SENT AS VICEROY TO PERU TO ENFORCE THESE LAWS.

IN early American history Las Casas is, undoubtedly, the principal figure. His extraordinary longevity has something to do with this pre-eminence. Very few men can be named who have taken a large and active part in public affairs for such an extended period as seventy years. Las Casas was an important person, in reference to all that concerned the Indies, during the reigns of Ferdinand the Catholic, of Philip the Handsome, of his son Charles the Fifth, and of Philip the Second.* Upon the mind of Charles the Fifth Las Casas seems to have had a peculiar influence. The Emperor had known him from his own boyhood; and such a discerning person as Charles the Fifth could not fail to have appreciated the character of Las Casas. He knew him to be a thoroughly disinterested man. It must have been with a smile that Charles read, in private letters, accusations of a personal nature directed against Las Casas by disappointed colonists, the Emperor well knowing how Las Casas, in his times of utmost poverty (when Charles, fresh from Flanders, used to call him "Micer Bartolomé"), had refused pecuniary aid, and abjured all thought of personal advancement.

* Even while Philip the Second was in England, Las Casas was in correspondence with the celebrated Carranza, who accompanied Philip as his confessor.

It will be recollected that Las Casas, after peaceably conquering and converting the province of Tuzulutlan, had gone to Mexico, and thence to the court of Spain, where he had been detained by the Council of the Indies, who wished to profit by his knowledge of Indian affairs. It may be imagined with what force he could then speak in favor of his Indians, having for once a great feat of practical success to appeal to in the peaceful conquest of Tuzulutlan—he who had never been daunted when the course of affairs had been apparently most decisive against him.

It was at the end of the year 1538 that Las Casas reached the court of Spain. The Emperor was absent in Germany, contending against Luther and the German princes who favored the views of the great Reformer. Las Casas employed his time in writing the work which, of all his works, has become most celebrated, namely, *The Destruction of the Indies.* It was afterward translated into several languages, and has been read throughout Europe. It gives a short account of what had taken place in each colony, and is one of the boldest works that ever issued from the press. At that time it was not published, but was only submitted to the Emperor and his ministers. It is possible that in this, its first form, it was a still more daring production than it appears to be now, for in the printed copies there is not a single name given of the persons inculpated. These are generally spoken of as this or that "tyrant." The work was not published in its present form until twelve years afterward, when it was addressed, with an epistle dedicatory, to Philip, the heir to the throne.

The above, however, was not the only, or perhaps the most important work, which Las Casas wrote about this time for the information of the Emperor and the Council of the Indies. He drew up a Memorial, which is in itself an elaborate work, consisting of twenty reasons, to prove that the Indians ought not to be given to the Spaniards in *encomienda*, in fee, in vassalage, or in any other manner. It appears from the title that this work was written by the Emperor's command, for the information of a certain great Junta which was to be held at Valladolid in the year 1542. There is one very striking passage in the Memorial, in which Las Casas states that the Indians were subjected to four masters, namely, first, his majesty the Emperor; secondly, their own caciques; thirdly, their *encomendero;* and, fourthly, his manager, "who," as Las Casas said, "weighed upon them more than a hundred towers."*

In all his pleadings for the injured Indians, Las Casas was greatly aided by the Dominican monks who had accompanied him from Mexico. He had need of all the aid that he could muster, for several of the great personages of the council were opposed to his views. Indeed, there was much to be said against them. In those days, when national debts had not been invented, it was a most difficult thing to provide compensation for vested interests. The path of reform has been greatly smoothed in modern times by the power of providing in a satisfactory manner for those who are injured by any great public measure. The riches of Spain, or indeed of all the countries that Charles the Fifth ruled over, could hardly have furnished funds to satisfy the conquerors of the New

* "Por manera que tienen quatro señores: Á vuestra Magestad, y á sus Caciques, y al que estan encomendados, y al estanciero que agora le acabo de dezir, que pesa mas que cien torres. Y podemos añadir con verdad a quantos moços y negros tiene el amo, porque todos no saben sino dessollarlos, oprimillos, y roballos."—*Veynte Razones*, p. 181, Sevilla, 1552.

World for the loss of their *encomiendas*. When a single conqueror, such as Gonzalo Pizarro, is stated to have possessed revenues larger than those of the Archbishopric of Toledo (one of the wealthiest sees at that time in the world), it is inconceivable that the Emperor's subjects in Spain, Italy, or Flanders would have suffered themselves to be taxed to provide adequate pensions or gratuities for all the conquerors of Mexico and Peru. Notwithstanding these difficulties, the views of Las Casas prevailed at this period. A great Junta was held at Valladolid. This Junta was but a continuation of other Juntas that had been held before upon the same subject. It consisted of several of the most important men in Spain. The members were the Cardinal Archbishop of Seville, who was President of the Council of the Indies; Don Sebastian Ramirez, who had been President of the Audiencia at Mexico; the governor of Prince Philip of Spain, the Emperor's secretary Francisco de los Cobos, the Count of Osorno, with several doctors of civil and ecclesiastical law. The Memorial of Las Casas, containing his sixteen remedies for the Indies, was laid before this council. What their conclusions were does not exactly appear, but it is probable that they were most favorable to the views of Las Casas. The Emperor, however, consulted his great Council of State and the Cardinal Archbishop of Seville separately, obtaining written opinions from them on the points at issue. Charles the Fifth was very much pressed at that time by European affairs. The King of France had brought five armies into the field against the Emperor. The Dauphin was besieging Perpignan. Embassadors from England had arrived while Charles was at Valladolid; and he was afterward obliged to proceed to Barcelona, to confer with his admiral, the celebrated Andrew Doria. The Emperor found time, however, to give some attention to the affairs of the Indies; for, while at Barcelona, he summoned another Junta, smaller, but perhaps more important than that held at Valladolid. The celebrated statesman Granvella, the Cardinal Archbishop of Seville, Doctor Guevara, Doctor Figueroa, the Emperor's confessor, and Francisco de los Cobos, were present at this Junta. Before them all the papers were laid, including, no doubt, the opinion pronounced by the former Junta and by the great Council of State. There is reason to think that this Junta was nearly divided in opinion; and the Emperor's secretary has left on record his objection to the abolition of *encomiendas.* Granvella, Dr. Figueroa, and the Emperor's confessor were, it appears, in favor of the views of Las Casas.* Charles the Fifth adopted their opinions; or, as it may be stated with more probability, received from them a confirmation of his own.†

The result was, that one of the most celebrated bodies of laws that was ever framed came forth under the sanction of the Emperor and his Council of the Indies, which laws were framed so entirely according to the spirit of Las Casas that they might have been dictated word for word by him. They have been known for generations by the name of the New Laws.

The principal clause, which affected the rights and interests of all the conquerors in the New World, is the following: "That after the death of the conquerors of the Indies, the *repartimientos* of Indians which

* At least they are not mentioned as dissentients.

† "El emperador como catholico y christianissimo, fue facilmente del frayle persuadido."—FERNANDEZ, *Hist. del Perú*, parte i., lib. i., cap. 1.

had been given to them in *encomienda*, in the name of his majesty,* should not pass in succession to their wives or children, but should be placed immediately under the king, the said wives and children receiving a certain portion of the usufruct for their sustenance."

Another most important clause was this: that the bishops, monastic bodies, governors, presidents, auditors, corregidors, and other officers of his majesty, both past and present, who held *repartimientos*, should be obliged to renounce them. It was well argued by the colonists that the foregoing clause was a punishment to men of good repute. As men of good repute, held to be trustworthy by their fellow-citizens, they had been appointed to certain offices, and now the possession of these offices was to have something of a penal character attached to it.

There was a third clause, especially affecting Peru, namely, that all the *encomenderos* of Peru, who were inculpated in the rebellious and factious proceedings of Pizarro and Almagro, should be deprived of their *encomiendas*.

Now it would be difficult to say that any person of note in Peru had not been concerned in those deplorable transactions. And in New Spain, the second clause, affecting those who had held offices under the crown, must have proved a large sentence of confiscation; so that, to use the words of a contemporary historian, "Those two clauses alone were as a dragnet which comprehended all the Indies."†

But this was not all. Personal service of the In-

* These words were carefully introduced to show whence the right had arisen.

† "De suerte que solas estas dos leyes eran como red barredera, que comprehendian todas las Indias."—FERNANDEZ, *Hist. del Perú*, parte i., lib. i., cap. 1.

dians was to be abolished altogether, and a fixed sum was to be settled for each *encomendero* to receive from his Indians, so that he might be unable to overtask them.

Too much praise can hardly be awarded to the humane intentions of those who promoted and framed this great code for the Indies. Too much censure can hardly be given to their utter want of foresight and worldly wisdom. Few people, however, know how to be moderate in reducing their opinions into action at the moment when those opinions are triumphant, and certainly Las Casas was not one of those few persons. The wonder is, that so cautious a monarch as Charles the Fifth should ever have consented to such untempered legislation. His sincerity in the matter is manifest. Persons of weight and ability were authorized by the court to proceed to the Indies and to see that these laws were carried into effect. Francisco Tello de Sandoval was sent as visitor to New Spain. Blasco Nuñez Vela was sent to Peru as viceroy and president of an *Audiencia*, with four auditors under him, their names being Cepeda, Zarate, Alvarez, and Tejada.

Before entering upon their proceedings in Peru, it must be related what the visitor, Tello de Sandoval, was able to accomplish in Mexico, where he had to act in concert with the prudent, humane, and experienced viceroy, Mendoza.

No caution was observed in communicating the intelligence to the New World that such laws, affecting deeply the interests of every colonist, had been framed. Indeed, it is not likely that when they were once known to Las Casas, they would be long in reaching the colonies through the agency of the monastic orders, which in those ages were the great means of conveying intelligence from country to country. Before the arrival of Don Tello de Sandoval, all the Spanish inhabitants of Mexico were in despair at what they had heard of the nature of the laws which he was coming to enforce. They had even resolved to go out of the city to meet him, clad in mourning robes as at a funeral. The wise viceroy, Mendoza, dissuaded them from this discourteous demonstration. When, however, Don Tello de Sandoval did arrive, his authority, combined with that of the viceroy, only sufficed to prevent the people from breaking out into open tumult. The visitor soon saw that it was impossible to enforce the new laws, and he prudently consented that an appeal should be sent to his majesty the Emperor against them.

If such was the result in well-ordered, long-colonized, discreetly-governed Mexico, originally conquered and settled by such a master of the arts of conquest and government as Cortez, what was to be expected in Peru, a country recently conquered, and torn by contending factions?

The *encomiendas* in Peru were at this time held by a tenure which was called in the Indies "the law of succession," by which the *encomiendas* were to be held for two lives, namely, those of the original conqueror and of his son. Moreover, it is very probable that the conquerors imagined that the law of succession gave the *encomienda* for two lives after the death of the first grantee, namely, for those of his son and his grandson. This was an entire mistake; but even a man so well informed as Las Casas had fallen into that error. This law had been passed as recently as 1536; and now, in 1542, these turbulent conquerors were to be told that there was no inheritance for their children and their grandchildren, but that some allowance was to be made to their wives and children when their hardly-earned possessions should, on their death, lapse to the crown. Besides, as before stated, nearly all of them had been concerned on one side or the other in the feud between the Pizarros and the Almagros, and thus their *encomiendas* were already liable to confiscation. Charles the Fifth seems indeed to have been an enthusiast, as perhaps he was, in thinking that such laws could be adopted peaceably in a distant colony.

Moreover, the person chosen to introduce this new code into Peru was as unfitted, both by his virtues and his defects, for the difficult task as could well be imagined. Blasco Nuñez Vela, the new viceroy, had held the honorable appointment of Inspector General of the Guards of Castile. In character he was an upright, narrow-minded, sincere, intemperate, loyal man. He was a favorite courtier of Charles the Fifth's, having hitherto executed his majesty's commands with a loving obedience and great exactitude. He was handsome, of noble presence, skilled in knightly arts, very pious, and very harsh. He perhaps resembled Bobadilla, whose unfortunate appointment by Ferdinand and Isabella had caused so much mischief in the early times of the Spanish Conquest.

Blasco Nuñez Vela took no delight in his appointment to the supreme command in Peru. He would much rather have remained in Spain with his wife and children; but, as he told the Emperor, since he had been born with the obligation to serve his majesty, he would do that which he commanded. The Emperor doubtless thought that as the main evil which had hitherto manifested itself in his colonies was that his officers had consulted their own interest and the interest of their friends, he could not do wrong in sending a viceroy to Peru who would neither favor himself nor his friends, but would be equally severe with all men, and would obey with an Eastern obedience the commands received from home. Charles the Fifth was to discover that want of judgment in his representative might be more dangerous to the state than even a corrupt subserviency to self-interest.

Blasco Nuñez Vela set sail from San Lucar on the 1st of November, 1543, arrived at Nombre de Dios on the 10th of January, 1544, and from thence went across the Isthmus to the town of Panamá. When there he lost no time in commencing to execute his instructions. At that town there were many Indians of service, as they were called, who had been brought from Peru. The viceroy caused them all to be sent back to their own provinces at the expense of their masters. These Indians amounted in number to three hundred. They were sent back in a vessel of insufficient tonnage, and many of them died on the voyage.

While Blasco Nuñez was at Panamá he was informed of the bitter feelings with which the Spanish inhabitants of Peru had heard of the new laws, and of the great danger there would be in carrying them into execution. This information, however, did not quell his ardor. Blasco Nuñez appears to have acted throughout like a fanatic, but it was with the fanaticism of obedience to the royal orders.* It was in

* As another illustration of the uncompromising character of the viceroy's obedience to the instructions he carried out, it appears from a letter of his, dated Panamá, 15th of February, 1544, that he seized "a quantity of gold and silver" belonging to persons who had contravened a certain provision in the original agreement made between the Emperor and Pizarro, which ordained that Indians should not be sent

vain that the auditors endeavored to allay his ardor and mitigate his obstinacy. He resolved to set forth on his voyage without them, declaring that they would know what sort of a man he was when they should find, on rejoining him, that the new laws were being obeyed in Peru. Setting sail from Panamá, he reached the port of Tumbez on the 4th of March. There he disembarked and pursued his journey by land, every where publishing the new laws, taking away *encomiendas* from some colonists, and settling the fixed payments to be made by those Indians whom he still left in *repartimiento.*

to work at the mines, and which provision, I imagine, had always remained a dead letter. Indeed, it is not improbable that the offending persons did not know of its existence. The following are the viceroy's words: "Maravillado estoy que el licenciado haya echado Indios á minas, cuando en los asientos que se tomaron con Pizarro se insertó provision que perdiese los Indios quien los echase á minas. Quanto á la Cedula que llevo yo para que los que en esto hubiesen escedido, pierden Indios y la mitad de sus bienes, he embargado aqui cantidad de oro y plata de algunos que aqui estaban, y supe haver contravenido."—*Coleccion de Muñoz*, MS.

CHAPTER II.

DISMAY OF THE SPANISH COLONISTS IN PERU. — VIOLENCE OF THE VICEROY.—THE MURDER OF THE FACTOR ILLAN SUAREZ DE CARVAJAL.

MEANWHILE the inhabitants of Lima, Cusco, and the southern cities of Peru, hearing of the severe proceedings of Blasco Nuñez Vela, were inclined not to receive him as their viceroy. Vaca de Castro's position became most difficult. The rebellious colonists wished to maintain him in power. He, however, did not yield to their wishes; and by his exhortations and those of the Factor Illan Suarez de Carvajal, it was agreed upon to receive the viceroy into Lima. As that officer journeyed onward, he came to a district called Guaura, where there was a tambo,* on the walls of which the viceroy saw these words written up: "The man who comes to thrust me out of my house and estate, I shall take care to thrust out of this world." The neighboring proprietor was a certain Antonio de Solar. The viceroy said nothing, but these words made a deep impression on his furious mind, and he resolved to deal with Antonio de Solar when opportunity should offer.

The viceroy's entry into Lima was magnificent. All the skill of the Indians, which was great in festal decoration, such as making triumphal arches of flowers, was exhibited; but, nevertheless, it was noted that the ceremony was more like a grand funeral than the welcome reception of a new governor. One of

* Probably one of the resting-places of the Incas.

the first things that the viceroy did was to throw the Licentiate Vaca de Castro into prison—a most intemperate proceeding, which was protested against by the principal persons of the city. They only succeeded, however, in persuading the viceroy to take Vaca de Castro out of the common prison, and to keep him in the palace, a hundred thousand *castellanos* being provided as bail for him. Then the principal inhabitants had a conference with the viceroy, and in temperate language represented to him the dangers that would follow from adopting the new laws. He interrupted their discourse by throwing down his bâton, and declaring that he must fulfill the will of his prince. It is true that the viceroy admitted that the laws were prejudicial to the kingdom, and that, if those who framed them had been eye-witnesses of the state of the country, they would not have advised his majesty to sanction such laws; but he had no power to suspend their execution. After they were executed he would write to his majesty and inform him how much it would be for his service that these ordinances should be recalled. This was a cold way of comforting men who had shown him their wounds (as they did at Truxillo) which they had received in conquering Peru, and who complained that, after pouring out their blood and wasting their estates in the conquest, their Emperor sought to take from them "these few vassals" whom he had granted to them. The soldiers had added (doubtless when out of hearing of the viceroy) that for the future they would not go to conquer new lands, since the hope of gaining vassals was taken from them, but they would plunder to the right hand and to the left whenever they could.*

* "Los Soldados decian, que no irian à conquistar otras tierras, pues les quitavan la esperança de tener vasallos, sino que robarian à

The auditors now arrived with the royal seal, and they also were received into the city with fitting demonstrations of respect. The discord between them and the viceroy, which had commenced at Panamá, broke out immediately at Lima on the subject of the new laws. In personal matters also he was very arbitrary in his conduct to the auditors.

The viceroy had not forgotten the threatening notice which he had seen on the walls of the tambo at Guaura. He sent for the suspected writer, Antonio de Solar, ordered the gates of the palace to be closed upon him, demanded a confession from him that he was the author of these words, called for a chaplain to confess the prisoner, and caused preparations to be made for hanging him in a corridor that opened out into the great square. But Solar would not confess. A rumor of what was going on in the palace spread through the city; and the archbishop, with others of the chief personages, hurried into the presence of the viceroy, imploring him to suspend the execution. He did so, but sent the man to prison, without making any charge, in writing or otherwise, against him. There Solar remained for two months, until one day the auditors, going their rounds of the prison, visited the cell of Antonio de Solar, and inquired of him the cause of his imprisonment. He replied that he did not know. On the following Monday the auditors protested against his imprisonment. The viceroy said that he had power to hang the man without being obliged to give them an account of it. They replied that there was no government except that which was in conformity with the general laws of the kingdom. On the succeeding Saturday (it appears that their

diestro, y à siniestro, quando pudiesen."—GARCILASO DE LA VEGA, *Comentarios Reales del Perú*, parte ii., lib. iv., cap. 2.

visits to the prison were weekly) they allowed Solar to change the prison for his own house as a place of confinement, and afterward they set him free altogether.

Such violent transactions on the part of the viceroy as the foregoing added greatly to the disfavor with which he was regarded by all men. More than ever, men's eyes began to turn to Gonzalo Pizarro as a leader under whom they might contend, even in arms, against the viceroy. Gonzalo, accordingly, was appointed by four cities as procurator of their grievances; and, leaving his estate at Charcas, he went to Cusco. There an army gathered round him.* The first man whom he appointed as master of his camp was Alonzo de Toro; but, on his illness, Pizarro gave this high post to the celebrated Francisco de Carvajal, a name that has ever since been memorable in the Indies.

Francisco de Carvajal was a man of great intelligence, clear resolve, and utter ruthlessness. He also presented the strange contrast of a humorous cruel man, for his witty sayings were as frequent as his cruel deeds. At the beginning of these troubles he was seventy-five years of age. He had been a standard-bearer at the battle of Ravenna, had also been present at the battle of Pavia, and at the sack of Rome;† and was an old soldier versed in the arts of war.

* A pretext for the raising of this army was that it was needed to chastise Manco Inca; but the new laws were the chief enemies that the Spanish colonists had now to dread or cared to encounter.

† It is related of Carvajal that, like many a good soldier, he was more intent upon fighting than upon plundering, and that in the sack of Rome he did not get any booty until three or four days after the troops had entered the city, when he went into the house of a notary and carried off six mule-loads of law-papers. The notary afterward bought these papers of him for more than a thousand ducats, and with this money he made his way to Mexico.

On emigrating to the New World, he had first gone to New Spain, and had been sent to Peru by the Viceroy Mendoza, when the Marquis Pizarro, alarmed at the general revolt of the Indians before described, had demanded succor from the viceroyalty of New Spain and the other colonial governments. Carvajal, though one of the most daring of men, was not reckless, and had from the first foreseen what confusion and danger were at hand for Peru. He had, therefore, done all he could to get himself elected as a procurator by the colonists, to represent their grievances at the court of Spain, his only object being to escape from the country in any way. Failing in this, he had afterward endeavored to get away as a private citizen without any public charge; but an embargo had been laid on all vessels both at Lima and Arequipa, and Carvajal found himself obliged to abide in Peru, upon which he retired to his own estate. He afterward, however, joined Gonzalo Pizarro, and was soon promoted to the high post of Gonzalo's master of the camp.

It must not be concluded that all those who gathered round Pizarro had done so with the intention of becoming at once rebellious against the viceroy. At first Pizarro had merely two hundred soldiers as a sort of body-guard. When this small force began to swell into an army, sundry reflecting persons, seeing what this would come to, resolved to fly from Pizarro's camp. Among them was Garcilaso de la Vega, the father of the celebrated historian.

It is almost impossible to imagine a more unfortunate state of things than that which then prevailed in Peru, or a more unfit man to deal with it than the Viceroy Blasco Nuñez Vela. His own disposition, being of the most severe kind, was exactly what was not wanted at this juncture in Peru. He was not, in the strict sense of the word, a tyrant. Had he succeeded to a settled government, his rule might have been strict and harsh, but it would have been just and upright, and his name would have entered into the catalogue of righteous governors. He would not have oppressed any man. He would have shielded the Indians from injustice. He would have guarded the Emperor's rights with the most scrupulous care and fidelity. He would not have taken any gifts, and would have left Peru no richer than he entered it. In battle he was unflinching. But what was wanting now was a most skillful diplomatist, who could bear and forbear, and who could put aside for the present all thoughts of his own dignity and of the Emperor's high prerogative.

Independently, however, of his own unfitness of disposition to cope with the present difficulties, the viceroy's ill fortune seemed to grow up even out of those circumstances which might have been most propitious. The inhabitants of Arequipa had seized upon two vessels fitted out by Gonzalo Pizarro in their port,* and had taken them to the viceroy at Lima. This transaction delighted him, and seemed to give a great addition to his strength. But it proved almost ruinous to his cause, for those principal men and captains who had fled from Pizarro's camp, which was then fixed at Sacsahuana, had relied upon these vessels as their means of escaping to the viceroy. When they arrived at Arequipa they found that the vessels had sailed. They resolved to build a vessel

* Arequipa is always spoken of as if it were a port, but it is far inland; and what must be meant when the port of Arequipa is spoken of is Quilca, the nearest port to Arequipa.

for themselves. It was hastily put together in forty days; but, as the wood was not seasoned, and there were not seamen to manage it, the ship went to the bottom before they had embarked in it. They then

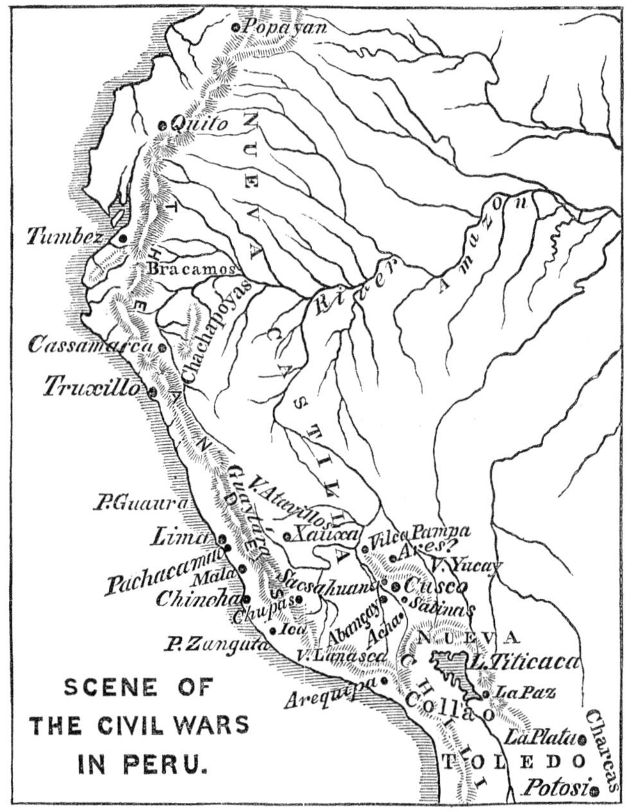

SCENE OF THE CIVIL WARS IN PERU.

determined to proceed by the coast, but before they arrived at Lima the viceroy's authority had suffered a fatal blow.

Meanwhile, however, Gonzalo Pizarro was so disheartened by this defection from his camp that he had almost determined to return to his estate at Charcas, or to fly into Chili with fifty friends who would not desert him. But, unfortunately, at this juncture he learned that Pedro de Puelles, an important personage in Peru, as he was lieutenant governor of the province of Huanuco, had revolted in his favor, and was coming to join him.

The viceroy, meanwhile, was not idle. He dispatched his brother Vela Nuñez to intercept Pedro de Puelles. But there was treachery among the followers of Vela Nuñez; and, far from intending to intercept Puelles, they had resolved to kill their own leader and to join Pizarro's camp. Some scouts that preceded this body met in their way with a friar, Tomas de San Martin, whom the viceroy had sent to negotiate with Pizarro, and who was returning from his embassage. One of these scouts took the friar aside, and told him what were the intentions of the main body. The friar instantly went to Vela Nuñez, and informed him of the intention of his men, whereupon Vela Nuñez fled that night with three or four of his friends whom he could rely upon. The main body went over to Pizarro.

There was nothing but treachery on both sides. Gaspar Rodriguez, an important person on Pizarro's side, together with some friends, resolved to quit Pizarro, and to betake himself to the viceroy. As, however, he had placed some artillery in Pizarro's hands, and as he knew of the severe disposition of the viceroy, he did not venture to go to Lima until he had received a safe-conduct and a pardon. Accordingly, he and his friends dispatched a certain friar, named Loaysa, to negotiate with the viceroy for a safe-conduct. The viceroy was already aware of their intentions, and most unwisely had not kept his knowledge of them to himself. Loaysa received the pardon and the safe-conduct, and set off with them to Gaspar Rodriguez. Now all the people of Lima knew well the nature of Loaysa's mission, and there were many friends there of Gonzalo Pizarro. Five-and-twenty of them resolved to set off secretly the following night, to pursue the Friar Loaysa, to capture him, and to take his dispatches from him. Among the five-and-twenty were three nephews of the Factor Illan Suarez de Carvajal. The enterprise was executed as it had been planned. The twenty-five pursuers came up with Loaysa, seized him, and carried him to Pizarro's camp. Pizarro, thus made aware of the treachery of Gaspar Rodriguez, put him and his friends to death.

This transaction was sufficiently calamitous for the viceroy; but, by his savage imprudence, he made it absolutely fatal. It may be remembered that the Factor Carvajal had been one of those who mainly persuaded the people of Lima to receive the viceroy peaceably and respectfully. He had, however, soon fallen under the suspicions of the viceroy. A letter had been sent to him from Pizarro's camp, written in cipher, by his brother the Licentiate Carvajal. This letter came into Blasco Nuñez's hands. He demanded that it should be read to him. It was read, and the substance of it was information about the intentions of Pizarro and the number of his army. It concluded by saying that the writer was coming over to the viceroy. This was probably the true deciphering of the letter, for the Licentiate Carvajal did escape from Pizarro's camp, and did come to Lima, but not until some time after a most deplorable transaction had occurred, which must now be related, and which was the culminating point of the viceroy's almost insane proceedings.

The twenty-five men who went in pursuit of the Friar Loaysa had not been so secret in their preparations but that some knowledge of their intention had reached the ears of the viceroy's master of the camp. The night of their departure, as this officer made his rounds of the city, he went to the houses of these men. He found that they were absent with their horses and their Indians of service. He proceeded immediately to the palace, awakened the viceroy, and told him (what the master of the camp really believed to be true) that most of the Spanish inhabitants had fled from Lima.

The viceroy was furious. He rose from his bed, ordered a general call to arms, summoned his captains about him, and sent from house to house throughout the city to find out who were absent. He soon discovered that the factor's nephews were among those who had gone upon this expedition. An additional circumstance against the factor was that these men lived with him in his house. The viceroy sent his brother, Vela Nuñez, with a party of arquebusiers, to bring the factor before him.

They found Illan Suarez in his bed, made him get up and dress, and brought him instantly to the palace of the viceroy. The viceroy was lying in his armor upon his bed. As the factor entered the room, the viceroy rose and thus addressed him: "So, Don Traitor, you have sent your nephews to serve Gonzalo Pizarro." The factor answered, "Let not your lordship call me traitor, for in truth I am not one." "I vow to God," exclaimed the viceroy, "that you are a traitor to the king." The factor boldly replied, "I vow to God that I am as good a servant to the king as your lordship is." Upon these words the viceroy sprang upon him, drawing forth a dagger. Some say that he struck him with this dagger. The viceroy always declared that he did not; but that his servants and halberdiers, hearing how rudely the factor answered, struck him down with their partisans and halberds, and slew him. The viceroy did not venture to send the body out through the guards who were in the principal vestibule, but it was put forth from a corridor which led into the great square. Some Indians and negroes were sent to receive it, and they carried it to the church and buried it there, the factor's purple robe serving as a shroud. The date of these important transactions, namely, the flight of the twenty-five and the murder of the factor, was on Sunday, the 13th of September, 1544.

The viceroy's anger was calmed, and from that moment grief took possession of him for that unjustifiable deed. He was wont to say that the death of Illan Suarez brought terror on his soul, and made him almost mad. He cursed his brother, who, knowing the fierceness of his temper, and seeing that it was provoked, had still conducted Illan Suarez before him on that fatal night. Though such were his inward terrors and regrets, the viceroy outwardly maintained a brave demeanor. He called the principal inhabitants of Lima before him, and justified the murder of the factor, attributing his death to the insolence of his language. Finally, the viceroy told them that nobody should be scandalized by this deed, for, whether he had done well or ill in it, he would render an account of it to his king and to his God. Brave words! but the deed itself was such as must have loosened still more the hold which Blasco Nuñez had upon those who remained in appearance loyal to him, and were unwilling to oppose their Emperor's representative. It is even said that Blasco Núñez himself admitted that this murder would be fatal to his authority.

CHAPTER III.

THE AUDITORS SEIZE UPON THE PERSON OF THE VICEROY AND EMBARK HIM FOR SPAIN. — GONZALO PIZARRO IS APPOINTED GOVERNOR.—DEFEAT AND DEATH OF THE VICEROY.

IN the mean time Gonzalo Pizarro had become more powerful. The traitors in his own camp had been discovered and punished; Pedro de Puelles, with some forces, had joined him; the twenty-five from Lima had come over to him; and—which was not the least circumstance in his favor—it was at this time that Francisco de Carvajal became his master of the camp, who ever afterward stood by him, and whose advice on most occasions was so judicious that, if followed, it might have placed upon Pizarro's head a crown of independent sovereignty.

The viceroy, hearing that Pizarro was gaining strength, and knowing well that he himself was losing it, resolved to suspend the new laws for two years. This was a wise step, but the viceroy could not do any thing in a wise manner. He made a protest, and registered it in the Minutes of the Council, stating that the suspension was a measure adopted upon compulsion, and that he would execute the royal ordinances when he should have pacified the country. The virtue of secrecy was unknown to the unfortunate viceroy, and this protest was noised abroad at the same time that the suspension of the new laws was made known throughout the country. The suspension, therefore, was naturally of little or no effect. The viceroy now gave notice by herald that leave was granted to put to death Pizarro and his followers, and he promised to assign their estates as rewards to any persons who should slay them.

After this the viceroy made preparations in anticipation of an attack upon Lima. He stored up provisions; he barricaded the streets, and formed several batteries. The news, however, of Pizarro's increase of force induced the viceroy to take a step of a different kind, which might have been feasible if attempted by a popular monarch or a triumphant general, but which could only hasten the downfall of a man so much dreaded and abhorred as Blasco Nuñez Vela. He resolved to dismantle the fortifications of Lima, to break up the mills, to carry off whatever could be of use to the enemy, to cause the women and children to embark in the vessels which he had in port, while he, with the men, should march by land up the coast northward. The auditors opposed this determination. The citizens of Lima sided with the auditors, and objected strongly to their wives and daughters being put on board these vessels, and left at the mercy of mariners and soldiers. The viceroy, always ready to take the most imprudent measures, seized upon the sons and daughters of the late Marquis Pizarro, and had them conveyed to the ships. He also had the former governor, Vaca de Castro, conveyed thither.

This step was the signal for a very great disturbance in the city. The auditors were more opposed than ever to the viceroy; and one of them, who was his friend, particularly begged of him to bring back Donna Francisca Pizarro, saying that it was not a decent or proper thing that a young lady should be left among the mariners and soldiers. The viceroy listened neither to him nor to any one else, but persevered in his intention to dispeople and desert Lima.

The auditors resolved upon resistance. They accordingly lost no time in coming to some concert with an officer, named Martin de Robles, who was the second in command of the army, and they urged him to seize upon the person of the viceroy. This officer was naturally much averse from such a proceeding. The auditors declared to him that it was for the service of his majesty and for the quiet of the whole country. He demanded an order, signed by them all, for the apprehension of the viceroy. This order they gave him. They also drew up a proclamation ordering the inhabitants of Lima not to obey the viceroy in the demand which he had made respecting the embarkation of their wives and daughters, and, on the contrary, to give all favor and aid to Martin Robles in securing the person of Blasco Nuñez Vela. They did not, however, publish the order or the proclamation. All that day the people of Lima were in the greatest confusion. The most prudent men could not determine what it was wise and right to do. It was the height of rebellion against their prince to seize upon the person of his viceroy. On the other hand, their interests and their feelings were wholly with the party of the auditors. Blasco Nuñez was soon made aware of the machinations of his enemies. At first he seems to have made light of the intelligence, for he observed to his master of the camp, who brought the news, that "he should not fear, for, after all, the auditors were only Bachelors of Law, and would not have the courage to come to blows."*

* "El Visorey respondió que no temiese, porque á la fin eran Bachilleres, y no ternian animo para cometer cosa ninguna."—ZARATE, lib. v., cap. 11.

Afterward receiving another warning from his master of the camp, the viceroy called his soldiers to arms in the great square, and there they remained until the middle of the night. Blasco Nuñez, prudent for once, or rather timid than prudent, did not arrest the auditors. They, as soon as they had heard of his call to arms, summoned their friends to support them. But few came; and they were fortifying themselves in the house of one of their body, the Licentiate Cepeda, and were expecting an attack from the viceroy, when one of their friends, Francisco de Escobar, exclaimed, "Body of me, let us go, señores, into the street, and let us die fighting like men, and not shut up like hens." This counsel of despair seemed good to them. They sallied out into the great square, not with any hope of success, but rather with the intention of meeting their fate at once.

By this time it was the middle of the night. The viceroy, at the instance of his captains, had retired to his palace, and gone to his chamber. His soldiers were under arms in the square; and, as they found themselves free from the influence of his presence, they made no attempt to seize upon the auditors and their party. Indeed, two of the commanders, Martin de Robles and Pedro de Vergara, came over with their companies to the auditors. After them came others, and then others, until at last the auditors, who had come out to die in despair, found themselves in command of all the viceroy's soldiers, excepting a body of one hundred, who were on guard at the palace.

The auditors did not even then venture to attack the viceroy. When morning broke, however, some arquebusiers fired from the corridor of the palace upon the revolted party in the great square. This enraged the revolters, and they determined to force an entrance into the palace, and slay all who should resist them. The auditors allayed the tumult among the soldiers, and sent messengers to the viceroy, telling him that they did not wish any thing else but that he should countermand the order to embark, and should meet them in the Cathedral, where they would wait for him. If he did not consent to this, his own life would be in peril, and the lives of all those who were with him. When these messengers reached the palace, the hundred soldiers of the guard, who were at the gate, made no resistance, but went over at once to the party of the auditors. The soldiers in the square, seeing that their entry would be unopposed, went into the palace, and began to pillage the apartments of the viceroy's servants. The messengers reached the viceroy's presence; and he, seeing that his own guard had deserted him, and that the revolted soldiers had effected an entrance, complied with the auditors' demand, went forth to the Cathedral, and delivered himself up as a prisoner. He was then conveyed to the house of the Licentiate Cepeda.

The difficulty was now what to do with the imprisoned viceroy. The auditors came to the conclusion that he should be embarked in a vessel and sent to Spain. They argued thus. If Gonzalo Pizarro should come and find the viceroy a prisoner, he would probably put him to death. Moreover, the relations of the murdered factor might cry for instant vengeance; and, whatever should happen to the viceroy, the blame would be laid upon them, the auditors. They elected the Licentiate Cepeda as their captain general, and then carried down the viceroy to the port. The admiral of the fleet, however, a brother-in-law of the viceroy, was stanch to his cause. He got his vessels ready for action, and demanded that Blasco Nuñez Vela should be set at liberty. The auditors refused, and shots were exchanged between their party on land and the fleet. The auditors then sent a message to the admiral, saying that if he would deliver up the armada and the children of the late Marquis Pizarro, they would deliver up the viceroy, and he might have one vessel to go back to Spain. The admiral did deliver up the children of the marquis, but did not place the armada at the auditors' disposal, neither did they give up the person of the viceroy. On the contrary, they declared that they would behead him if the fleet were not surrendered to them. They returned, therefore, with the viceroy into the city.

The captains of the fleet, hearing that the revolters were meditating an attack upon them, and seeing that they could not obtain the person of the viceroy, set fire to four of the small ships that they might not be followed, and with the six remaining vessels set sail. They proceeded up the coast, and put into the port of Guaura, eighteen leagues from Lima, to take in wood and water, and there they resolved to await the issue of the affair. The auditors suspected that the fleet would not go far, and leave the viceroy in such great peril. Accordingly, they launched and manned two barks, which, having been drawn up on land, had not been burnt when the smaller vessels were set fire to, and these barks they put under the command of a skillful mariner, ordering him to follow the fleet. This captain arrived at night near Guaura, and anchored his vessels behind a small island, so that they were unperceived by the fleet. The auditors had also sent a body of troops by land to the same point. These troops began to fire upon the fleet. The captains misunderstood this hostile movement, and supposed it to be a signal from the viceroy, who had, they thought, escaped. His brother, Vela Nuñez, put out in a boat to learn the news. This boat was captured by the commander of the two barks, who then sent a message to the admiral, saying that if he did not give up the fleet, they would put to death both the viceroy and his brother Vela Nuñez. The admiral at last consented, and placed his vessels at the disposal of the auditors. They were now able to send off the viceroy to Spain. The auditors resolved that one of their own body, the Licentiate Alvarez, should take charge of the prisoner, and this Alvarez proceeded by land to Guaura. The viceroy was sent from Lima by sea; and now the auditors might congratulate themselves, as they had good reason for thinking that they had at last got rid of their chief in the best way they could. But in this deplorable business there is a complexity of treachery which is almost inconceivable. The Licentiate Alvarez set sail with his prisoner immediately after he had arrived at Guaura, not even waiting for the final dispatches of his brother auditors, which it had been agreed that he was to wait for. Soon after they had set sail, Alvarez entered the viceroy's cabin, told him that his intention in accepting this charge had merely been to serve him, and with a wish to rescue him out of the hands of Cepeda and Gonzalo Pizarro; that he there and then delivered up to him the vessel, placed himself under his authority, and besought his pardon for having been concerned in his imprisonment. The viceroy thanked him much, accepted the offer of liberty, and took the command of the vessel. It was impossible, however, for this misguided man to do any thing graciously and wisely. He might have relied upon the Licentiate Alvarez as a man fatally injured with the other side; but the viceroy soon began to affront him, calling him a scoundrel and a revolter, swearing that he would hang him but for the necessity which he had of his services. The vessel proceeded up the coast to Truxillo, where the viceroy disembarked.

The auditors who remained in Lima were in a most painful position. They had reason to suspect the treachery of their colleague Alvarez and to dread the return of the viceroy. On the other hand, they had to fear the approach of Gonzalo Pizarro with his army. They accordingly resolved to send the contador, Augustin de Zarate (the historian), with a certain Antonio de Ribera, to Gonzalo Pizarro, to tell him that since they had suspended the execution of the obnoxious new laws, had granted leave for an appeal to be made against them, and sent the viceroy back to Spain, they had done all that Pizarro and his men were in arms to effect, and consequently they (the auditors) were entitled to demand that he should now disband his followers. If he wished to come to Lima, he might do so, accompanied by fifteen or twenty horsemen as a guard for the safety of his person, but without his army. When the message was brought to Pizarro he called a council of his captains. The witty Carvajal said that as to what the auditors had permitted with respect to the fifteen or twenty men, it was to be understood that Gonzalo Pizarro should enter the town with a squadron formed in lines of fifteen or twenty. After a debate, the council of captains came to the resolve that it was for the common good that Pizarro should be elected Governor of Peru, and that if this were not agreed to, they would put the inhabitants of Lima to the sword.

This conclusion was doubtless communicated to the auditors.

The position of those persons who had fled from the camp of Pizarro to serve the viceroy was most perilous. The auditors were not their friends, though they might wish to save them. Some, therefore, hid themselves in the Indian villages or fled to the Andes; but there were others who remained in Lima.

Meanwhile Pizarro approached within a quarter of a league of the city, and, as he found that the auditors delayed to send him the appointment of governor, he sent forward his master of the camp, Carvajal, with twenty arquebusiers, who, entering the town, took and put in prison twenty-eight of those unfortunate persons who had fled from Pizarro's camp. The auditors still resisted. But they were powerless, as in all the city there were not more than fifty soldiers to obey their commands. The rest had gone over to Pizarro, who now found himself at the head of twelve hundred well-armed men. The next morning some of Pizarro's captains entered the town and threatened the auditors that if they did not dispatch the necessary document appointing Pizarro as governor, the citizens of Lima should be put to the sword, and the auditors would be the first to be slain. They still, however, resisted, declaring that they had no power to do what was demanded of them, upon which the cruel Carvajal took out of prison three of those men who had deserted to the viceroy, and in half an hour's time hanged them on a tree that was close to the city. In his usual atrocious manner of jesting he allowed the principal person of the three to choose from which branch he should be hung. The auditors were subdued. They hesitated no longer in drawing up a document declaring Pizarro to be Governor of Peru until his majesty, Charles the Fifth, should appoint otherwise.

Pizarro entered the town with all due solemnity at the end of October, 1544, forty days after the seizure of the person of the viceroy. Pizarro, who was not a cruel man, issued an order of pardon for those who had fled from his camp to join the viceroy. One of his first cares was to send messengers to the Emperor to plead his cause. These were called procurators. Carvajal protested against this measure, saying that the best procurators were soldiers, arms, and horses; and that the best thing that could be done would be to seize the auditors themselves and send them to his majesty, that they might give an account of the imprisonment of the viceroy, as they were the persons who had done that deed. Another commander, named Hernando Bachicao, coincided in this opinion; but more moderate counsels prevailed, and it was resolved that one of the auditors, Doctor Tejada, together with Pizarro's master of the household, Francisco Maldonado, should go to Spain. The necessary instructions were prepared for them, and they were to set off in the only vessel that remained in the port of Lima. The former governor, Vaca de Castro, was confined in that vessel. Fearing what might happen if he were brought on land, he persuaded the mariners to sail away furtively with him. This caused a great disturbance. It was supposed that those who had fled from Pizarro to the viceroy were concerned in the escape of Vaca de Castro. They were accordingly seized and imprisoned; and one of them, the Licentiate Carvajal, was ordered to be put to death. This man was the brother of the murdered factor. Great efforts were made to save him, but they were of no avail until his friends bethought them of bribing Francisco de Carvajal, which it is said they did with a bar of gold weighing 2000 *pesos.* Francisco de Carvajal then interposed, and the licentiate, with the rest of the prisoners, were set free.

Meanwhile a brigantine had arrived from Arequipa. The command of it was given to Bachicao, and the procurators were sent to Spain in it. Bachicao went up the coast and came to Tumbez, where the viceroy was. The viceroy fled at his approach, and Bachicao seized two vessels which were in the port. This was the beginning of the formation of that fleet which was afterward fatal to the cause of Pizarro. As he went on, Bachicao seized upon other vessels, and, sailing for Panamá, made himself master of that town. The procurators proceeded to Spain. The auditor, Doctor Tejada, died on the way; but Francisco Maldonado reached Spain, and thence went without delay into Germany to give an account to the Emperor of his embassage. The commander also of the viceroy's fleet, Don Alvarez Cueto, reached the Emperor's court at the same time, so that Charles the Fifth had the means of learning, from the representatives of both parties, some of the sad events which had happened in Peru.

The viceroy retreated to Quito. Gonzalo Pizarro resolved to follow him. The viceroy had been wont to say that the king and the Indian Council had given him four auditors, one of whom was a youth, another a madman, a third a blockhead, and the fourth a fool. The Licentiate Cepeda was the youth, Alvarez the madman, Tejada the blockhead, and Zarate the fool. Cepeda seems to have been entirely gained over to Pizarro's cause, and to have thrown himself into it with all the impetuosity of youth. Before proceeding to attack the viceroy, Pizarro demanded that the auditors should authorize him to drive the viceroy out of the kingdom. Zarate would not consent to sign any paper giving the authority, and Pizarro was obliged to content himself with the signature of Cepeda. But this youthful partisan went much farther; and, as there was a disposition to substitute Pizarro's independent authority for that of the King of Spain, Cepeda argued that the authority of all kings descended from a tyranny, that the nobility had their origin in Cain, and the common people in the just Abel. This was manifest, he said, from the dragons, serpents, flames, swords, severed heads, and other sad and cruel insignia which figured upon the armor of the nobles.* Carvajal mightily approved this saying of the auditor, adding that it would be well to look into Adam's will, and see whether he had left Peru to the kings of Castile. These sayings also pleased Gonzalo Pizarro; but he never had the courage to put the crown upon his head. Having appointed Lorenzo de Aldana governor of Lima in his absence, and carrying with him the royal seal, Pizarro commenced his pursuit of the viceroy, accompanied by the Licentiate Cepeda, Pedro de Hinojosa, Carvajal the master of the camp, and other principal personages.

It is not necessary to relate in detail the flight of

* "Arguya Cepeda, que de su principio y origen todos los Reyes descendian de Tyrania. Y que assi la nobleza tenia principio de Cayn: y la gente plebeya del justo Abel. Y que esto claro se veya y mostrava, por los blasones é insignias de las armas: por los dragones, sierpes, fuegos, espadas, cabeças cortadas y otras tristes y crueles insignias que en las armas de los nobles se ponian y figuravan. Aprovava mucho esto Francisco de Carvajal, y discantava diziendo, que se viesse tambien el testamento de Adam, para vér si mandava el Perú al Emperador Don Carlos, ó á los Reyes de Castilla. Todo lo qual oya Gonçalo Piçarro de buena gana: puesto que con palabras tibias lo dissimulava."—FERNANDEZ, *Hist. del Perú*, parte i., lib. i., cap. 34.

the viceroy and the pursuit of Pizarro. The viceroy left Quito, wandered over desolate country, the enemy hanging ever on his rear, came back to Quito, and, after a forced march by night, when he and his men were totally unfit for battle, he went out to meet Pizarro on the plain of Anaquito. He fell after fighting valiantly, and his head was cut off by a negro belonging to the Licentiate Carvajal, the brother of the murdered factor. The licentiate had been thoroughly reconciled to Pizarro, and was intent upon this act of vengeance.

About this time two incidents occurred, which, though apparently unimportant, led afterward to great results. One was, that Bachicao with his fleet came from Panamá to join Pizarro, and that the command of this fleet was afterward given to Pedro de Hinojosa, who proceeded with it back to Panamá. Panamá was the key of Pizarro's position, as it was the way in which all persons came from Spain to Peru. The other incident was that a certain Diego Centeno raised the royal standard in the south of Peru. Francisco Carvajal was sent to oppose him, and succeeded in conquering him and dispersing his adherents. Centeno was reduced to hide himself from his enemies in a cave.

Gonzalo Pizarro was now without a rival in Peru; but he still hesitated to take upon himself royal authority, for he had always the hope that he should obtain the government of Peru peaceably from the Emperor; and there is a statement that Charles the Fifth had given the government of Peru to the marquis for two lives, allowing him to leave it to whomsoever he pleased, and that, in the exercise of this power, he had named his brother Gonzalo as his successor.*

For all that had happened since the death of the marquis, Gonzalo thought that the just blame would fall upon the impetuous imprudence of the viceroy, Blasco Nuñez Vela, now numbered with the dead.

When it is said that Gonzalo Pizarro remained without a rival in Peru, it may be asked, What had become of the rightful heir to the throne of the Incas, who had, not long before, threatened the Spaniards with extermination? This prince, Manco Inca, had, for some time after the memorable siege of Cusco, maintained a desultory warfare with the Spaniards. Finding, however, that he was no match for them, and that he had lost forty thousand of his own men, he had retired behind the Andes to a place called Villcapampa. After the battle of Chupas, in which the young Almagro and his followers were defeated by the governor Vaca de Castro, some of the Almagristas had taken refuge at the Inca's court, and were kindly entertained by him. When the viceroy, Blasco Nuñez Vela, came to Peru, the Inca entered into a negotiation with him through one of these Spanish fugitives named Gomez Perez, the same man who had been sent back by Juan de Rada because he walked round the pool of water instead of through it, when the conspirators were going to murder the Marquis Pizarro. It is said that the Inca offered to submit himself to the King of Spain, that the viceroy was much delighted at receiving this offer, that he pardoned the Spaniards who were at the Inca's court,

* "Demás, de que avia dado Cedula á su Hermano el Marqués, para que despues de sus dias fuese Governador el que él nombrase, y que su Hermano avia hecho nombramiento en él."—GARCILASO DE LA VEGA, *Comentarios Reales del Perú*, parte ii., lib. iv., cap. 51.

and sent a very gracious answer to the Inca, thinking that the Indian prince might prove a most serviceable ally. This piece of good fortune, like several others which occurred to that viceroy, was rendered of no use to him by the rapid breaking up of his power after the murder of Illan Suarez and the viceroy's quarrel with the auditors.

Gomez Perez returned to Villcapampa with the viceroy's message. It has been noticed before that the Indians were more ready to acquire the games of the Spaniards than any other branch of their teaching, and the game of bowls had found favor at the Inca's court. Gomez Perez was a rude man, and did not hesitate to quarrel with his host on any little point* of difference that occurred in the course of the game. The polite Inca had hitherto borne this rudeness very well. After the return, however, of Gomez Perez, who was probably elated by his reception from the viceroy as the bearer of such good news as the Inca's submission, the Spaniard was more rude than ever in his treatment of the Indian prince. One day, when they were playing at this game of bowls, his insolence rose to such a height that the Inca could bear it no longer. He gave Gomez Perez a blow or a push, saying, "Go hence, and consider to whom you are speaking." Gomez Perez hurled the bowl, which was in his hand, at the Inca, and it struck him with such force that he died upon the spot.† The Inca's followers who were present immediately attacked Gomez Perez and the other Spaniards, and avenged

* "Sobre qualquiera ocasioncilla."

† "Gomez Perez, que era tan colerico, como melancolico, sin mirar su daño, ni el de sus compañeros, alçó el braçó con la bola, que en la mano tenia, y con ella le dió al Inca un tan brabo golpe en la cabeça, que lo derribó muerto."—Garcilaso de la Vega, *Comentarios Reales del Perú*, parte ii., lib. iv., cap. 7.

the death of their sovereign by the slaughter of them all.

Thus died the Inca Manco Capac by as ignoble a blow as that which ended the days of his conqueror, the Marquis Pizarro.

BOOK XIX.

THE RECONQUEST OF PERU BY THE PRESIDENT GASCA.

CHAPTER I.

APPOINTMENT OF THE LICENTIATE DE LA GASCA.—HE SAILS FOR PERU.—HIS NEGOTIATIONS AT PANAMÁ.

CHAPTER II.

CORRESPONDENCE BETWEEN THE PRESIDENT AND GONZALO PIZARRO.—THE PRESIDENT GAINS OVER THE CAPTAINS OF PIZARRO'S FLEET.

CHAPTER III.

PIZARRO PREPARES FOR WAR.—ALDANA ARRIVES AT LIMA.—DESERTIONS FROM PIZARRO'S CAMP.

CHAPTER IV.

THE PRESIDENT ENTERS PERU.—PIZARRO DEFEATS THE ROYALISTS UNDER CENTENO AT HUARINA.

CHAPTER V.

PIZARRO OCCUPIES THE CITY OF CUSCO.—THE REBELS AND THE ROYALISTS PREPARE FOR BATTLE.

CHAPTER VI.

THE BATTLE OF SACSAHUANA.—GONZALO PIZARRO AND CARVAJAL ARE DEFEATED.

CHAPTER VII.

THE CONDEMNATION AND EXECUTION OF GONZALO PIZARRO AND CARVAJAL.

CHAPTER VIII.

THE PRESIDENT'S ALLOTMENT OF ENCOMIENDAS.—OTHER ACTS OF HIS GOVERNMENT.—HIS RETURN TO SPAIN.

CHAPTER IX.

THE REBELLIONS OF SEBASTIAN DE CASTILLA AND FRANCISCO HERNANDEZ DE GIRON.

CHAPTER I.

APPOINTMENT OF THE LICENTIATE DE LA GASCA.—HE SAILS FOR PERU.—HIS NEGOTIATIONS AT PANAMA.

IN their way to Germany Pizarro's representatives had gone to Valladolid, where Philip, Charles's son, had charge of the government of Spain. Immediately a council was assembled under the presidency of the prince, to take into consideration the alarming state of Peru. Some of the council were of opinion that Gonzalo Pizarro and the other rebels should be conquered by force of arms; but the majority were for dexterous negotiation. They urged the impossibility of sending a sufficient number of men, horses, and arms to such a distance as sixteen hundred leagues from Spain. Indeed, this distance must be traversed before touching at the first port, Nombre de Dios. Moreover, such an expedition would have to undertake a second conquest of the country—a conquest, not of unwarlike Indians, but of desperate Spaniards, occupying all the strong positions in the country. The council determined, therefore, that Peru was to be reduced by gentle means;* and that, as a fitting agent to effect this purpose, the Licentiate Pedro de la Gasca should be chosen. He was already well known for his skill both in civil and military affairs. He had been distinguished in the preparations that he had made for the defense and fortification of Valencia and other maritime towns against the fleet of

* "Por buenas medias."

the Turks under Barbarossa, and that of France. He had also been concerned in very intricate and difficult business for the Holy Office; and he was at this moment engaged in their affairs.

The council communicated with the licentiate, who came to Madrid to meet them there. At this time it was not known that the viceroy, Blasco Nuñez Vela, had fallen on the field of battle; and Gasca's commission was to mediate between the revolters and the viceroy, and to reinstate him and the *Audiencia* in their authority. Gasca did not hesitate to undertake the commission, but observed that he wondered they should think of sending him with such small authority to settle an affair which was already so serious, and which threatened to become worse before he reached Peru. He therefore asked for the largest powers to be given him that could be given—as large, in fact, as his majesty himself possessed. The following were the powers that he claimed: First, that he should have all the men, money, ships, and horses that he might require; secondly, that he should have at his disposal all the vacant *repartimientos*, and all the offices of government in Peru; thirdly, that he might be allowed to give orders for new expeditions into unconquered countries; fourthly, that he might be allowed a plenary power of pardoning, and that those whom he pardoned should be protected not only from the government prosecutions, but also from those instituted by the injured parties;* fifthly, that he might send home the viceroy if it seemed good to him;

* "Y no solo, para que contra los delinquentes y criminosos que se perdonassen, no se pudiesse proceder en lo criminal, de officio; pero ni aun á instancia de parte: que dando quanto al interesse de hazienda que uviessen robado, ó damnificado, á cada uno su derecho á salvo."—FERNANDEZ, *Hist. del Perú*, parte i., lib. ii., cap. 16.

sixthly, that he might expend any portion of the royal estate for the pacification of Peru, and in its government after he should have pacified it.

For himself, he did not wish any salary, and he would take with him but few attendants, in order that the revolters might observe that the chief means which he had were his clerigo's robe and his breviary. For his personal expenses and for those of his suite, he would not receive any money himself, but requested that an officer might be appointed by his majesty to take charge of the requisite funds, and to disburse them for these purposes.

The council approved of all these requirements except one, namely, the power of pardoning in so ample a manner that those who were guilty of the great excesses which had been committed in Peru should not in any way suffer for their deeds. They doubted whether the prince could grant this. They therefore referred the point to Charles the Fifth in Germany. At the same time they expressed their wish that his majesty would confer a bishopric upon Gasca. The licentiate protested strongly against their making this suggestion, saying that it would not be right for his majesty to give a church to a man who was going so far as to "the other world."

Charles the Fifth acceded to all that Gasca had demanded; and being at Venloo on the 16th of February, 1546, the Emperor signed the requisite dispatches, together with many letters in blank for the licentiate to fill up in such a manner as he might find necessary. The Emperor also wrote letters to Gonzalo Pizarro, to Bachicao (thinking that this commander was at the head of Gonzalo's fleet at Panamá), to the Viceroy of New Spain, and to the other governing authorities in the Indies, ordering them to assist the

Licentiate Pedro de la Gasca in any manner that he might demand of them.

It is a characteristic thing of this remarkable man, the Licentiate Gasca, that, before he set out, he completed with care the business for the Holy Office that he had on hand in Spain. The title that he went under was that of President of the *Audiencia*, though he had no intention of remaining in Peru after he should have pacified it.

Gasca's personal appearance was not imposing. He was very small, and somewhat deformed. From the waist downward he had the person of a tall man; and from the waist upward his body was not more than a third, it is said, of the height it should have been. On horseback he presented a strange appearance, the body sunk down in the demipique saddle like that of a dwarf, and the legs like those of any other cavalier, so that he appeared to be all legs. His countenance, too, was very ugly.* His natural disposition, however, seems to have been as well composed as his body was ill formed. Of his powers of mind there is but one account: all those who describe him speak of his penetrating sagacity and astuteness. A common soldier once asking him for some gratification which the president said he was not able to confer upon him, the soldier in despair replied, "Let your lordship then give me that cap of yours, with which you have deceived so many persons; with that I shall consider myself paid, and shall be content." The president

* "Era mui pequeño de cuerpo, con estraña hechura, que de la cintura abajo tenia tanto cuerpo, como qualquiera hombre alto, y de la cintura al ombro, no tenia una tercia. Andando á cavallo, parescia aun mas pequeño de lo que era, porque todo era piernas: de rostro era mui feo."—GARCILASO DE LA VEGA, *Comentarios Reales del Perú*, parte ii., lib. v., cap. 2.

merely looked at him, and bade him go away in God's name.

The president set sail from Spain on the 26th of May, 1546. He went first to Santa Marta, where he was informed of the death of the viceroy. Those who accompanied the president were greatly disturbed by this news; but he said that, though he grieved for the viceroy, he thought that his death was rather an advantage than otherwise in the pacification of Peru. In truth, it is often better to deal with three enemies than with one perverse ally.

It may be remarked that in the powers conceded to the president, no special mention was made of the revocation of the new laws. The truth is that they had already been abolished in consequence of the opposition made to them at Mexico and in other provinces in the Indies; and the ordinance canceling these laws is dated Malines, 20th of October, 1545.* Still the news of this revocation does not appear to

* "Copia de algunos capitulos de carta de EMPERADOR al CONSEJO DE YNDIAS. Copia simple sin fecha, solo en la cubierta está 1545.

"Revoquese espresamente la prematica de quitar los indios í ponerlos en nuestra cabeza, que ha sido el fundamento de las alteraciones, y de los indios quede como se estaba antes de las nuevas ordenanzas. Asi se publique en las Yndias con palabras generales que ya pensaremos con maduro acuerdo como queden las cosas, dando á los de alli parte de los tributos. Suspendase tambien la execucion de todas las otras ordenanzas que han causado alteracion, como la de que no sirvan Yndios á Governadores, Oficiales, ídemás."—*Coleccion de* MUÑOZ, MS., tom. lxxxiv.

Muñoz had not discovered the exact date of this letter, but from the collection of laws made by PUGA it appears to have been the 20th of October, 1545. "Avemos acordado de revocar la dicha ley y dar sobre ello esta nuestra carta en la dicha razon: por la qual revocamos y damos por ninguna y de ningun valor y efeto el dicho capitulo y ley suso incorporada, y reduzimos lo todo en el punto y estado en que estava antes y al tiempo que la dicha ley se hiziesse. Dada en Malinasa, á veynte dias del mes de Octubre, de mill y quinientos y quarenta y cinco años."—PUGA, *Provisiones.*

have reached Peru, and the president was, perhaps, the first person to bring it.

He proceeded on his voyage to the Gulf of Acla, and thence to Nombre de Dios, where he arrived on the 26th of July, 1546. There he found a captain of Pizarro's, Hernan Mexia, of whom he soon made an ardent friend, skillfully urging upon him as an inducement that it would be sure to prove a great thing for him if he were to be the first person to come over to the royal cause. From Nombre de Dios the president went on the 11th of August to Panamá, where Pedro de Hinojosa was stationed with Pizarro's fleet. That officer received the president courteously, but with such a disposition of his troops as left the president doubtful whether it was done to honor him or as a demonstration of force. Pedro de Hinojosa kept a frigate ready to dispatch to Pizarro to inform him of the arrival of the president and the nature of his powers. To ascertain these powers, Pedro de Hinojosa came to see the president and to make the requisite inquiries. The president replied that he was the bearer of great tidings for all the Spanish inhabitants of Peru, especially for those who possessed Indians, since his majesty, being informed that the new laws were not suitable, had recalled them. He brought the revocation of those laws, and also a full pardon for all that had happened in Peru. Pedro de Hinojosa replied that he was aware of this (he had learned it probably from Hernan Mexia), but that it grieved him to perceive that the president did not say any thing about the appointment of Gonzalo Pizarro as Governor of Peru. Upon this point Hinojosa would like to be informed. This question had already been asked of the president, and had greatly perplexed him. He was a man, however, of the utmost skill in negotiation, and he replied that the commands which he brought were those of his sovereign, and must be treated with all the honor and reverence which was due to the person who had given them. This honor and reverence would not be shown by him if he were to declare his majesty's commands before the proper season of doing so had arrived. He could only say, therefore, that the welfare of Gonzalo Pizarro and of his followers would consist in responding to the natural obligation which, as vassals, lay upon them, of obeying first and before all other things that which their sovereign commanded them; that those who did this should not only be preserved in their honors and estates, but would be favored as those persons were accustomed to be favored who served his majesty—as, indeed, those had done who had been concerned in the conquest and pacification of that land. If Pedro de Hinojosa were a friend to Pizarro, he would represent these things to him. The interview ended, and Pedro de Hinojosa was shrewd enough to perceive that the president was not going to confer the government on Pizarro. Accordingly, he wrote to Pizarro, saying that he did not believe that the appointment of governor had come for him. He did not venture to recommend strongly that Pizarro should submit himself, fearing lest Pizarro might suppose that he was not so firm a friend as he had been. Throughout these transactions it does not appear that Pizarro was one of those persons to whom unpleasing advice, however wise, might safely be offered.

In the same vessel that carried this dispatch from Hinojosa, the president contrived to send a friar with letters to the prelates and to the chief persons in the principal towns of Peru, telling them that he had come with the revocation of the new laws, and with full powers of pardon.

While the president was at Panamá, uncertain whether Pedro de Hinojosa would allow him to proceed to Peru, he learned from those who arrived at Panamá the exact state of the country, and the pretensions of Pizarro. He then dispatched messengers to the Viceroy of New Spain suggesting that he should not allow horses or arms to go out of the country for Peru, and that he should keep his navy ready, to see how things would go, whether they would settle down peaceably, or whether it would be necessary to commence a war.* If a war should be requisite, it would be upon New Spain that his majesty would chiefly have to rely.

* "Tambien me paresce, que vuestra Señoria deve ser seruido de no mandar salir los galeones, ni navios de armada que, me dizen, vuestra Señoria tiene en el mar del Sur, sino que vuestra Señoria mande adereçarlos, y que estén á punto, y se detenga hasta ver á que vienen las cosas. Porque en breve daran señal, si se pueden assentar por bien, ó si será necessario allanarlas con gente de guerra."—FERNANDEZ, *Hist. del Perú*, parte i., lib. ii., cap. 28.

CHAPTER II.

CORRESPONDENCE BETWEEN THE PRESIDENT AND GONZALO PIZARRO. — THE PRESIDENT GAINS OVER THE CAPTAINS OF PIZARRO'S FLEET.

WHEN Gonzalo Pizarro learned from Hinojosa of the arrival of the president at Panamá, it does not appear that he was exceedingly disturbed by the intelligence. He summoned, however, a council of his principal officers, and there the matter was much debated. Some said that they should let the president come on to Peru, and if he did not do what they wished, they could kill him, or send him back to Spain. Others were of opinion that on no account should they allow him to enter the country. It was said that there were some who advised that the president should be poisoned at Panamá. Finally it was agreed that an embassy should be sent to Spain, to represent to Charles the Fifth the state of affairs, and to petition that the government should be confirmed to Pizarro; and, meanwhile, that Hinojosa should detain the president at Panamá. Delegates from the different cities of Peru were summoned, who wrote a letter to the president, saying that it was their general opinion that he must not be allowed to enter the kingdom. They said that even if Hernando Pizarro, who was the man having the highest repute in Peru, had been sent in the president's place, they could not have allowed him to enter the country. Rather would they all die. They intimated to the president the nature of the desperate men he had to deal with.

In this country, they said, there was nothing that was thought less of than risking life and estate even for things of no great value; how much more readily, then, would great hazards be encountered in a case like this, where life, honor, and estate were all concerned.* This letter bears date the 14th of October, 1546.

The envoys chosen to represent the Pizarro party were the Bishop of Lima, the Bishop of Bogotá, the Provincial of the Dominicans, Lorenzo de Aldana, and Gomez de Solis, the steward of Pizarro's household. It was afterward alleged that instructions were given to the Provincial of the Dominicans to proceed to Rome, and see whether he could not obtain from the Pope the throne of Peru for Pizarro. There is no doubt, I think, that this plan of obtaining an investiture directly from the Pope was in the minds of Pizarro's followers, and it shows the dangerous nature of the rebellion.

It was thought that Lorenzo de Aldana should proceed at once to Panamá with instructions for Hinojosa, and it appears that Pizarro's friends entertained some hope of bribing the president to further their wishes by a gift of fifty thousand *pesos*.

They little knew the man they had to deal with. He was occupied at Panamá in gaining over the captains of Pizarro's fleet, one by one, to the royal cause; and so skillful was this Cortez in priestly garments, that he succeeded not only in gaining these captains, but in restraining them from action until the proper time for acting should arrive. Hernan Mexia offered

* "Porque no ay cosa que en el mundo se tenga en menos que en esta tierra arriscar la vida y hazienda, aun por cosas no de mucho peso. Quanto mas en esto que nos vá, vida, honra, y hazienda."—FERNANDEZ, *Hist. del Perú*, parte i., lib. ii., cap. 33.

his men to the president in order to force Hinojosa to comply with the president's wishes. Another captain, named Palamino, offered to kill Hinojosa. The president temporized with them all. It gave him great trouble and anxiety to see such an ardent desire to act upon a determination so recently taken,* and his difficulty was to prevent his own partisans from committing themselves until he had won over all the partisans of Pizarro. He appears to have taken as much pains in gaining Pizarro's principal captain, Hinojosa, as if he had him alone to deal with. And, indeed, Gasca was unwilling that any blood should be spilled that could possibly be avoided.

The crafty president, still doubting whether Hinojosa would allow him to proceed, at any rate until a reply had been given by Gonzalo Pizarro, made excuses for staying at Panamá. Of his brother auditors whom he had brought out to replace the defunct auditors, one was dead, and the other was very ill. This formed a good excuse for the president's delay; but he thought that he must write to Gonzalo Pizarro; and accordingly he dispatched a certain man, named Paniagua, to Lima, with Charles the Fifth's letter, and also with a letter from the president himself to Gonzalo Pizarro.

The Emperor's letter is little more than a statement of the facts respecting the rebellion in Peru, an authorization of the President Gasca, and an assurance on the part of his majesty that he keeps in mind, and will keep in mind, the services which had been rendered both by the Marquis Francisco Pizarro, and by Gonzalo himself. Gonzalo is strictly or-

* "Le dava congoxa y pena, ver tan ardiente desseo en determinacion tan moça."—FERNANDEZ, *Hist. del Perú*, parte i., lib. ii., cap. 38.

dered to do whatever the President commands as if it were commanded by Charles himself.*

The president's letter is a long and very skillful production. He thought that if Pizarro kept this letter to himself, that reserve would be a suspicious circumstance in the eyes of his followers; and if he caused it to be read aloud in the presence of his officers, it should give such a statement of the case as would show them the peril into which they were rushing. The president begins by stating that the Emperor's view of the disturbances which had taken place in Peru since the arrival in that country of Blasco Nuñez Vela was that they did not manifest a spirit of rebellion as regarded his regal authority, but had reference only to the rigor of that viceroy, as was proved by the terms in which Pizarro had written to his majesty when he informed him of his acceptance from the *Audiencia* of the governorship of Peru. Such being his majesty's opinion of the events in that country, he had sent him, the president, to pacify it by the revocation of the new laws, by the promulgation of a general pardon, and by consultation with the several towns of Peru as to what measures would best promote the service of God, the good of the country, and the welfare of the colonists.

He then urges Pizarro to look at the whole question in the spirit of a Christian, a hidalgo, a prudent man, and of one who wishes for the good of the country. Loyalty was a subject which could be well handled in those days and to those men; and the president impresses upon Pizarro that the man who is unfaithful to his sovereign not only loses his fame, but disgraces his lineage. If this letter were to be read aloud, the president knew well the effect that

* "Como si por Nos os fuese mandado."

it would produce upon the hidalgos in Pizarro's camp.

He then turns to prudential considerations; and, in dilating upon the power of the Emperor, shows how the Grand Turk had not been able to withstand it. Indeed, in his retreat from Vienna, that potentate, finding himself no match for Charles the Fifth, had sacrificed thousands of horsemen in order to cover his retreat.

Again: Pizarro must not suppose, because he had found allies to assist him against the viceroy, who was hated and feared by many persons, that the same alliances would hold good now.*

The president then gives a very skillful turn to the fact that no new armies had been sent out by Charles, namely, in order that there might not be more Spaniards sent to that country than were necessary, so that it might not be destroyed. This was a weighty argument; for, had Charles the Fifth sent an army, each man of them would have required to be gratified by grants of Indians when the war should end, and all these grants would have to be made at the expense of the present conquerors and colonists.

The president then addresses himself to the most important part of his letter, which is to tell Pizarro plainly that if he does not obey, there is no soul whom he can venture to trust—not a child, nor a friend, nor a brother. To confirm this, the president relates an

* "Y tambien debe V.m. considerar, quan otra seria la negociacion de aqui adelante, de lo que ha sido hasta agora, porque en lo pasado los quem á V.m. se allegaban, le eran buenos, por el Enemigo, con quien lo havia, í por la causa que trataba contra el Enemigo, que era Blasco Nuñez, a quien cada una de los que á V.m. seguian, tenia por proprio Enemigo, por tener creido que Blasco Nuñez no solo la hacienda, pero la vida deseaba quitar á todos los que le eran contrarios." ZARATE, *Historia del Perú*, lib. vi., cap. 7. BARCIA, *Historiadores.*

anecdote of two Spanish brothers. The one was at Rome, a good Catholic; the other a Lutheran in Saxony. The one at Rome, thinking that his brother dishonored him and his lineage, resolved to convert him or to slay him. He set out for Saxony, found his brother, reasoned with him for fifteen or twenty days, and, not being able to convince him, slew him—that, too, in a town where all were Lutherans. The president presses this argument home, and skillfully shows that those very men who had hitherto most closely followed Pizarro, thinking themselves on that account in most danger of blame from their sovereign, would be the most likely persons to destroy him. No word or oath of theirs could be relied on, since to take such an oath would be unlawful, and to keep it much more so.

For Pizarro to persevere in rebellion, now that the new laws were revoked, would make the inhabitants of Peru think that he did this for his own interest and not for theirs, as if he wished to keep them in continued disquietude instead of allowing them to enjoy their estates.

The president then shows that new discoveries can not be made, and the Spaniards thus be profitably employed, while these internal dissensions remain unhealed.

The president speaks of himself as a man who desires nothing in the enterprise he has undertaken but to serve God and procure peace. Finally, begging Pizarro to consult with persons desirous of the service of God, and praying that God may enlighten him and his councilors so that they may bring this business to such an end as should be good for their souls, their honor, their lives, and their estates, and that God may have the illustrious person of Pizarro in his sacred keeping, the president concludes this remarkable letter.

There never was a better instance of the truth that it is often wise to be plain-spoken in diplomacy than in the president's clearly warning Pizarro of the treachery he would have to encounter, even from his nearest and dearest friends, this being the sole means which the president, without any armed force of his own, had then to rely upon.

Paniagua, after encountering some difficulties, ultimately reached the presence of Gonzalo Pizarro and delivered his dispatches. Pizarro called into council the Auditor Cepeda and Francisco de Carvajal; and when the three had read the letter over two or three times, Pizarro asked for the opinion of the other two. Carvajal said, "My lord, these are very good bulls. It appears to me that there is no reason why your lordship should not receive them, and we may all do the same, for they bring great indulgences." Cepeda, on the other hand, contended that the letter contained mere promises without any security; and that the president, once allowed to land, would win over all men to him, and would do whatever he pleased. He was not sent as a simple plain-minded man, but because of his great craft and astuteness. In fine, Cepeda's opinion was, that in no way should they receive the president, as it would prove the destruction of them.

Meanwhile, Lorenzo de Aldana arrived at the port of Panamá on the 13th of November, 1546, and, without visiting the president, went to take up his quarters with Hinojosa. What he heard from that officer seems at once to have determined Aldana in the course that he should pursue. He read the private dispatches from Pizarro that night, and burnt them, without Hinojosa being able to prevent him. The next morning he went with Hinojosa to the president, when a great discussion took place between the three, in the course of which Aldana went over entirely to the president's side. Hinojosa still resisted. He could not bear to be a traitor to Pizarro, nor to take any step against him, until he should be assured that he would not obey the Emperor's commands. When they were alone together, however, Aldana seems to have convinced his friend Hinojosa that it would be hopeless to persevere in this course of neutrality, for the next day he went in company with Aldana to the president, declared that he would be a faithful servant to his majesty, and would surrender himself, his men, and his ships to the president. A *junta* of the officers was called, and the fleet was delivered up to the president, who appointed Palamino to the supreme command. As there were still, however, some partisans of Pizarro who were not gained over, leave of absence was given to those men, and their places were filled by adherents of Palamino.

This important transaction, the defection of Pizarro's captains, still remained a secret. It was given out that Aldana had required the president to produce all the dispatches and powers which he had received from his majesty, in order that copies of them might be sent to Pizarro. It was also given out that Pizarro had ordered that the sails and the rudders of all the fleet should be taken on board one vessel. And, accordingly, they were unshipped, and brought to the galleon commanded by Palamino. The fleet was now completely at the president's disposal.

The president then made answer to the letter which had been sent him by the delegates of the various towns of Peru. Addressing it to Pizarro, he expressed his wonder that a clerigo of such little account as he was should be forbidden to enter Peru; and said that, as Hinojosa and Aldana had demanded, on Pizarro's behalf, to see the orders he had brought from his majesty, he now furnished him with copies of these documents, which he also sent to the principal towns. His object was to keep Pizarro still in ignorance of what had happened at Panamá, and to make known throughout Peru intelligence which would sow discord between Pizarro and his followers.

Hinojosa was very anxious that these missives should be sent directly to Pizarro. The president was obliged to dissemble with him, and contrive that the missives should be sent to the several towns of Peru unknown to Hinojosa. Then a public and formal act took place, in which a general amnesty was proclaimed, and was accepted by Hinojosa, by all the other captains, and also by the sailors of the fleet, which was now placed publicly under the orders of the president. He did every thing in his power to gratify the soldiers and sailors, providing them liberally with money and with clothes.

Great debates now took place as to whether the fleet should move on to Peru. Some were for postponing the enterprise for a year, but Hinojosa and the president were for immediate action. The president determined, however, to send on Lorenzo de Aldana, with four vessels, in order to secure the town of Lima before Pizarro should discover that his fleet had come over to the royal cause. Aldana set sail for this purpose on the 17th of February, 1547.

It appears that at this period Pizarro had resolved to carry his rebellion to the uttermost limits, and to make himself king.* Intelligence, however, reached him, which must soon have lowered his hopes of attaining to royal dignity. The fact that Lorenzo de Aldana and his squadron did not touch at Tumbez excited the suspicion of Pizarro's lieutenant in that city, who instantly sent word to Gonzalo of what he suspected. Moreover, the squadron fell in with a vessel in which one of Pizarro's adherents was coming to take the government of Truxillo. Aldana gained over the principal part of the ship's company, but some found means to escape and to return to Pizarro, who must now, therefore, have been fully aware of the defection of his captains at Panamá.

* A letter from Carvajal to Pizarro, dated March 17th, 1547, seems to prove this: "Y esto suplico á vuestra Señoria, que se hierre por mi cabeça: porque para la corona de Rey, con que, en tan breves dias, emos de coronar á vuestra Señoria, avra muy gran concurso de gente. Y para entonces, yo quiero tener cargo de adereçarlas, y tenerlas como conviene."—FERNANDEZ, *Hist. del Perú*, parte i., lib. ii., cap. 49.

CHAPTER III.

PIZARRO PREPARES FOR WAR. — ALDANA ARRIVES AT LIMA. — DESERTIONS FROM PIZARRO'S CAMP.

HIS fleet lost to him, his captains false, the way to the capital now thoroughly open to his enemies, Gonzalo Pizarro was aware that a struggle for life or death, for infamy or empire, was now inevitable. He lost no time in making preparations. The first thing he did was to settle his military appointments. He named the Auditor Cepeda, of whose adherence he was well assured, his lieutenant and captain general. He appointed the Licentiate Carvajal as general of the cavalry. Juan de Acosta, with two other captains, were to command the arquebusiers. Martin de Robles, with two adjutants, were to command the rest of the infantry. Antonio Altamirano was appointed as Pizarro's principal standard-bearer. For his master of the camp there could be no other than the practiced soldier, devoted adherent, and wise councilor Francisco de Carvajal. It was the custom in Spanish armies for this high officer to have no company of his own. As soon, therefore, as the other captains knew of Carvajal's appointment, they all wrote insinuating letters to him, begging him to make over to them his men and ammunition. He received their messengers courteously, read each letter one by one, put them carefully one upon another, laying them upon a table. Then, in the presence of many of his soldiers, he took all the letters up, and holding them as if they were a tambour, and pretending to play upon them with his fingers, sang a well-known song—

"Para mí me los querria,
Madre mia,
Para mí me los querria."*

He then took paper and ink, and wrote a letter to Pizarro, saying that his soldiers were formed after his fashion, and that they would be very reluctant to serve another captain, or follow any banner but his; wherefore he prayed Pizarro to allow him to retain his company; and Pizarro, wisely putting aside the usual practice, complied with Carvajal's request. Carvajal was at this time at some distance from Lima.

During his absence Pizarro had taken a step which proved very injurious. It is not given to every commander to imitate a Cortez. But Pizarro made the attempt, for he burnt or sank every vessel that he had in the port of Lima. His object in this rash step was to prevent his followers from deserting to Lorenzo de Aldana. When Carvajal entered Lima he expressed strong disapproval of this act, saying that he could have put himself in these vessels with a great company of arquebusiers, and would have encountered Lorenzo de Aldana, whose men, as there was every reason to think, would arrive sick and sea-worn, and whose powder would probably be damp. Pizarro's chief councilors, however, maintained that what had been done had been well done; and they sought to persuade their chief that Carvajal would have passed over to the enemy with the ships. But Pizarro, who was of a generous nature, did not cease to confide in his master of the camp, committing all the arrangements for the war to him.

Orders were given to Pizarro's lieutenants at Cusco,

* Fernandez, *Hist. del Perú*, parte i., lib. ii., cap. 54.

at La Plata, and at Arequipa, to join their master with whatever men and ammunition they possessed.

A general review was held, when it appeared that there were nine hundred soldiers at Lima, all in the highest state of warlike equipment, and richly clad in silk, brocade, and gold. In such a review the Indians were not reckoned, though they may have amounted to thousands.

The pedantic Cepeda insisted upon having a junta formed of all the *letrados* at Lima. Before them he instituted a formal suit against the President Gasca and his adherents. In such an assemblage the auditor was sure to be successful, and futile sentences of condemnation were duly pronounced. The president was condemned to have his head cut off; Lorenzo de Aldana and Pedro de Hinojosa were condemned to be drawn and quartered. The Auditor Cepeda attached his signature to this sentence;* but when Pizarro required that the other *letrados* should sign it, they resisted, saying that it would be bad policy as regarded these captains, since they might return into allegiance to Pizarro, and, as regarded the president, they themselves would run the risk of being excommunicated if they were to pronounce a sentence of death upon a man in priest's orders. These argu-

* Cepeda is here, and in other places, made to act a very violent part. It is but just to mention that ILLESCAS, the author of the *Historia Pontifical*, says that he had in his possession a legal paper written by Cepeda in his defense, which Illescas thought to be completely conclusive of Cepeda's innocence. His plea, I imagine, would be that he was not his own master under the tyranny of Gonzalo Pizarro. The following is the passage in Illescas: "Defendiase Cepeda por muchas y muy vivas razones . . . . Yo huve en mi poder una elegantissima informacion de derecho que tenia hecha en su defensa, que cierto quien la viere no podra dexar de descargarle, y tenerle por leal servidor de su Rey y Señor."—ILLESCAS, *Hist. Pontifical*, tom. ii., lib. vi., p. 254. Barcelona, 1595.

ments prevailed with Pizarro. Carvajal, as his manner was, mocked at the whole proceedings. "Señor Licentiate," he said, addressing Cepeda, "if the other *letrados* sign these sentences, will all these cavaliers die instantly?" Cepeda answered "No; but that it was well that it should be all settled for them when they should take them." Carvajal laughingly replied that Cepeda seemed to think that a process of law was like a thunderbolt, and carried execution with it. As for his part, if he caught these gentlemen, he would not give a nail for the sentence or the signatures.

Among Pizarro's advisers there was one faithful monk, who suggested to the governor that he should take quite a different course, and submit himself to his sovereign. But Pizarro replied that he might lose his soul but that he would be governor.*

At last the vessels of Lorenzo de Aldana, which had suffered much from storms, made their appearance on the coast, fifteen leagues from Lima. Pizarro instantly took a step which showed how apprehensive he was of treachery. He gave notice by his heralds that every one should quit the city, for he dreaded any communication with the vessels. Great was the dismay in Lima. Some of the inhabitants went forth and hid themselves in caves; some in cane-brakes or in dense forests. Pizarro himself marched out with all his men-at-arms as Aldana's fleet appeared, and pitched his camp at a league's distance from the city, between it and the sea. Immediately communications were opened between Aldana and Pizarro. On the part of Pizarro, a certain inhabitant of Lima, named Juan Fernandez, was sent

* "Le respondió que el diablo le avia de llevar el anima, ó avia de ser governador."—FERNANDEZ, *Hist. del Perú*, parte i., lib. ii., cap. 62.

to negotiate with the fleet; on the part of Aldana, a captain, named Peña, came as hostage and negotiator to the camp of Pizarro.

Pizarro sought by magnificent offers to bring over Peña to his side, but his overtures were indignantly rejected. Aldana, on the other hand, was successful in corrupting the faith of Pizarro's messenger; and when the hostages were exchanged, Fernandez told Pizarro how Aldana had sought to gain him over, and had intrusted him with copies of certain proclamations of the president for distribution, which he begged to hand to Pizarro. By this statement Pizarro was completely deceived, and the treacherous Fernandez was enabled to circulate other copies of these documents so dangerous to Pizarro's cause.

And now commenced a series of treacheries almost unrivaled in the history of a falling cause, having all that ludicrous character which seems to belong to this kind of baseness. Many of the principal men fled at once. Aldana had taken care to inform them, in letters carried by the crafty Fernandez, where they might find small vessels on the shore, in which they could join him. One of these men, named Hernan Bravo de Laguna, was captured and brought to Pizarro. He handed him over to Carvajal to be instantly executed, when a lady, named Donna Inez Bravo, a cousin of the prisoner (the wife, moreover, of one of those who had succeeded in escaping to the enemy), threw herself at Pizarro's feet, and, with tears and clamorous entreaties, prayed for a remission of the sentence. At last she succeeded in softening the heart of Pizarro, and he made haste to stay the execution, sending his cap with a medal in it as an undoubted token that the message came from him. It was but just in time, for Carvajal, who was always prompt when any thing severe was to be done, had already ordered out the unfortunate man for execution. He had the rope round his neck, and was under the fatal tree. Carvajal, however, obeyed Pizarro's command, and Hernan Bravo de Laguna was set free. A by-stander, named Alonzo de Caceres, was so much touched by Pizarro's generosity that he kissed him on the cheek, exclaiming loudly, "Oh Prince of the World, may ill happen to him who shall deny thee, even unto death."*

In three hours' time Alonzo de Caceres, Hernan Bravo de Laguna, and some others, were in full flight to the enemy, and they all succeeded in escaping.

After such defections from the camp, it was closely and severely guarded. But traitors will always find the means to fly; and the next great treachery which Pizarro had to endure was contrived with singular ingenuity. There was a certain captain, named Martin de Robles, who had been largely trusted by Pizarro, but who was now most anxious to go over to the other side. He sent word to an old man, named Diego Maldonado, commonly called "the rich," that Pizarro intended to kill him, and had consulted upon the matter with his captains; that he, Robles, advised Maldonado to conceal himself, and that he could do him no greater service than thus informing him of what was about to happen. Maldonado gave ready credence to this message. He had been one of the late viceroy's partisans; on a previous occasion he had suffered torture on account of certain letters of his which had been discovered; and his intimate friend, the standard-bearer, Antonio Altamirano, had just been put to death upon suspicion.

* "Le besó en el Carrillo, diciendo á grandes voces: O Principe del Mundo! mal aia quien te negare, hasta la muerte."—GARCILASO DE LA VEGA, *Comentarios Reales del Perú*, parte ii., lib. v., cap. 12.

No sooner, therefore, had Maldonado received the message, than, without any attendant, without even waiting to saddle a horse, he rushed away from the camp, and, though he was sixty-eight years old, walked nine miles to some cane-brakes from whence Aldana's fleet could be seen. There he found an Indian who took him to the ships in a raft.

The next morning, very early, Martin de Robles went to Maldonado's tent to see how his message had been taken. Finding that Maldonado had fled, Robles went immediately to Pizarro, and said to him, "My Lord, Diego Maldonado has fled. Your lordship must see how the army diminishes hour by hour. It would be prudent to strike our tents and march at once to Arequipa as we have resolved, and your lordship must not give permission to any one to go to the city on the pretext of providing necessaries, for by such devices they will all contrive to fly; and in order that my company may not ask for this permission, but may afford an example to the rest, I should like to go to the city, if your lordship sees fit, with some of my men in whom I can most confide, in order that in my presence they may provide what is necessary for them, without my losing sight of them. On the way I think of going to the Dominican convent, where, according to report, Maldonado lies hid, and I will take him out and bring him to your lordship, that you may order him to be publicly punished, and that from this day forward no one may dare to fly from the camp."

Pizarro at once assented. Martin de Robles had been engaged in the capture of the viceroy, Blasco Nuñez Vela, and was deeply implicated with Pizarro in all the late deplorable transactions in Peru. Probably not a thought of suspicion arose in Pizarro's mind. Martin de Robles went from his presence, and the first thing he did was to seize upon the horses which Maldonado had left behind, treating them as the confiscated goods of a traitor. He then summoned to him the companions whom he could most rely upon, about thirty in number, put them upon his own and upon Maldonado's horses, and took the road to Lima. He did not stay a moment in that city; and declaring publicly that he was going to seek the president, and that Gonzalo Pizarro was a tyrant, he set off for Truxillo.

Nothing now was left for Pizarro but to adopt the course which the traitor Robles had suggested. But this was not done before some of the most important men in the camp, such as Gabriel de Rojas and the Licentiate Carvajal, with many others, had succeeded in escaping. Pizarro did not attempt to pursue them, as he could not venture to trust any one out of his presence. In fact, the camp was in such a state of fear and ferment that men did not dare to look at one another,* as each man saw treachery in the other's eyes. The master of the camp, Francisco Carvajal, contented himself with prophesying evil to most of the traitors that had fled, and singing an old ballad,

> "Estos mis cabellicos, madre,
> Dos á dos me los lleva el ayre."†

However, like a good soldier, he carefully collected all the arquebuses which the traitors had left behind. The followers of Pizarro had fled in such numbers, that after he had commenced his march to Arequipa, and had proceeded sixty leagues from Lima, he found that he had only two hundred followers left to him.

* "No se osavan mirar los unos á los otros."

† These my hairs, mother,
Two by two the wind carries them away.

CHAPTER IV.

THE PRESIDENT ENTERS PERU.—PIZARRO DEFEATS THE ROYALISTS UNDER CENTENO AT HUARINA.

AT this juncture of affairs in Peru there were four principal centres at which important transactions were taking place. The president, who probably knew that his success in negotiation must by this time have reached Pizarro's ears, set sail from Panamá on the 10th of April, 1547. He encountered dreadful storms. Many of his company were for returning to Panamá, and prosecuting the enterprise the next year. They had much to say in favor of their views. Experienced captains were ready to declare that the troops which had come from Spain, or from Nombre de Dios, would be sure to feel the effects of the Peruvian climate, whereas Pizarro's troops were hardened and trained men, accustomed to the climate and the warfare of Peru. Hinojosa, however, sided with the president, and these two were ready to prosecute the enterprise with one vessel only. Their strong resolve prevailed. The motives which influenced the president were of great force and cogency. If he did not persevere, and the armada were to return to Panamá, he would leave unsupported the fleet which he had sent on before. What would be still worse, he would leave unprotected all those persons who in the various towns of Peru might, in obedience to his requisitions, have taken up the royal cause, and already have committed themselves by making some demonstration against the *de facto* government of Gonzalo Pizarro. Having these motives in his mind, the president proceeded almost to foolhardiness in his determination to sail on. In the midst of a gale he would not allow the sails to be furled, although his vessel, which was over-freighted, labored heavily in the storm, and shipped much water. As long as he remained on deck, his orders were obeyed; but when he went down into his cabin, at three o'clock in the morning, not to sleep, but to secure his papers from the water which had made its way into the cabin, the mariners took advantage of his absence, and began to furl the sails. When he came upon deck again he could not make his orders heard for the noise that prevailed; and, moreover, the orders were such that the sailors were glad to have any excuse for pretending not to hear them. Just at that moment, however, those luminous appearances were seen upon various parts of the vessel which the sailors in the Mediterranean think to be a manifestation of Saint Elmo. On seeing these lights they knelt down and began to pray. There was thus a little silence. The president took advantage of this silence to reiterate his orders, and this time he was obeyed. He then made a speech, in which he explained to the chief men in the vessel what Aristotle and Pliny thought about these luminous appearances—namely, that they were a good sign, and indicated that the storm would soon abate; and, although it was not a favorable time for the narration of fables,* he related the well-known story which the ancient poets had invented about these lights—how Jupiter had been enamored of the beautiful Leda: how from their amours three children had sprung, Castor, Pollux, and the fairest of women, Helen:

* "Aunque el tiempo era incomodo para novelar."

how the two brothers, Castor and Pollux, had been great pilots, and by land and sea had accomplished notable enterprises: how, when they died, Jupiter had placed them in the heavens; and their constel-

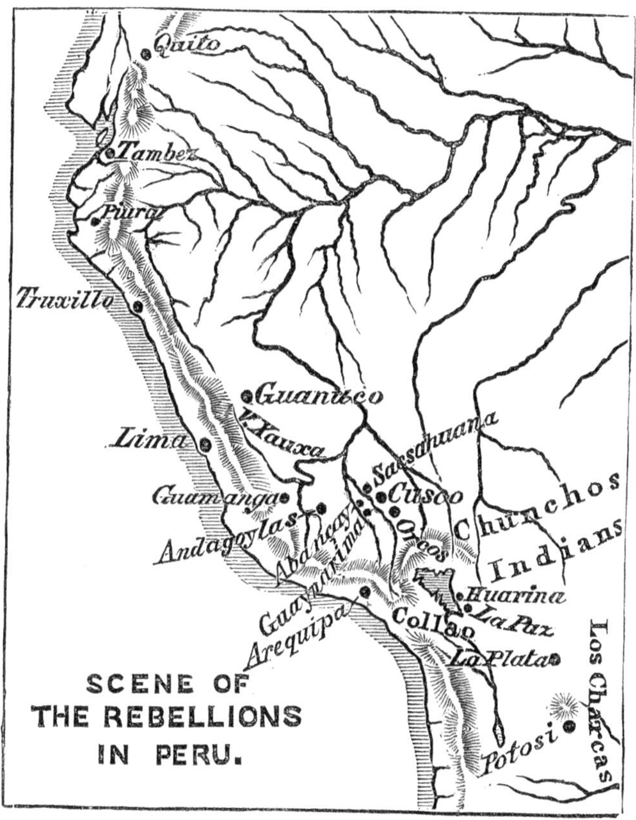

SCENE OF THE REBELLIONS IN PERU.

lation was that which is called the Twins. Having been pilots when they lived in this world, upon their translation to the skies it became their great concern to console mariners in peril. And thus, when several luminous appearances were seen together, these lights were, in many parts of the world, called Castor and Pollux. As they had been loving brothers, so these lights were a sign of peace and concord. If, however, one light only were seen, it was the sign of Helen, and the storm would increase instead of abate, for had she not been the cause of abundant discord when she dwelt upon the earth? The president took care to add that all these things were an allegory, but that the conclusion was that the sign which they had just beheld was a favorable one. Thus he comforted the mariners, and persuaded them not to slacken sail.

The armada made its way to Gorgona, Tumbez, and Truxillo; thence the president, with his army, marched to the valley of Xauxa.

Another centre of action was that which Aldana occupied with his fleet, being ready to enter Lima as soon as Pizarro should be far away.

Then there were Pizarro and his faithful Carvajal, moving with what forces were left to them toward the southwest, strong in desperation, and resolved to force their way into Chili, or across the Andes, if no other means of safety remained for them.

Lastly, there was a celebrated captain of those times, named Diego Centeno, whose proceedings, although they had already great influence on Pizarro's fortunes, have not been more than briefly alluded to, for fear of complicating the narrative.

Centeno had been one of the few who had remained faithful to the viceroy and the royal cause, and who, after being defeated by Carvajal, had taken refuge in a cave, where he remained for a whole year. It was now the time for him to emerge. A small band of faithful men gathered round him, and he resolved upon the daring exploit of attempting to surprise Cusco, which was held by a lieutenant of Pizarro's, named Antonio de Robles, who had under his command a considerable body of men. Before making his attempt, Centeno contrived to communicate his intention to many of the inhabitants of Cusco, and found them not averse to favor his assault. He accordingly commenced his march to Cusco, and approached that city about four hours before daybreak on a clear moonlight night, being the eve of Corpus Christi. Centeno and his principal men dismounted, and, kneeling, offered up their prayers, commending themselves to God and to the Virgin Mary, taking her for their advocate.* They then commenced their difficult attempt. In an account that was sent to Spain of Centeno's proceedings, it is stated that the object of dismounting was to render the enterprise a desperate one, leaving no alternative but victory or death. But one who was almost an eye-witness, who at least was in Cusco a few days afterward, says that the horses were wanted for a stratagem of war, which had signal success. When they came near the town they hung lighted matches from the saddle-bows and from other parts of the harness of the horses, and made the Indians drive these animals into the principal street, which was called the Street of the Sun, and which led straight to the great square, where Pizarro's lieutenant had placed his men, expecting the

* "Quatro horas antes que amanesçiesse, con una luna bien clara, víspera de Corpus Christi, se apearon de sus caballos é les quitaron los frenos é los dexaron allí, porque ninguno tuviesse respecto más de á vençer ó morir, é se hincaron de rodillas é hicieron su oraçion, encomendándose á Dios é á su gloriosa Madre; é tomándola por abogada començaron á caminar."—OVIEDO, *Hist. Gen. y Nat.*, lib. xlix., cap. 14.

assault. The horses plunged in, with the Indians after them, making a fearful noise and creating much confusion. Meanwhile Diego Centeno and his men entered the town in another direction, and shouting "Cæsar, Cæsar," rushed into the great square, discharged the few guns they had with them, attacked Pizarro's men vigorously, and, almost at a blow, succeeded in gaining the victory. The only person seriously hurt was the commander, Centeno, and he received his wound from a very corpulent peaceable citizen of Cusco, who was repeating his prayers at the moment when Centeno and his men were entering the town. Hearing the alarm, he put his Breviary under his vest, girt on his sword, took a pike in his hand, and sallied forth to the square, where the first person he met was Centeno, whom he pierced more than once with the pike, but did not wound him fatally, as the weapon was of a very ancient character, made at the end like a fleur-de-lis, a weapon befitting such a peaceful man. Centeno's page fired upon this citizen, but the bullet only penetrated a certain distance into the Breviary, and so the good man was saved. This was the great adventure of the night, and thus was Cusco taken for the royal cause. Many of Pizarro's followers placed themselves under Centeno's banner; and that commander, finding himself at the head of a considerable force, resolved to bar the way and prevent Pizarro's escape into Chili.

On hearing of Centeno's outbreak, Pizarro, before he marched from Lima, had sent Juan de Acosta with three hundred men to counteract the movements of Centeno. Juan de Acosta rejoined Pizarro at Arequipa. Before, however, venturing to attack Centeno, Pizarro made the greatest efforts to gain that commander over to his side. He suggested that they should unite their forces, resist the president, and divide the country between them. Centeno declined these overtures, and remained faithful to the royal cause. Desertions still continued to take place from Pizarro's camp. The army, however, moved on to Huarina. Before giving battle to Centeno, Pizarro sent one of his chaplains, bearing a cross in his hand, to demand of Centeno that he should allow free passage to Pizarro and his troops; adding, that if this request were not granted, all the loss and the slaughter that might ensue would be upon Centeno's head. This messenger was treated as a spy, and was immediately conveyed to the tent of the Bishop of Cusco, Juan Solano, who was in Centeno's camp. Indirectly, however, the sending of the message did great service to Pizarro, for, being construed as a sign of weakness on his part, it emboldened the other side to recklessness.

It may be remembered how carefully Francisco de Carvajal, the master of the camp, had collected the fire-arms of the deserters. He was enabled, therefore, to furnish each of his arquebusiers with three or four arquebuses. As they could not attack, carrying three or four weapons, the main hope of Carvajal was that the enemy should attack him. He had addressed a discourse to his men which was singularly characteristic. Carvajal was not the person to talk of heroism, or glory, or even of duty. But no man was more skillful in teaching his soldiers how to manage their fire. "Look you, gentlemen," he said, "the ball which passes too high, although it be but two fingers above the enemy, is entirely lost, while that which goes too low drives up against him all that it carries with it. Besides, if you hit your enemy in the thighs or legs, he will fall, which is all we want; whereas, if you hit him in the arms or in the body, if it be not a mortal wound, he remains on foot." In a word, he ordered them to fire low, and he also insisted that they should not discharge their arquebuses until the enemy had approached within one hundred paces.

It was particularly unfortunate for the royal cause that Centeno was at this juncture very ill of a calenture, and obliged to be carried about in a litter. The whole burden of command fell upon his master of the camp. His troops advanced upon Pizarro's men confident of victory. The crafty Carvajal caused some of his arquebusiers to fire off their guns when the enemy were at a considerable distance. This tempted them onward: they commenced firing all their guns. Again, a second time, they gave a general volley, but it was at a distance of three hundred paces. None of Carvajal's men fell. It was only when the enemy approached to within one hundred paces that they returned the fire. It had a fatal effect: they poured in another volley, using their spare arquebuses, and the enemy gave way at once, and fled.

Centeno's cavalry made a gallant effort to retrieve the day, and with such effect that they had almost captured Pizarro himself. But, being unsupported by their infantry, they were obliged to retreat, and, after one of the bloodiest battles that had taken place in South America, the fortune of the day remained wholly with Pizarro.

Diego Centeno, seeing the defeat of his forces, bade his bearers carry him out to die in the enemy's ranks. But they put him on a horse and hurried him off the field. Finally, he reached the president's camp, where he was well received as a most faithful though unfortunate servant of his majesty. The battle of Huarina took place on the 20th of October, 1547.

CHAPTER V.

PIZARRO OCCUPIES THE CITY OF CUSCO.—THE REBELS AND THE ROYALISTS PREPARE FOR BATTLE.

THIS great victory gained by Pizarro was well followed up. Carvajal lost not a moment in organizing a rapid pursuit of the enemy. But Pizarro's army must have been deficient in cavalry, for many of Centeno's principal men escaped. Forty, however, were captured by a party of Carvajal's arquebusiers. Among these prisoners was a man of much repute, named Miguel Cornejo, who was well known to the master of the camp.

When Carvajal first came to Peru, there were no inns for travelers throughout the country. Arriving at Cusco, he had taken up his place patiently in a corner of the great square, with his wife and family, and had remained there for three hours, no man taking any notice of him. As Miguel Cornejo, however, was going to the Cathedral, he saw Carvajal standing in this corner, went up to him, heard his story, invited him home, and treated him and his family hospitably, until the Marquis Pizarro gave Carvajal a *repartimiento* of Indians. Carvajal was one of those whom Mendoza, the Viceroy of Mexico, had sent to assist the Marquis Pizarro when he was in great straits on account of the rebellion of Manco Inca.

When Carvajal discovered that his former host was among his prisoners, he took him apart and said to him, "Señor Miguel Cornejo, your honor thinks me an ungrateful man, and that I am unmindful of what you did for me when you saw me in the great square, with my wife and family, not knowing where to go. But the benefits which I then received from you are never to be forgotten. Now know how much I have ever remembered them, and remember them still, when I tell you that I have had certain knowledge that Diego Centeno hid himself in a cave on your estate, and was supplied with provisions by your Indians; all which I kept to myself, in order not to bring upon you the enmity of the general. Since then, for your honor's sake, I have respected so great an enemy as Diego Centeno, how much more would I respect your person, your friends, and the city in which you dwell. Wherefore I give you liberty, and, for your sake, exempt your companions from all punishment. Go to your house; look to your safety with all quiet and content; and do what you can to pacify the city." Such was the substance of the speech which Carvajal addressed to Cornejo, and then dismissed him.

There is a story, entirely false, of Carvajal's having gone about the field of battle, accompanied by two negroes, armed with clubs, to dispatch the wounded. There is also another story that he had boasted of having killed a hundred men in battle. What he meant was, that his good disposition of the arquebusiers had had this effect. But his enemies represented him as a monster, and, occasionally, his acts justified their sayings of him. On this occasion, though he was exceedingly kind to the wounded, and was guilty of no cruelty in reference to the battle, he persisted in hanging from her own window a lady who had uttered injurious sayings against Pizarro. He was also very bitter against the Bishop of Cusco, who, he said, instead of going to battle with Centeno's army, ought to have been in his cathedral, praying that peace might be restored among the Christians. There is no doubt that he would have hanged the bishop, could he have caught him.

Carvajal's chief attention was given, not to persecuting his vanquished enemies, but to providing every kind of warlike munition, especially arquebuses, which arm he especially admired, saying that it was not in vain that the Gentiles had assigned to their god Jupiter a weapon that could injure at a distance as well as close at hand.

Carvajal was well aware that the great contest had yet to come; and, at all hours of the day and night, he might be seen doing his own work and that of other commanders. He even carried his hat in his hand, so that he might be excused the ceremony of kissing hands to the parties of soldiers whom he met as he was going to and fro. A common proverb was ever on his lips, "Do not put off until to-morrow that which you can possibly do to-day;" and if asked when he found time to eat and to sleep, he answered, "To those who are willing to work there is time and to spare for all things."*

Meanwhile Gonzalo Pizarro was approaching Cusco by slow journeys, being encumbered with his wounded men. During this tedious march the Licentiate Cepeda urged Pizarro to enter into negotiation with the president. But Pizarro declined to do so, asserting that it would be a sign of weakness, and would discourage the friends whom he had in Gasca's camp. At last Pizarro entered Cusco, under triumphal arches, with ringing of bells, the joyful notes of military music, and loud acclamations from the Indians, who accounted him as an Inca.

* "Á los que quieren trabajar, para todo les sobra tiempo."

The news of the battle of Huarina was not long in reaching the Royalists' camp. The president felt the defeat deeply, but dissembled all he felt. It is said that when he heard how considerable an army Centeno had collected, he had been anxious to diminish the number of his own followers. This showed the forecasting sagacity of the president, who knew well that each adherent would have hereafter to be gratified, and would probably become a disappointed man and somewhat of an enemy. The president had manifested a similar wisdom before. Having written to the Viceroy of Mexico and other governors for aid, the moment he felt himself strong enough to do without it, he had dispatched messengers to them, countermanding his former orders. He now, perhaps, regretted that he had taken these steps.

It is said that, on receiving the news of Centeno's defeat, the president hesitated as to whether he should proceed farther.* This may be doubted; but, at any rate, he recommenced and increased his preparations for war. He sent for all the artillery that remained at Lima; and he took care to encourage and protect the caciques who were friendly to him. This is almost the first time that the Indians have been mentioned in this contest, though, no doubt, they bore a great part of the burden, and suffered much of the slaughter. The reason for protecting the caciques was, as the chief historian of Gasca's proceedings points out, that whoever had the caciques on his side gained thereby intelligence, Indian followers, and provisions.†

* "Ex quo non mediocri dolore affectus, aliquandiu hæsitavit an ulterius procederet."—Benzoni, *Hist. Nov. Orb.*, lib. iii.

† "Que todos fuessen á Guaylas, á dar calor y animar á los Indios,

When all his preparations were made, the president quitted the valley of Xauxa and moved to Andagoylas, where the defeated Centeno, with sixty horsemen, met him.

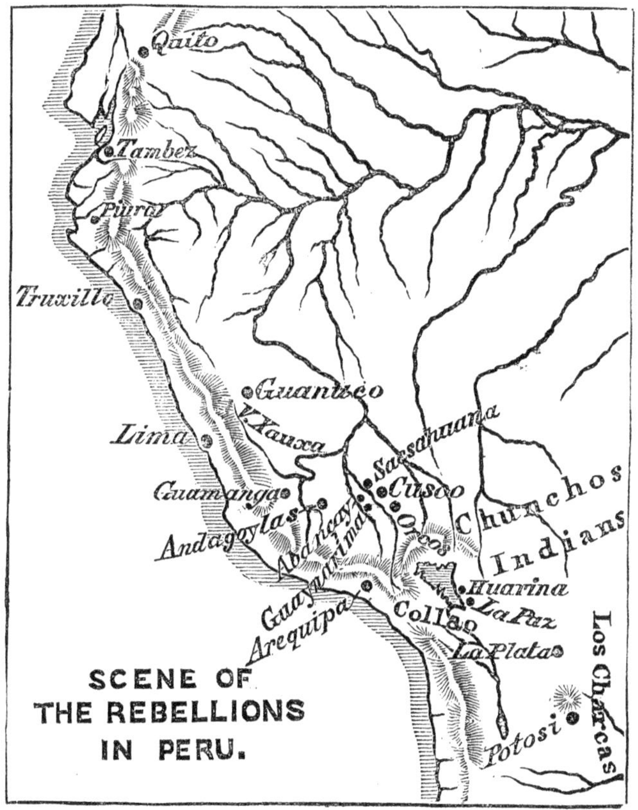

SCENE OF THE REBELLIONS IN PERU.

para que no acudiessen á Piçarro, y le alçassen los mantenimientos. Y assimismo, para que deffendiessen que los de Piçarro no llevassen los Caciques: y que ellos los recogiessen á Guaylas. Por razon, que quien tiene los Caciques, tiene los avisos, y los Indios, y los mantenimientos."—Fernandez, *Hist. del Perú*, parte i., lib. ii., cap. 82.

The greatest addition to his strength, however, which the president received at this time was from the arrival at his camp of Pedro de Valdivia, the conqueror of Chili. This commander was esteemed one of the best soldiers in the New World. He was a worthy opponent to Francisco de Carvajal.

In honor of such welcome arrivals, and also to comfort Centeno, a great tournament was held. It was now winter, and the rains had set in. The Royalists, therefore, were obliged to remain at Andagoylas for three months. A large part of the army fell ill, but the president was indefatigable in succoring the sick.

When the rainy season had passed, the president moved on to Abançay, where he arrived on the 18th of March, 1548, and prepared to pass the Apurimac by means of rope bridges. The passing of this river was a most difficult feat. The extent of the difficulty appears from the president's own dispatches; and it is clear that he expected to meet with much greater opposition than he encountered. In order to distract the enemy's attention, he made preparations for crossing the river at four different places, and then suddenly chose the passage at Cotabamba, where, however, a few of Pizarro's followers (not more than three of them being Spaniards) contrived in one night to do much mischief to the bridge, when partially constructed. If Gonzalo Pizarro had made himself strong in the confines of the Apurimac, the president might easily have been repulsed, if not defeated. At one time he must have been in a state of the utmost alarm,* for a part of his army had passed the river

* "No poca pena me dió por el peligro que parecia que corrian el general y los que con ellos estavan, no yendose á juntar con ellos mas gente, si acaso Gonzalo Pizarro viniesse, con todo su campo sobre ellos."—GASCA, *Relaciones*, MSS.

and were left unsupported, the bridge having given way. Moreover, it would have been almost impossible for Pizarro's men to have deserted when a river lay between the two camps. At the point where the president crossed, the banks of the Apurimac were so precipitous that the horses were thrown down into the water, and left to take their chance of being able to swim across. Several of them perished in the transit. The danger of the royal army was such that no man spared his labors, not even the president or the Bishop of Cusco.

After the president's army had crossed the Apurimac, Juan de Acosta, at the head of a body of Pizarro's troops, arrived upon the spot, but was unable to check the advance of the royal army.

While the president was slowly approaching, Pizarro's most sagacious follower, Francisco de Carvajal, was counseling him to retreat. The attempt to stop the royal army in its march to Cusco had been ill sustained; but Gonzalo Pizarro, who had scarcely ever known defeat, placed his reliance upon another great battle, which he was confident would end in a signal victory. Carvajal, on the other hand, felt that the slightest reverse would be fatal to the side that was justly open to the charge of rebellion. He therefore took an opportunity of addressing a long dis-

These valuable *Relaciones* of the President Gasca to Charles the Fifth are to be found in the family papers of the Counts of Cancelada, descendants from the house of Gasca. General Don Manuel de la Concha, who is married to the Countess of Cancelada, gave permission for the *Relaciones* to be copied; and Don Pascual de Gayangos, well known for his eminent scholarship and for the assistance he has rendered to several English and American students of Spanish history, has kindly furnished me with copies which have been made under his superintendence.

course to Pizarro, in which he laid before him his view of the manner in which the contest should be conducted. "Your lordship," he said, "to obtain a victory over your enemies, should go out of this city, leaving it dispeopled, the mills broken, the food and merchandise carried off, and every thing burned that can be consumed. Two thousand men are coming against your lordship: one half of them are sailors, ship-boys, and such like people. They are half naked, shoeless, hungry. They hope, by occupying Cusco, to supply all their deficiencies. When they find it deserted and destroyed, they will be dismayed; and the president, not being able to support his men, will endeavor to get rid of them.

"Again, by the course I counsel, your lordship will be freed from Centeno's men, who, as conquered people, will never be fast friends. You will have with you five hundred men, choice soldiers, upon whom you can rely. You will throw out two exploring parties, one to the right and the other to the left of your march, whose business it will be, for thirty leagues on each side, to burn or destroy all that they can not carry off. Your own people will be fed on the fat of the land as they go along.

"The enemy can not pursue us with a combined force of a thousand men. They will have to divide their army, and you can then fall upon whichever division it may please you to attack. If you do not wish to fight with them, you can go rejoicingly from province to province, keeping up the war, making it very brilliant (*mui galana*), until you wear out the enemy and force him to surrender, or to offer you advantageous terms."

Pizarro, who was much guided at this time by the younger captains in his army, refused to adopt this advice, saying that it would tarnish (literally "ungild") his former victories, and would annihilate the fame and honor which he had already gained.

"No," replied Carvajal, "adopting such a course is not to lose honor, but to add to it, following the example of renowned captains dexterous in war, who, with great military skill, have diminished the number of their enemies, and broken up their ranks without the risk of a battle."

Carvajal then referred to the battle of Huarina, which, he said, God had gained for them; and he added, using an unwonted kind of argument for him, that it was not right to tempt God, expecting Him to perform such miracles on every occasion. Pizarro answered in the same strain, urging that since God had given him success in so many battles, without ever permitting, up to this time, that he should be conquered, He would not deny him this last and crowning victory.

Thus ended the conference; and such was the counsel of Francisco de Carvajal, "a man never sufficiently understood, either by his friends or by his enemies." GARCILASO DE LA VEGA, after describing Carvajal in the foregoing terms, adds that the master of the camp had lost influence with Pizarro ever since that day when he put the letters of the president on his head, and said, in his humorous manner, that they were very good bulls—a remark which Pizarro had considered to be very like treason to his cause. With regard to the point at issue between Pizarro and his lieutenant, it may here be noticed that the choice of the fields of battle in the course of these civil wars in Peru seems to have been singularly infelicitous. In no case does any commander avail himself of the advantage of fighting in or near a town. The battles of Salinas, Chupas, and Huarina are instances of this neglect; and Gonzalo Pizarro was now about to give another example of the temerity of coming out to meet an enemy, and abandoning a position strong by nature and by art. It seems almost inconceivable that such a fortress as that of Cusco, which to this day affords strong lines of defense, should have been thought useless in those times in which it could only have been partially destroyed. Pizarro had a large force of arquebusiers, but only a small body of cavalry. In such circumstances it appears as if it would have been the most natural course for him to have made himself strong in the city or the fortress of Cusco. But such a plan is never even mentioned; nor, in any of the foregoing instances, is a remark made by the writers of that age as to the folly, if it were so, of abandoning good defenses, and risking every thing upon a battle in the open field.

It was soon after the ill success which Pizarro had met with in attempting to check the advance of the president's army, especially in the passage of the River Apurimac, that Pizarro came to the conclusion of going out to meet the president in battle. He accordingly issued a proclamation that on a certain day all his men should be ready to march to Sacsahuana, four leagues from Cusco. Pizarro did this without consulting his master of the camp. Carvajal was greatly vexed, and went to remonstrate with Pizarro. "It is in no manner fit," he said, "that your lordship should go out to receive the enemy, which is merely lightening so much of his labor. I entreat your lordship to believe me, and to trust somewhat to me." Pizarro replied that, in occupying Sacsahuana, he should have a position so admirable for giving battle that the enemy could not attack him except in front;

and that, by means of his artillery, without coming hand to hand, he hoped to disperse them. "My lord," said Carvajal, "there are many of these strong positions at every turn in this country, and I know where

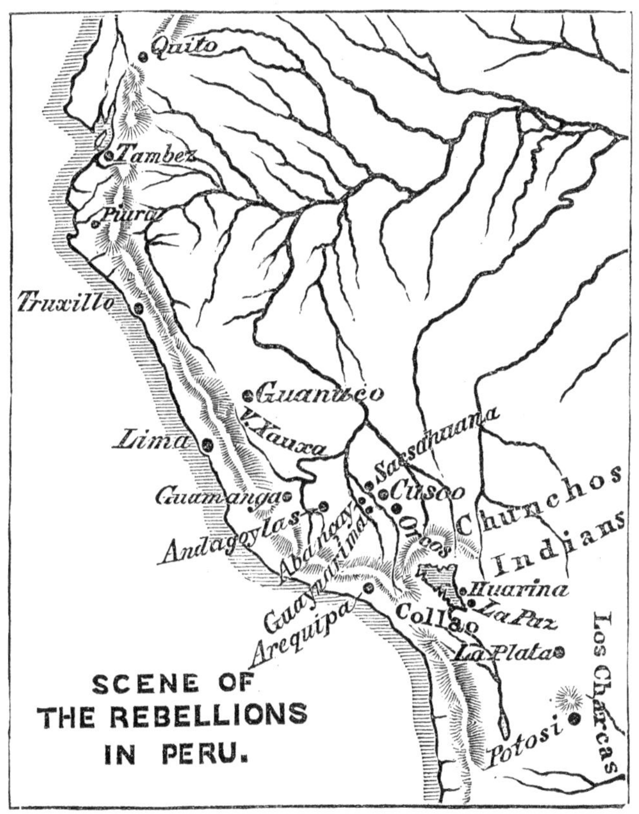

SCENE OF THE REBELLIONS IN PERU.

to choose one, if your lordship would allow me, which would assure us the victory.

"What I contend is, that, instead of marching out these four leagues to receive your enemy, your lordship should fall back to a position named Orcos, five leagues from Cusco, on the other side; and your lordship will see the confusion and trouble which this retreat of five leagues will cause the enemy; and when you have seen that, you can decide whether it is better to give him battle or to continue your retreat." Carvajal then reminded Pizarro that the astrologers had pronounced that this was the year of his life in which he would run the greatest risk of losing it; and they had added that if he escaped that danger, he would live many other years in great felicity. "Besides," he urged, "what is the necessity for giving battle now, when we can go delighting ourselves from land to land, to the grief and cost of our enemies—at least until this astrological year has passed." It may be much doubted whether the shrewd old man cared any thing about astrologers or their predictions; but it was his final opportunity for endeavoring to persuade Pizarro to listen to good counsel.

Pizarro replied in few words that it did not become his honorable reputation to retreat, little or much, far or near; but that he must follow his fortunes, and abide by that which he had determined—which was, to await the enemy at Sacsahuana, and give battle to him there, wthout regarding the moon or the stars.

Meanwhile the president pursued his painful way, so encumbered with baggage, artillery, and provisions that he could not advance more than a league a day, which served to show how wise was the counsel which Carvajal had offered to his chief.

Pizarro hastened his departure from Cusco to Sacsahuana, this step being highly approved by the younger captains, and as much disapproved by the more experienced, who looked upon Carvajal as an oracle in military matters. They could not but reflect that it was a circumstance pregnant with danger that a considerable portion of their force consisted of Centeno's men, who had been so recently conquered that many of them still wore the bandages upon wounds inflicted by those who now marched side by side with them.

It was about the end of March, 1548, that Pizarro and his army moved out from Cusco, and in two days' time reached the plain of Sacsahuana.

CHAPTER VI.

THE BATTLE OF SACSAHUANA.—GONZALO PIZARRO AND CARVAJAL ARE DEFEATED.

THE position that Pizarro had determined to occupy at Sacsahuana was indeed a strong one. It lay in a corner of the valley where a river came close up to the foot of a sierra, so that they joined, as it were, in a point. There were some very deep ravines between the river and the sierra. In the rear of these ravines, and at some distance from them, Pizarro caused the tents for his soldiery to be pitched, in order that he might leave quite free a plain that lay between the ravines and the sierra, on which he intended to form his cavalry. Three days after Pizarro had taken up his position, the president and his army arrived upon the sierra, and afterward descended into the plain. Some skirmishes of no moment took place; but, for the most part, the armies gazed at each other without coming into action, the chief care of Pizarro's captains being lest any of their men should escape and pass over to the president. Already Carvajal's advice was fully justified. The armies were not ill matched. Pizarro's men were fewer, but they were not fatigued by a long and difficult march. Their position was excellent; and they were accompanied by large numbers of Indians, for the natives were greatly attached to Gonzalo Pizarro, and reverenced him as one of the original conquerors and as a child of the Sun.

There was discussion on the president's side whether they should give battle or not. But, as they were greatly deficient in provisions, in wood, and even in water, it was decided that they could not delay, and the day after that on which the council had been held was fixed for the battle.

Pizarro sent two priests, one after the other, to require the president to declare whether he possessed any instruction from the Emperor to the effect that Pizarro should lay down the government. If he could produce the original of any such document, he, Pizarro, was ready to yield obedience to it, to lay down his office, and to quit the country; but if not, he stated that he would offer battle, and the consequences must be laid to the president's charge, and not to his. The president seized these priests, considering them as spies. He sent, however, an answer to Pizarro, stating that if he surrendered he would pardon him and all his followers; pointing out what honor Pizarro would gain in having caused the Emperor to revoke the new laws, if at the same time he should remain a faithful servant of his majesty, and also what obligation they would all be under to him if he yielded himself without a battle, some for their pardon, others for their estates being secured to them, others for the preservation of their lives. But to reason in this way with Pizarro was, as GARCILASO observes, like preaching in the desert, so determined was he to risk his fate upon a great encounter.

The night before the battle, Juan de Acosta resolved to surprise the president's camp. He took four hundred arquebusiers with him, and might have caused a great reverse to the Royalists, when he suddenly discovered that one of his men, a soldier of Centeno's, was missing. Acosta, rightly conjecturing that the man had gone over to the enemy and was awakening them, desisted from the enterprise. The president kept his men under arms all that night; and so severe was the cold, that the lances dropped from their stiffened hands. Pizarro gave himself little concern at the failure of Acosta's design. His wish was for a decisive battle in the field, and not for skirmishes or nocturnal surprises. "Juan," he said to Acosta, "since we have the victory in our hands, do not let us risk it." Perhaps no man ever fails greatly until misled by large and continuous success. Pizarro, by no means an inferior man, was blinded by the bright reflection of his former triumphs.

On the morning of the 9th of April, 1548, the commanders of both armies made ready for battle. They brought their artillery into position, and threw out their companies of arquebusiers. To the Licentiate Cepeda was intrusted the arranging of the army on Pizarro's side. The arrangements on the president's side must have been skillful, for Carvajal remarked "that either Pedro de Valdivia or the devil was in the opposite camp." Men's hearts now beat with expectation, and the young captains of Pizarro might soon have the opportunity, which they had longed for, of distinguishing themselves, and winning another battle such as that of Huarina. Suddenly, at this moment, Garcilaso de la Vega, the father of the historian, seemed to have missed his lance, for he ran down toward the river calling loudly after the Indian who had charge of the lance. When partially concealed from observation by a ravine, Garcilaso quickened his pace, dashed through a marshy piece of ground that divided the armies, ascended another ravine, and then, in the presence of both armies, made his way to the president, who welcomed the deserter warmly. This must have been a sad sight for Pizarro; but sadder sights for him were yet to come. The Licentiate Cepeda, whose arrangements for battle must have afforded some amusement to the critical eyes of the accomplished soldier Carvajal, seemed to wish to make some change in the disposition of one of his squadrons. Accordingly, he moved a little way out from the squadron he was arranging, and then, suddenly dashing spurs into his horse, made for the marsh which Garcilaso had safely passed through. His intention was immediately divined. He was followed on horseback by a devoted partisan of Pizarro named Pedro Martin de San Benito, who rapidly gained upon the fugitive. Just as Cepeda reached the marsh, Pedro Martin succeeded in wounding with his lance the horse, and afterward the horseman. They both fell into the marsh; and the treacherous Cepeda would have lost his life if he had not immediately been succored by four horsemen of the opposite party, who had been placed near that spot for the purpose of protecting fugitives. Cepeda, having floundered out of the marsh, made his way to kiss the hands of the president, who, all muddy as the fugitive was, embraced him and kissed him on the cheek, considering that, by the flight of one who had hitherto been so devoted a partisan, Pizarro's cause was lost. The next two persons who took to flight must have created some amusement for both camps. They were two horsemen, and one of them was a very small man on a very small horse, more fit for prancing about in the streets of Madrid than for the field of battle. The resolute Pedro Martin rushed after them. The larger horseman succeeded in pushing through the morass; but, finding that his little friend had foundered in it, he returned to protect him, and compelled

Pedro Martin, the pursuer, to retreat. While this episode was going on and attracting attention, some of Pizarro's soldiers were stealing off here, and some there; and almost every man was thinking how he could safely and speedily contrive to desert. Carvajal began to sing

"Estos mis cabellos, madre,
Dos á dos me los lleva el ayre."*

And now came a more serious defection. Thirty arquebusiers, of those that had been thrown out on the right, made as if they were going to attack the enemy suddenly; but their simulation of attack was only the prelude to a flight that proved successful. These, and all the rest of the deserters, advised the president's commanders not to attack, but to remain quiet; for very soon, they said, all the rest of Pizarro's army would cross over, and leave him undefended. The president consented to this, though he much feared that the chief criminal, Pizarro, would thus be enabled to escape by flight. But, on Pizarro's army continuing, notwithstanding the desertions, to advance, the wings of the president's army, and his pickets also, moved forward and discharged their firearms.† The deserters, however, had not misunderstood the intentions of their companions, for immediately a body of Pizarro's arquebusiers on the left moved off in the direction of the president's camp. They marched in good order, and showed that they were ready to resist any attempt to follow them. Still Carvajal continued to sing

"Estos mis cabellos, madre,
Dos á dos me los lleva el ayre."

* These my hairs, mother, two by two the breeze carries them away.

† Such is the president's own account. Garcilaso makes no mention of any movement of the kind.

Then the pikemen threw down their pikes, and began to fly in different directions. This was the decisive point of the battle, if battle it can be called, in which only one man was killed on the president's side, and fourteen on Pizarro's,* chiefly by their own companions, such as Pedro Martin and a few other stanch men, who endeavored at first to prevent the desertion.

Pizarro, turning toward Juan de Acosta, said to him, "What shall we do, Brother Juan?" Acosta replied, "Let us charge upon them, my lord, and die like the ancient Romans." But Pizarro answered, "It is better to die like Christians;" and, having said this, he also took his way to the royal camp, accompanied by four of his captains. As he was riding toward his enemy's quarters, he met with Pedro de Villavicenzio, the sargento mayor in the president's army, who, seeing him accompanied by several men of distinction, asked him who he was. Pizarro replied, "I am Gonzalo Pizarro, and I give myself up to the Emperor." Saying this, he delivered up to Villavicenzio a rapier, for he had thrown his lance after some of his flying people. The party then went together to the spot where Gasca was stationed. On Pizarro's approach, several of the commanders who stood round the president withdrew. It was not pleasant to look upon the man whom they had betrayed.

The president, according to his own account of the interview, endeavored to console Pizarro, but at the same time represented to him his guilt. He asked the prisoner if it appeared to him that he had done well in having raised the country against the Emperor, made himself governor of it against the will of his majesty, and slain in battle his viceroy?

* The artillery had played on both sides, but evidently at too great a range, and with no effect.

Pizarro replied that he had not made himself governor, but that he had been appointed by the auditors, at the request of all the cities of Peru, and in confirmation of the grant which his majesty had made to the marquis his brother, by which he had allowed him to name the governor who should succeed him. He said that it was a matter of public notoriety that his brother had named him, and it was not much that he who had gained the land should be governor of it. As to the viceroy, the auditors had commanded him, Pizarro, to drive that man out of the kingdom, saying that it was necessary for the peace and quiet of the country, and for the service of his majesty, that this should be done. He said that he had not slain the viceroy; but that the murders and outrages which that officer had committed, so utterly without excuse or cause, had forced the relations of the murdered and injured persons to avenge themselves. "If," Pizarro added, "my messengers had been allowed to proceed to the Emperor, and to give an account to his majesty of the events that have happened (but these messengers are the persons who have sold me, and have caused me to be declared a traitor), his majesty would have been convinced that what I have done has been good service to him, and would have ordered the government accordingly; for all that I have done and commanded to be done has been by the persuasion and at the demand of the representatives of all the cities of this realm, and with the opinion and by the advice of men learned in the law, who have resided in Peru."

The president replied that Pizarro had been very ungrateful for the benefits which his majesty had conferred upon the marquis his brother, by which he had enriched all his brothers, who had been poor men formerly, but had been raised by the marquis from the dust of the earth. That, as for the discovery of Peru, he, Gonzalo Pizarro, had not had any thing to do with it.

Pizarro replied, "To discover the land, my brother alone sufficed; but to gain it, as we have gained it, at our risk and cost, all the four brothers were necessary, and the rest of our relations and friends. The reward which his majesty conferred upon my brother was only the title and name of marquis, without giving him any estate. If not, tell me what the estate is? And he did not raise us from the dust of the earth, for since the Goths entered Spain we have been cavaliers and hidalgos of known descent. Those who are not, his majesty, by offices and commands, can raise from the dust in which they are; and if we were poor, that was the cause why we went out into the world and gained this empire, and gave it to his majesty, for we could have remained with him, as many others have done, who have gained new lands."

The president was angered by this bold speech, and exclaimed loudly, "Take him away from here. Take him away; for he is as great a tyrant to-day as he was yesterday." Then Diego Centeno took him away, having asked from the president that he might be his keeper. The other captains of Pizarro who had not deserted were also put under arrest, and guarded.

Francisco de Carvajal had no thought of attacking, alone, two armies, or of surrendering himself while there was the least chance of escape. He wished to prolong his life beyond the eighty-four years which he had already attained to. Accordingly, when he saw that the contest was all over, he ceased his ballad-singing, and sought what safety he could in flight.

He rode an old horse, which had been a good one in its time, and to this he trusted as his only hope. Coming to a rivulet, he rushed down the descent, through the water, and up the other bank. But, as he was old and corpulent, and as the horse went very fast, he could only cling to its mane. In this way he swayed over to one side, brought the horse down, and they both fell into the brook, the horse falling upon Carvajal's leg, so that he could not rise. There some of his own men, who were flying, found him, and took him prisoner. They were much delighted with their prize, and agreed to convey him, bound, to the president, thinking the presentation of such a prisoner would insure the pardon of his captors for their own misdoings.

Francisco de Carvajal was borne along in a sort of triumphal procession, for his captors shouted out his name as they went along, and many of the president's army came to see a man so famous as Carvajal, and to vent their hatred upon him. Their mode of tormenting him was by inserting lighted matches between his armor and his breast. As he was being haled along in this ignoble manner, he happened to observe Centeno, who had just placed Gonzalo Pizarro in security in his own tent, and was returning to head-quarters. Carvajal, seeing Centeno pass without taking any notice of him, called to him with a loud voice, and said, "Señor Capitan Diego Centeno, does your honor take this as a little service that I should thus present myself before your honor?" He meant that he now gave Centeno an opportunity of triumphing over one who had before so greatly triumphed over him. The gracious Centeno, turning his head and perceiving who it was that thus addressed him, exclaimed that it grieved him much to see Carvajal in such distress. Carvajal replied, "I believe that your honor, being a cavalier and a Christian, will act as becomes such a man. But let us talk no more about this; only just order that these gentlemen should not continue to do what they have been doing." Centeno, now perceiving their cruel mode of torturing Carvajal (which the soldiers did not desist from, thinking that it would rather gratify Centeno), ashamed of such barbarity, darted in upon the crowd, dealt about him several blows with the flat of his sword, and, rescuing Carvajal, gave him in custody to two of his own soldiers who accompanied him. As they went along they met with Pedro de Valdivia, who, learning that their prisoner was Carvajal, begged that he might be allowed to bring him before the president. Centeno complied with this request, and Valdivia conducted Carvajal into Gasca's presence. Even when there, his persecutors were hardly stayed from slaying him on the spot. Carvajal himself would have been delighted at such a speedy death, and begged that these, his personal enemies, might be allowed to kill him. But the president's authority sufficed to quell the tumult.*

The president then reproached the prisoner for his tyrannies and his cruelties. But Carvajal did not utter a single syllable in reply. Neither did he humiliate himself before the president, but made as if he did not hear a word of what was said, or as if the discourse had no reference to him. He looked first at one side of the tent and then at the other, in a grave,

* E luego me truxo Valdivia á Fran^{co} de Carvajal maestre de campo de Gonzalo Pizarro, y tan cercado de gentes que del avían sido ofendidos que le querian matar, que apenas le puede defender; el qual mostró que holgára que le matáran allí, é ansi rogava que dexassen á aquellos matarle: entregósele en guarda á Villavicencio.—GASCA, *Relaciones*, MS.

composed manner, as if he was lord over all those who were in his presence. The president, seeing what a hardened recusant he had to deal with, sent him away in Villavicenzio's custody, and he was carried to Centeno's quarters, and placed in a tent by himself.

All these events took place before ten o'clock in the morning of the 9th of April; and probably there never was an occasion in which a battle was determined (for we can not use the word fought), and the many results of a battle settled, in so brief a time. The president sent two captains immediately to Cusco to prevent any disturbance from arising in that town, and also to seize upon any fugitives who might have escaped thither from the field of Sacsahuana.

CHAPTER VII.

THE CONDEMNATION AND EXECUTION OF GONZALO PIZARRO AND CARVAJAL.

A COUNCIL was summoned by the president to try the prisoners. The condemnation of Pizarro and Carvajal was quickly resolved upon. Pizarro was held to be guilty of high treason, and the sentence was that he should be beheaded; his houses be pulled down; the ground whereon they stood be sown with salt; and a stone pillar be set up, commemorating his crime and its punishment. Carvajal was to be hanged and quartered, and his houses and lands were to be treated in the same manner as Pizarro's.

Pizarro bore his fate in a dignified manner: he remained alone, walking up and down for hours, very pensive.* There has seldom been a greater fall than that of this man, who had many fine qualities, and especially that of mercy.

When they notified the sentence to Carvajal, he merely said, without any change of countenance, "It is sufficient to kill,"† for he was always an enemy to many words. It is said that he inquired how many persons had been executed; and when they told him not one, he remarked, "Very merciful is the lord president; for, if the victory had been ours, there would have fallen on this spot nine hundred men." GARCILASO DE LA VEGA disbelieves this story, and others

* "Lo gastó en pasearse á solas, mui imaginativo."
† "Basta matar."

of a similar nature that were told of Carvajal at this juncture. It appears certain, however, that he retained his droll humor, if not his ferocity, to the last. A merchant came to see him, demanding payment for the goods of which Carvajal's men had despoiled him. Carvajal handed him the empty scabbard of his sword. Some young men came to offer him good advice: they themselves did not happen to bear the best of characters, and so he replied to one of them, "I beg your honor to take for yourself the same advice which fits me so well too, and do me the favor to hand me that jug of liquor which those Indians are drinking." To another he replied, "Your honor has spoken like a saint, as indeed you are; and so that saying is true, that when youths are great scamps, afterward becoming men, they turn into very worthy and respectable persons." Another man came to him and exclaimed, "I kiss your honor's hand, my lord master of the camp; and, although you wished to hang me upon a certain occasion, I come now to see whether I can be of any service to you." Carvajal replied, "What can your honor do for me, that you make this offer with such pomp and grandeur? Can you give me life? When I thought of hanging you, I could have done it; but I did not hang you, because I never put to death such a contemptible person as your honor; and now, why do you wish to sell me that which you do not possess? You can do nothing for me; go away, in God's name."

Carvajal sent for the president's secretary, and had a conference with him. He gave him three emeralds of great value. Two of them were for the heirs of other people; the third was to be sold, and to be given for masses to be said for his own soul. The secretary must have been much touched by Carvajal's noble bearing, for he offered, out of his own estate, to advance 10,000 *pesos* to be given to any one to whom Carvajal might wish to make restitution. Upon this, Carvajal condescended to offer a justification of his conduct. "Señor," he said, "I did not raise this war, nor was I the cause of it. On the contrary, in order not to engage in it (for I was on the road to Spain), I fled many leagues; but, not being able to escape, I followed the side which fell to my lot, as any other good soldier might have done, and as I did in the service of the Emperor, when I was *sargento mayor** to the Licentiate Vaca de Castro, who had the government for his majesty in this country. If there have been spoliations on the one side and on the other, it is inevitable that such things should occur in war. I did not rob any body. I took that which was freely given to me. And now, at the end of my time, they take away from me this and that: I mean to say, this which has been given me, and that property which I possessed before the war. All which things I remit to the infinite mercy of God our Lord, whom I pray, considering how merciful he is, to pardon my sins. May he guard and prosper your honor, and reward you for the generosity which you have shown to me, for I esteem the kind offers which you have made as such nobleness deserves."

So the conversation ended, and the secretary took his leave. After midday he sent a confessor to Carvajal, who detained the priest in conference until late in the evening, so that two or three times the officers of justice came to hurry him. Carvajal's object in lengthening out his confession was that he might not

* It is always difficult to give the exact modern equivalent for an officer's command in any ancient army. *Sargento mayor* may be translated by lieutenant general.

be brought out for execution until daylight had departed, hoping, doubtless, to avoid being baited by the rabble, for this is an indignity which even the bravest may be glad to escape. At last the execution could no longer be delayed, and Carvajal was brought forth, and drawn by two mules to the fatal spot in a sort of pannier into which he was sewed, so that his head only appeared, upon which he humorously remarked, "The infant in a cradle, and the old man in a cradle."* As he was dragged along, he recited prayers in Latin; and two priests who were by his side exhorted him to commend his soul to God. "So I am doing," he said; and afterward he spoke no more. He was then hanged and quartered, and the quarters were sent to different cities of Peru.

Thus ended one of the most remarkable soldiers of fortune of those times. Like many others, he was carried along by the stream of faction. Had he remained in Spain and served under a settled government, he might have been the founder of a family, and have been justly pre-eminent in great European wars. Charles the Fifth would have known how to estimate, employ, and reward such a man, if he had once had him near his person. It is probable that Carvajal's cruelty was not purposeless; but that, in every instance, he thought that, upon military principles, the execution he ordered was necessary. Even in that atrocious case where he hanged the lady in Cusco, he had warned her twice before, and he doubtless felt that in the critical circumstances in which his party was placed, there was need for swift and extreme punishment when a principal personage, in an important town, persevered in uttering the boldest and most injurious sayings against their chief and commander,

* "Niño en cuna, y viejo en cuna."

Pizarro. He knew that Pizarro would be sure to be merciful, as was his wont, and therefore took the execution upon himself. Some explanation of this kind is to be looked for when a wise and witty man, who has nearly reached the end of life, continues to stain his soul by acts of cruelty; and it must be owned that, in times of faction, cruelty has, by better men than Carvajal, been often supposed to be the only sound policy.

The president's army had now to witness the execution of the sentence pronounced upon Gonzalo Pizarro. He also spent the greater part of the day in making his confession, until the officers of justice in his case, as in that of Carvajal, were impatient to commence their work. When brought out for execution, he was placed on a mule. His hands were not tied, but, instead, a rope was placed round the neck of the mule, and so the law was held to be complied with. In his hands he carried an image of "Our Lady," of whom he had always been a most devout worshiper. Midway he asked for a crucifix; and having kissed, with great affection, the hem of the garment of the image, he gave that to a priest, and took the crucifix in his hands. With this he ascended the scaffold, and then addressed the concourse of spectators in the following words: "Señores, your honors well know that my brothers and I gained this kingdom. Many of your honors possess *repartimientos* of Indians which were given to you by the marquis, my brother. Many others possess *repartimientos* which were given to you by me. Besides, many of you owe me money which I have lent you; others have received gifts of money from me. I die so poor that even the garments I have on belong to the executioner who is to cut off my head. I have not the wherewithal to do good for my soul. Wherefore I supplicate your honors that those who owe me money, out of that which they owe me, and those who do not owe me money, out of their own means, may charitably afford me all the masses which they can, to be said for my soul. And I hope that God, through the blood and the passion of our Lord Jesus Christ, his Son, and through the charity spent in masses which your honors may expend for me, will pity me and pardon my sins. May your honors remain with God."

He said no more to the crowd, and a sound of lamentation rose up from the spectators. Pizarro then knelt before the crucifix. The executioner came to put a bandage on his eyes, but Pizarro said, "It is not necessary; put it down;" and when he saw the axe, he said to the executioner, "Do your office well, Brother Juan." The executioner promised that he would do it well; and as he spoke, lifting aside the large beard which Pizarro wore, he struck off the head at a single blow, and the body remained for a little time without falling. Thus ended Gonzalo Pizarro. They took the body to Cusco, and buried it with those of the Almagros in the convent of "Our Lady of Redemption" in that city.

Pizarro and Carvajal were executed on the day after the battle of Sacsahuana. Other executions among Pizarro's principal commanders followed, and the President Gasca now saw himself in the position to carry out the Emperor's commands, and to settle the government of Peru.

CHAPTER VIII.

THE PRESIDENT'S ALLOTMENT OF ENCOMIENDAS.—OTHER ACTS OF HIS GOVERNMENT.—HIS RETURN TO SPAIN.

THE President Gasca had hitherto been most successful in his mission. He is reckoned among the four or five distinguished men by whose services the crown of Spain obtained its dominion over the West Indies, Mexico, and a large part of South America. Indeed, he might fairly lay claim to take rank after Columbus, Cortez, Vasco Nuñez de Balboa, and the Marquis Pizarro; for, if the president did not discover or conquer a new country, he reconquered Peru, and stifled the most formidable rebellion that the Spanish crown had yet had to encounter in its colonies.

Stealthily, but with unvarying success, never planting his foot but upon firm ground, he had advanced from Nombre de Dios to Panamá, from Panamá to the south of Peru, always gaining over those whom he met with, avoiding obstacles rather than trampling them down, and apprehensively foreseeing and providing against the difficulties in government which were peculiar to the country.

But now was to arise a difficulty which the most dexterous man in the world could hardly be expected to overcome. The president had no longer to persuade individual captains to adopt the royal cause, nor to insinuate his way through hostile squadrons, nor to conquer experienced veterans in arms. But he had to divide the largest amount of spoil which, it is said, any man has ever had to apportion since the days of Alexander the Great. The empire of Peru and its inhabitants were in this man's gift, to be parceled out in any manner that might seem good to him. It is not to be wondered at that he should have sought to diminish, or, at least, not to increase the number of the royal armies; for the politic Gasca was well aware that each soldier who should fight for him against the rebels might fight against him whenever the critical time should come for dividing this immense amount of booty.

In order fully to appreciate the difficulty which the president had before him, it may be well to compare his position with that of some other great divider of spoil, such as William the Conqueror. In the Norman Conquest there were but two distinct parties, the conquerors and the conquered. In this second Peruvian conquest there were not only the original inhabitants who were to be allotted out in *encomiendas*, but there were two rival parties, the Royalists and the followers of Pizarro, each of whom had great claims upon the president, especially since the battle of Sacsahuana had been decided not by vigorous fighting, but by unexampled desertion on the part of the beaten side. A few chiefs, such as Gonzalo Pizarro, Carvajal, and Juan de Acosta, were the only persons thoroughly compromised; and the president found himself surrounded by a tumultuous body of soldiers, each of whom had peculiar services to recount and especial gratifications to look for. Moreover, the president was but a man of peace, a simple priest, and not, like William the Conqueror, a chief who was equal, if not superior, in personal prowess, to any of his barons.

In a day or two after the battle of Sacsahuana, which occurred upon the 9th of April, 1548, the president set off for Cusco, which was four leagues from the camp; and there he busied himself in giving or-

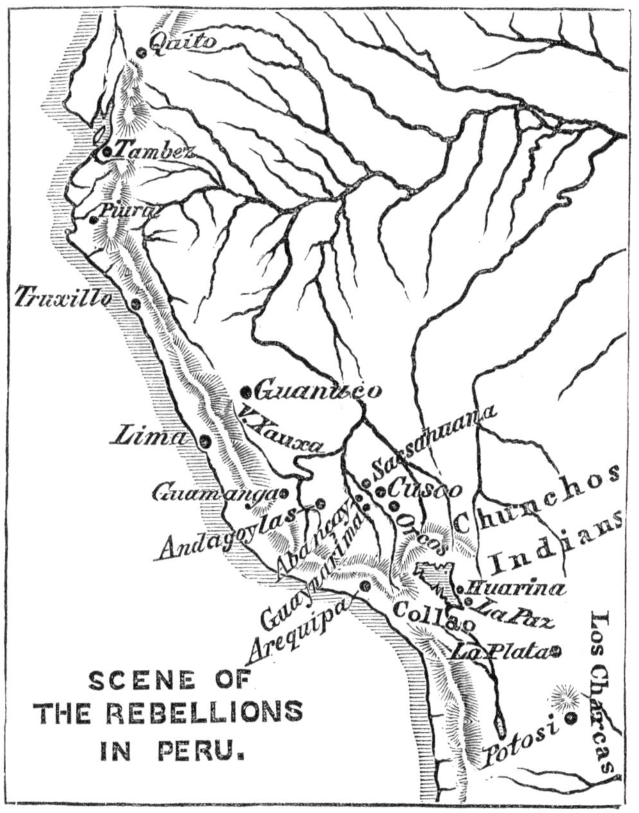

ders relating to religious matters, and also to the teaching and kind treatment of the Indians. He committed the chastisement of the rebels to the Licentiate Ciança and the Mariscal Alonzo de Alvarado.

To the former he gave very large powers, both judicial and executive, over the cities of Cusco, Arequipa, Guamanga, and Plata. He then betook himself, accompanied by Loaysa, the Bishop of Lima, to a place called Guaynarima, twelve leagues from Cusco; and there, in comparative solitude, and at least free from the incessant importunities which had beset him at Cusco, he framed his celebrated Act of Repartition. The value of the rents from *encomiendas* which he had to distribute amounted to one million and forty thousand *pesos*. It must be remembered that the mines of Potosi had not been long discovered,* or, at least, had not long been worked, and that the before-named amount in *pesos* would have been equal at that period to the rental of a large part of the mother-country.

There is a notable adjunct to this repartition made by the president, namely, a permission for a tenth part of the Indians to be employed in the mines.† The Indians appointed for this hard service came under the general name of Mitayos. The permission thus granted by the Spanish government contradicted the previous legislation on the subject; but doubtless the president thought it better to legalize, and thus in some measure to restrain, a practice which would be sure to be adopted, and which was already in constant operation.

The president's great labors were at last ended; and in the month of August he dispatched his coadjutor, Loaysa (who had in the interim been appointed Archbishop of Lima), to proclaim at Cusco the contents of this long-hoped-for document, which was to

* They were discovered in 1545.

† Pudiendo andar la decima parte de Indios en las minas.—*Relaciones* de GASCA, MS.

decide the amount of possessions that each of these hungry conquerors looked forward to as his family estate, and on which his future position in the colony, and that of his descendants, were to be founded.

The president himself did not venture to make his appearance at Cusco. He feared to hear the insolence of a disappointed soldiery, for he knew the world too well to suppose that even if his Act of Repartition had been an inspired document, and had contained within it the essence of the most thoughtful justice, it could have satisfied the hopes of all these turbulent men, each of whom was unaccustomed to consider any man's claims or interests but his own.

On the 24th of August the Archbishop of Lima proclaimed the terms of the repartition; and immediately a furious clamor arose of men so disappointed that they almost openly declared their readiness for a new revolt. They began to consult about putting the Licentiate Ciança and the Archbishop of Lima to death.

One great cause of offense was that *encomiendas* had been given to some of the principal followers of Gonzalo Pizarro. Moreover, those who would otherwise have been well satisfied with their own shares became dissatisfied when they compared them with the shares of others who in their opinion had less claim. The archbishop and the Licentiate Ciança did what they could to appease the malcontents, and for this purpose they did not hesitate to draw upon the royal chest, and to bestow great largesses of money. This measure, however, being thought to proceed from fear, rather increased than diminished the fervor of the discontented. Among the malcontents was a man of station, named Francisco Hernandez de

Giron. To him had been assigned the *repartimiento* of Sacsahuana, which had belonged to Pizarro. Other malcontents gathered round him, as he was a person of popular manners and of known courage. Ciança forbade any one to quit the town; but Francisco Hernandez, whether to avoid being placed at the head of a rebellion, or to form one more at his ease, quitted Cusco in order to proceed to Lima. He was, however, brought back and placed in custody. Finally he was sent to Lima, where he was not ill received by the president, who intrusted him with the conquest of a new territory among the Indians called Chuncos. He afterward became a very noted personage.

As regards the main body of the malcontents, their ire continued to smoulder, but did not come to any outbreak so long as the president held the supreme command in Peru.

Meanwhile the president, having finished his great work of repartition, and having given orders for the foundation of a new town half way between Arequipa and Los Charcas, to be called La Paz, in remembrance of the pacification of Peru, made his solemn entry into Los Reyes. This was done with exceeding pomp. The royal seal was placed in a rich coffer, which was set upon a white horse covered with a cloth of brocade that swept the ground. Both the president and the royal seal were under a canopy. Lorenzo de Aldana, the corregidor of the town, held the bridle of the white horse; Geronimo de Sylva, the principal alcalde, led the president's mule. The other officers of the town, and those who held the poles of the canopy, wore long crimson robes of state, and went along bareheaded. The guard of the town, and others who were to celebrate the games and dances, were in silk liveries of different colors. The most striking part of the ceremony was a solemn and beautiful dance, in which each dancer represented one of the principal towns of Peru. The order in which they occur is as follows: Lima, Truxillo, Piura, Quito,

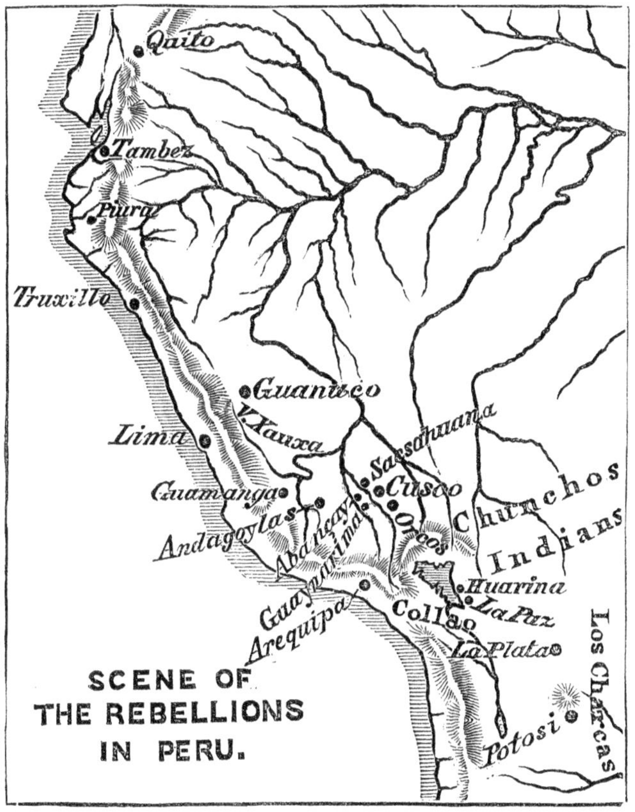

Guanuco, Guamanga, Arequipa, Cusco, and Los Charcas. Each dancer recited a stanza in honor of the town he represented. It is probable that the name of Lima now began to prevail over that of Los Reyes, originally given to the town by its founder, the Marquis Pizarro; for, in the stanza celebrating the town, it is named as Lima.* Henceforth it will always be called Lima.

The president, after his entry, labored to bring the affairs of the kingdom into good order. He made arrangements, as he had done before at Cusco, for the teaching and conversion of the Indians. He ordered a general inspection of *encomiendas* to be undertaken, in order to settle the tribute which the Indians should pay to their *encomenderos*. He gathered a large sum of money (a million and a half of *castellanos*) to carry back with him to the Emperor. And, finally, having remained about seventeen months at Lima, during which time many *encomiendas* had become vacant, he prepared a second Act of Repartition, which was not to be opened until eight days after his departure. He was thus enabled to leave every body in hopes of obtaining some gratuity, and, for his own part, to escape personal importunity and blame.

Two days before he left Lima there arrived a dispatch from Charles the Fifth, in which the Emperor ordered that all personal service among the Indians should be abolished. But the cautious president, seeing that "the state of the country was brittle as glass,"† and knowing how ready the Spanish colonists were for rebellion, took upon himself to suspend the execution of the royal order about personal service.

* "Yo soy la ciudad de Lima,
Que siempre tuve mas ley,
Pues fue causa de dar cima
A cosa de tanta estima
Y contino por el Rey."

FERNANDEZ, *Hist. del Perú*, parte i., lib. ii., cap. 93.

† "Que la tierra estava tan vidriosa."

This he did on the ground that he was going to inform his majesty of the state of the country, and would learn from the Emperor's own lips what he might determine in this matter.

The president set sail at the beginning of February, 1550. He narrowly escaped being seized on his way to Spain by the brothers Contreras, sons of the late Governor of Nicaragua, and grandsons of Pedrarias Davila, who were in revolt. The president's good fortune, however, held by him to the last. The brothers Contreras were defeated, and the president, with all his treasure, reached Spain in safety. The Emperor had already, in his absence, conferred upon him the Bishopric of Palencia. Philip the Second afterward translated him to the Bishopric of Siguenza, which he held until his death in 1567, being one of the few conquerors (for so he may be termed) of the New World who died peaceably, in the enjoyment of a well-earned reputation.

CHAPTER IX.

THE REBELLIONS OF SEBASTIAN DE CASTILLA AND FRANCISCO HERNANDEZ DE GIRON.

SOME of the Spanish historians have an easy way of accounting for the troubles which continued to beset that unfortunate country, Peru. They say that these troubles proceeded from the instigation of the devil, who thus sought to prevent the propagation of "the true faith." More obvious causes, however, were at work to prevent the pacification of Peru. There had been one rebellion about that clause in the new laws which revoked the grant of *encomiendas*, and there was now to be another rebellion about the clause which forbade the personal service of the Indians.

The president's second repartition was not more successful than his first; and, in truth, it would have been impossible to satisfy the conquerors of Peru. There might have been a few of them who had been true to the royal cause throughout, but these were probably very obscure persons. Almost every person of any note had been concerned in some transaction that was very questionable; and, in the feuds of the Almagros and Pizarros, the attack upon the royal authority in the person of Blasco Nuñez Vela, and, finally, the rebellion of Gonzalo Pizarro, there had been such a complication of violence, treachery, and treason, that every man had some reason to urge why another man should not meet with much favor from the crown. The royal officers might have availed themselves of this diversity of opinion, and, observing the old maxim, "*Divide et impera,*" might have succeeded in governing these turbulent colonists had there not been one subject which tended to unite them. They all wished to get as much labor and profit as possible out of the conquered races. The captain who had been true to Gonzalo Pizarro might look upon Pedro de Hinojosa and Lorenzo de Aldana as shameful traitors, but he had no doubt that they should have all possible usufruct from their *encomiendas.* Who was to build, to plant, or to work at the mines but the native Indian? On the other hand, the court of Spain was religiously determined to favor and protect the Indians in every possible way. It was inevitable that another collision must come.

The viceroy, Antonio de Mendoza, who had governed New Spain admirably, was, by the advice of the President Gasca, chosen by Charles the Fifth for a new command, and was ordered to proceed from Mexico to Peru, and to take the government of that country. He arrived on the 12th of September, 1551, but unfortunately in a state of health so broken that his great experience and sagacity were not long employed for the benefit of Peru.

He had been but a short time in Lima when a certain man, named Baltazar de Zarate, brought to him a royal order, which in fact legalized a monopoly, declaring that this man alone should be empowered for the next ten years to bring camels to Peru. This royal order was grounded on the supposition that there was no longer any such thing as personal service in that country. It was therefore supposed in Spain that these camels would be especially useful as beasts of burden, to replace the services of the Indians. It will be remembered that the president, just before he left Lima, had received a royal order touching personal service, and had ventured to suspend the execution of it. There came also, according to HERRERA, a letter from Las Casas to the head of the Dominicans in Peru, in which he said that he wondered that the auditors had not executed the royal order about personal service. This letter was shown to the auditors. They resolved that the emperor's original order should be promulgated. The Viceroy Mendoza remonstrated, thinking that the time had not yet come for the publication of so dangerous a document; but, the auditors pressing the question, he replied that he would neither approve nor disapprove; that they must do in the matter what seemed good to them; and, accordingly, the obnoxious document was promulgated. This occurred on the 23d of June, 1552. The viceroy died in the following month, and the auditors were left to bear the consequences of their bold publication of the royal order. As might be expected, this proceeding caused great discontent. A general remonstrance was drawn up by the Spanish colonists; but the auditors very foolishly blamed the man who presented it, on account of the remonstrance being a general one, saying that if any man had to complain against this order about personal service, he should make his complaint for himself alone. From previous experience, they probably feared the effect of any assemblage of men in such a troubled country as Peru.

Meanwhile, at Cusco, a most dangerous conspiracy was being formed among the common soldiers. Many of these men were in a state of desperation. In all parts of the kingdom there had been homicides, duels, street-fights, and all the violence and confusion which are likely to arise among unemployed soldiers without a leader. Many of them were flying from justice. Some had taken refuge in the churches and monasteries; others infested the Indian villages. The expedition of Francisco Hernandez de Giron had never taken place, in consequence of constant feuds that had arisen between him and the royal authorities at Cusco. The men who should have joined it were now idling about the town. The proceedings at a meeting of them which took place in the Dominican monastery of that town have been recorded. The speeches at this assemblage give great insight into the state of feeling of the soldiery and the colonists. Egas de Guzman, one of the principal conspirators, stood at the door of the apartment where they were all assembled, so that he could prevent any surprise from without, and yet could address those who were within. When they were all seated, one of them, whose name is not given, rose and made the following speech.

After the usual civilities and expressions of modesty with which speeches are wont to begin, he thus proceeded: "Your honors are well aware of the prosperity which there has been in this kingdom up to the present time, and now, for our sins, it has come to such misery as your honors understand and see. The reason is, because the royal auditors have oppressed the land, putting in execution his majesty's commands, so that even if there are any of the colonists who would wish to serve or favor your honors, they are not able to do so on account of the burdens which are laid upon them."* (He meant that the

* "Y es, porque estos señores Oydores, han estrechado tanto la tierra, poniendo en execucion lo que su Magestad manda; que si algunos vezinos avia que á vuestras mercedes hiziessen algun bien y

tributes of the Indians had been so reduced as to impoverish the colonists); "and if their necessities are great now, every day they will become greater; for, by reason of the pressure which the auditors put upon them, scarcely can they sustain themselves, their wives, and their children. Now you well know, my friends, that since Peru has been discovered, there have never been so many and such good soldiers as there are at present, nor any so entirely ruined. To what a pass things have come your honors may see, not only from the misery which exists among yourselves, but among others who are wandering about in Condesuyo, Callao, and Potosi, avoiding towns solely because they have not fit clothes to wear, and going among the Indians, eating their chuño* and food of that kind, which certainly is a disgraceful sustenance for such persons. Moreover, I say that the land will come to such distress that men like your honors will seek whom to serve in a menial capacity, and will not find any one; for, even if you were willing to demean yourselves to service of this kind, people, knowing who your honors are, would not like to employ you, neither would your honors like to be so employed. Such is the state of things; and there is Don Sebastian Castilla, whom you well know to be of an illustrious family, the son of the Conde de la Gomera. He, deploring our necessities, is willing to take upon himself the charge of providing a remedy for all of us. So, in concert with certain of his friends, he has determined, on whatever day shall seem good to you, to slay the Mariscal Alonzo de Alvarado. Señor Egas de Guzman, with another band of cavaliers, will put to

favor, tassandolos ya como los han tassado, no lo pueden hazer."—FERNANDEZ, *Hist. del Perú*, parte ii., lib. ii., cap. 1.

* Bread made of *papas*, which are a kind of pig-nut.

death the Licentiate De la Gama, Juan de Saavedra, the Captain Juan Alonzo de Palomino, with others who, as it appears to us, should die for our security."

The soldier then concluded by asking them to give their opinion upon his proposal. They all exclaimed that he had spoken very well.

Then Egas de Guzman took up the discourse, and said that they must show no lukewarmness; that they were such cavaliers that each one of them was fit to govern the kingdom of Peru. Did they not remember how few were the men of Chili who went to the palace of the Marquis Pizarro and slew him, and that, too, in the middle of the day?

Many of the soldiers now expressed their opinion upon the details of the enterprise. Some complained of the youthfulness of Don Sebastian. Egas de Guzman defended the choice, and said that if Gonzalo Pizarro had possessed such qualities as Don Sebastian, his cause would not have been lost. He also declared that even among the principal colonists there were many who favored their cause, especially a certain Vasco de Godinez, who had three hundred soldiers ready to support them in the town of La Plata.

Then a Biscayan, named San Juan, rose and said that he knew that Egas de Guzman was right; that, in fact, they would all obey a cat, much more a cavalier like Don Sebastian de Castilla; and if they would not have him, they might take out a skull from this monastery and swear obedience to it. Finally, he said that if that coward Francisco Hernandez had chosen to lead them, they would have had a remedy for their grievances, and so they would have now; "for I know," he added, "that from Potosi to Lima the good will to revolt is such that the revolters would obey a cat if it were set up as a leader; and I declare that the retail traders and the bad women are strong enough to drive the auditors out of Lima, and to raise the standard of rebellion."

The conspiracy proceeded, but the issues of it were very different from those that were expected or designed by the conspirators. They did not slay the Mariscal Alonzo de Alvarado; they did not surprise Cusco or Lima; but they murdered Pedro de Hinojosa, who had been sent as captain general to Potosi; and there they raised the standard of revolt. Their enterprise was unsuccessful. Don Sebastian was murdered by his own followers, and after the revolt had been quelled, the Mariscal Alonzo de Alvarado, much noted for his severity, was employed by the auditors to punish the delinquents. He was heard to say that the branches had been destroyed at Potosi, but that the roots of the conspiracy must be dug up at Cusco. This saying caused great alarm to the inhabitants of that city, and among others to Francisco Hernandez de Giron, a man to whom all the discontented had looked up ever since the publication of the first repartition of the President Gasca. Giron resolved to rebel. The time was most favorable. Discontent had reached its climax in Peru. The royal order about the personal service of the Indians was conceived in the tenderest spirit of kindness toward the natives. The Spaniards were not allowed to make terms with the caciques, but only with the Indians individually. They were to pay them a settled amount of wages; were not to employ them for more than three months at a time; and many other provisos were made, all in favor of the Indians, and so framed as to protect them from excessive work, or even from work to which they had not been accustomed.* In Cusco a Junta was

* "Primeramente, que el concierto que se hiziere con los Indios,

held of the colonists, and a remonstrance drawn up against the royal order respecting personal service. When this was presented to the corregidor of the town, he tore it up in the presence of the remonstrants. Their fury now knew no bounds; and Francisco Hernandez was surrounded by men who were ready and willing to throw off their allegiance to the king.

The 13th of November, 1553, was the day chosen for the outbreak of the conspiracy. There is a graphic account of this outbreak from the pen of the historian GARCILASO DE LA VEGA, who, as a boy of fourteen, was a witness of the most striking incidents of the revolt. That day was chosen because it was the day fixed for a grand marriage in Cusco between Alonzo de Loaysa, nephew of the Archbishop of Lima, and Donna Maria de Castilla, a noble lady. After the marriage-breakfast had taken place, there was a tournament* held in the street. GARCILASO says, "I looked at the festival from the top of a stone wall which is in front of the house of Alonzo de Loaysa. I saw Francisco Hernandez in the dining-room which looks out upon the street, sitting in a chair, his arms crossed and his

ha de ser con los propios Indios que han de servir: y no con el Cacique, ni principales. Y que á los mismos Indios se les pague, y se les dé á entender, quando se concertaren, que libremente lo pueden hazer, é que no se les ha de hazer fuerça para ello: é que el concierto ha de ser por tres meses, é no mas, é passados se les pague, é se buelvan á sus tierras. Y que á los Indios con quien se concertaren, para traer yerva, leña, servicio de su casa, huertas, charcarras, y guarda de ganado; se pague á cada uno, por cada mes (á lo menos) un peso y quatro tomines, y un quartillo de mayz, cada dia par su comida."—FERNANDEZ, *Historia del Perú*, parte ii., lib. ii., cap. 27.

* It was the *juego de alcanzia*, which was played on horseback, with balls of earth dried in the sun, which balls contained cinders or flowers, and were thrown by the assailants, while those who acted on the defensive endeavored to protect themselves with their shields.

head bent down, more abstracted and pensive than Melancholy herself. He must have been thinking about what he was to do that night."*

After the tournament came the supper. Don Baltazar de Castilla, the uncle of the bride, was the master of the ceremonies. "I went," says GARCILASO, "to the marriage-feast just about the end of the supper, in order to return with my father and my mother-in-law, who were among the guests." The corregidor, a good-natured man, saw the boy, observed that there was no seat for him, and called to him to come and share his seat, at the same time ordering conserves to be brought, which is what boys like, as GARCILASO remarks. At this moment it was announced at the farther end of the hall that Francisco Hernandez de Giron was entering. The master of the ceremonies, who was near the door, exclaimed, "How late your lordship has waited to do us this honor;" and he commanded the doors to be thrown wide open. Then appeared a sight very unusual at marriage feasts; for Francisco Hernandez entered with a drawn sword in one hand and a buckler in the other. On each side of him was one of his followers, with a partisan in his hand. The guests rose. Giron thus addressed them: "Let you honors be quiet, for this is for the good of all."

The corregidor, without waiting to hear any more, opened a door that was close to him, and fled into the apartment where the ladies were supping sepa-

* "Yo miré la Fiesta de encima de una pared de canteria de piedra, que está de frente de las casas de Alonzo de Loaysa. Vide á Francisco Hernandez en la sala, que sale á la calle, sentado en una silla, los braços cruçados sobre el pecho, y la cabeça baja, mas suspenso, í imaginativo, que la misma Melancolia. Debia de estar imaginando en lo que avia de hacer aquella noche."—GARCILASO DE LA VEGA, *Comentarios Reales*, parte ii., lib. vii., cap. 2.

rately. By that door, and by another on the same side, many of the loyal personages fled. One or two were murdered in the room. Garcilaso's father, with twenty-five others, and Garcilaso himself, escaped by the door which the corregidor had opened. They found that they could make their way through another house into a back street, and the elder Garcilaso besought the corregidor to accompany him. But he would not do so, and fell into the hands of the rebels. After capturing him, they went out into the great square, released the prisoners from the public prison, and took possession of the city.

Francisco Hernandez appointed his master of the camp, and filled up the other offices in his army. He then wrote letters to various towns, and even to one of the Auditors of Lima, justifying his proceedings. In his letter to the town of La Plata he enters largely into the subject of the grievances occasioned to the colonists by the remission of personal service. He says that the auditors had acted not so much from religious zeal as from a kind of envy, "taking away from us that which the Indians can righteously and religiously afford us, and giving it to them for their idolatries and drunken feasts—depriving us of liberty, and conferring it upon them, so that they may never come to the knowledge of the faith—doing away with personal service, which caused them so little mischief, and brought them so much profit. For, without adventuring any thing," he writes, "the natives increased their estates and changed their customs, taking up ours. Moreover, the auditors command that the Indians should return to their native places, and go forth from the farms and estates of the Spaniards where they had taken root."*

* "No mas de por un genero de invidia, mas que religioso zelo de

These arguments of Francisco Hernandez had much weight in many parts of Peru, and his rebellion became most formidable. As a fitting emblem, he wore in his cap a medal, on which was the inscription "*Edent pauperes et saturabuntur*," wishing it to be understood that he had taken up this enterprise that all might have sustenance and liberty.*

It would be interesting to follow in detail this rebellion of Francisco Hernandez de Giron, if it were not that the men, and even the geography of the campaigns, would be so unfamiliar to most European readers that the whole story would be sure to be forgotten almost as soon as it had been read. The fortunes of the Pizarros have some hold upon our memories on account of their relation to the great discoverer of Peru. The rebellion of Giron was, in some respects, similar to that of Gonzalo Pizarro, and was extinguished in a similar manner. The most noteworthy point about it is that a like result ensued as regards the liberties of the Indians. Pizarro's rebellion caused the Spanish court to give up the revocation of *encomiendas*. And one of the surest means which the au-

servir á Dios, y poner en orden la tierra. Evitando á nosotros lo que justa y religiosamente nos pueden dar los Indios: dandose lo á ellos, para sus ydolatrias y borracheras. Mandando en sus provisiones, que los Indios fuessen libres y exentos: quitando la libertad á nosotros, y dandosela á ellos para que nunca vengan en conocimiento de la fé. Quitando el servicio personal, que tan poco trabajo aventuravan en el, y tan gran prouecho se les seguia; pues sin aventurar nada augmentavan en sus haziendas los naturales, y mudavan sus costumbres, tomando las nuestras. Y ansi mismo mandavan que los Indios se volviessen á sus naturales, y saliessen de donde estavan arraygados y poblados en las haziendas, y tierras, y estancias de todos los vezinos."—FERNANDEZ, *Hist. del Perú*, parte ii., lib. ii., cap. 27.

* "En otra medalla de Oro traya al rededor un retulo que dezia, *Edent pauperes et saturabuntur*, dando á entender que porque todos comiessen, y por la libertad de todos, avia tomado la empressa que traya."—FERNANDEZ, *Hist. del Perú*, parte ii., lib. ii., cap. 32.

ditors took to suppress this rebellion of Giron was to suspend for two years the law remitting the personal service of the Indians.* They appointed the Mariscal Alvarado their captain general, but he was defeated by Giron, as Diego Centeno had been defeated by Gonzalo Pizarro. Giron unconsciously imitated the conduct of Pizarro. Engaging in a second battle under disadvantageous circumstances, he was finally defeated by the royal officers; and afterward, being captured, was put to death for his treason. The victors pressed the royal Audiencia to make a new *repartimiento*, but the auditors refused to do so, and meanwhile a new viceroy arrived in the person of Don Hurtado de Mendoza, the Marquis of Cañete.

This viceroy, acting at first with great severity, and afterward with singular mildness, succeeded in reestablishing the royal authority in Peru. It was at this period that the abdication of Charles the Fifth, and the assumption of royal authority by Philip the Second, were notified to the colonies. Henceforth we may consider the royal authority as firmly established throughout the Spanish possessions in America, and it will only remain to trace the progress of those humane and benevolent laws which emanated from time to time from the home government, rendering the sway of the Spanish monarchs over the conquered nations as remarkable for mildness as any, perhaps, that has ever been recorded in the pages of history.

* "De ay á veynte y cinco dias, le llegaron al Mariscal dos provisiones del Audiencia Real. Una para que fuesse Capitan General, é hiziesse gente, y gastasse de la Real hazienda, y de la de particulares, lo que fuesse necessario para la guerra, y castigo de Francisco Hernandez. Y otra provision, en que suspendian el servicio personal, por dos años."—FERNANDEZ, *Hist. del Perú*, parte ii., lib. ii., cap. 40.

BOOK XX.

THE PROTECTORS OF THE INDIANS: THEIR EFFORTS AND ACHIEVEMENTS.

CHAPTER I.

LAS CASAS AS A BISHOP.

CHAPTER II.

THE CONTROVERSY BETWEEN SEPULVEDA AND LAS CASAS.

CHAPTER III.

FINAL LABORS AND DEATH OF LAS CASAS.

CHAPTER IV.

LAWS RELATING TO ENCOMIENDAS AND PERSONAL SERVICES.

CHAPTER V.

LAWS REGULATING NEGRO SLAVERY, AND PREVENTING THE SLAVERY OF THE INDIANS.

CHAPTER VI.

RESULTS OF THE SPANISH LEGISLATION IN FAVOR OF THE INDIANS.

CHAPTER I.

LAS CASAS AS A BISHOP.

AMONG the achievements of the statesmen, churchmen, and lawyers who distinguished themselves as Protectors of the Indians during the first half of the sixteenth century, those of Las Casas are incomparably the most prominent. It can not even be said of any other protector, as was said of the second competitor in the race in VIRGIL'S *Æneid*, that he was next to the foremost man, "though next after a long interval;"* for Las Casas was entirely alone in his pre-eminence. It is desirable, therefore, to follow to its close the life of that man who, during his lifetime, was the prime mover on almost all the great occasions when the welfare of the Indians occupied the attention of the court of Spain.

Gonzalo Pizarro's rebellion in Peru, which the remarkable sagacity of Gasca only just sufficed to quell, was directly traceable to the influence of the new laws. It has been seen that the two minor rebellions which followed were also caused by these same ordinances. The new laws had been a signal triumph for Las Casas. Without him, without his untiring energy and singular influence over those whom he came near, these laws would not have been enacted.

* "Primus abit, longeque ante omnia corpora Nisus
Emicat, et ventis et fulminis ocior alis.
Proximus huic, longo sed proximus intervallo,
Insequitur Salius."—*Æneid*, lib. v., 318.

The mere bodily fatigue which he endured was such as hardly any man of his time, not a conqueror, had encountered. He had crossed the ocean twelve times. Four times he had made his way into Germany to see the Emperor. Had a record been kept of his wanderings, such as that which exists of the journeys of Charles the Fifth, it would have shown that Las Casas had led a much more active life than even that energetic monarch. Moreover, the journeyings of Las Casas were often made with all the inconvenience of poverty, and were not in any respect like a royal progress.

The narrative of his life is resumed at the year 1543, when he was at Barcelona, whither he had gone to thank the Emperor for the promulgation of the new laws. His joy was suddenly interrupted by an offer which would have delighted most other men, but which to him was singularly unwelcome. One Sunday evening, while at Barcelona, he was surprised by receiving a visit from the Emperor's secretary, Francisco de los Cobos, who came to press upon his acceptance the Bishopric of Cusco, vacant by the death of Bishop Valverde. There were weighty reasons why this offer of a bishopric should be unwelcome to Las Casas. To prove that he was moved by no private interest in his advocacy of the cause of the Indians, he had publicly and solemnly renounced all personal favor or gratification that Charles the Fifth could bestow upon him.* Moreover, his flock was already larger than that in any bishopric; and to become a bishop was, for Las Casas, a limitation of the sphere of his philanthropic endeavors. Accordingly, he refused the Bishopric of Cusco, and quitted Barcelona.

* See *ante*, vol. ii., book ix., chap. ii., p. 66.

He was not, however, to escape being raised to the episcopal dignity. The province of Chiapa had recently been constituted into a diocese, and the first bishop who had been appointed had died on his way to the seat of his bishopric. The Council of the Indies felt that it would be desirable to have a bishop in that diocese who would look to the execution of the new laws. The province of Chiapa was at a great distance from Mexico, where there was an *Audiencia*, and also from Honduras, where a new one was about to be constituted, to be called the *Audiencia* of the Confines. Chiapa, therefore, might be much misgoverned unless it had a vigorous bishop. The Council resolved that Las Casas should have this bishopric pressed upon him. The heads of the Dominican Order were of opinion that Las Casas ought not to refuse this offer; and, after being exposed to entreaty of all kinds, it being pressed upon him as a matter of conscience that he should accept the bishopric, he at last conquered his repugnance, and submitted himself to the will of his superiors.*

Having accepted the bishopric, Las Casas instantly set off for Toledo, where a chapter of his Order was about to be held, and where he resolved to ask permission to carry out with him a number of Dominican monks, who might assist him in Christianizing his diocese. The permission was granted. Several monks were chosen, who, with Las Casas, prepared themselves for their journey and voyage to the New World. Las Casas was consecrated at Seville; and

* "Le pusieron en conciencia el favor de los naturales con la dignidad Episcopal y á pura muchedumbre de ruegos y porfias, exortaciones, amonestaciones, exemplos y seguridad del dezir de las gentes, con la repugnancia que hasta entonces avia hecho; le hizieron aceptar el Obispado."—REMESAL, *Hist. de Chiapa y Guatemala*, lib. iii., cap. 13.

on a Wednesday, the 4th of July, 1544, the new bishop, with his friend Rodrigo de Ladrada, and some clerigos, took his departure from Spain. The monks who accompanied him were forty-four in number, and were under the orders of their vicar, Thomas Casillas. They all set sail from San Lucar; and, after touching at the Canary Islands, arrived at the island of Hispaniola. The bishop was exceedingly ill received there. Indeed, he was the most unpopular man in the New World, as being the one who had done most to restrain the cruelty and curb the power of the Spanish conquerors. We can not pursue the voyages and the journeyings of the bishop and the monks until they reached the province of Chiapa, and were installed in the town of Ciudad Real, the capital of that province. There exists, however, a minute account of all their proceedings, which is most interesting, and serves to show the hardships which such men underwent at that period before they could establish themselves in the Indies.

The episcopal dignity made no change in the ways or manners of Las Casas. His dress was that of a simple monk, often torn and patched. He ate no meat himself, though it was provided for the clergy who sat at table with him. There was no plate to be seen in his house—nothing but earthenware; and in all respects his household was maintained in the simplest manner.* He had lost all his books, which had

* "En su persona se trató siempre como frayle, un habito humilde, y algunas vezes roto y remendado. Jamas se puso tunica de lienço, ni durmió sino en sabanas de estameña, y una fraçada por colcha rica. No comia carne, aunque para los clérigos que assistian á su mesa se servia con mucha moderacion, como se ha dicho. Comia en platos de varro, y las alhajas de su casa eran muy pocas."—REMESAL, *Hist. de Chiapa y Guatemala*, lib. vi., cap. 2.

been on board a vessel that had sunk in Campeachy Bay. This was a great grief to the good bishop, who, amid all his other labors, was a diligent student, giving especial attention to the voluminous works of Thomas Aquinas, which were a needful armory to all those who had any controversy to maintain in that age.

It was only at rare intervals that Las Casas achieved success or knew happiness; and the sufferings of the Indians oppressed his soul here, in Chiapa, as they had done in other parts of the New World. The members of his household could often hear him sighing and groaning in his own room at night. His grief used to reach its height when some poor Indian woman would come to him, and, throwing herself at his feet, exclaim with tears, "My father, great lord, I am free. Look at me; I have no mark of the brand on my face, and yet I have been sold for a slave. Defend me, you, who are our father." And Las Casas resolved to defend these poor people. His way of doing so was by forbidding absolution to be given to those Spaniards who held slaves contrary to the provisions contained in the new laws. This bold measure raised a perfect storm in his diocese. Some of the colonists and conquerors put the question as a point of honor. "If we dismiss these Indians," they said, "and cease to buy and sell them as we have hitherto done, they will say that we have been tyrants from the beginning, and that we can not do with them what we have done, since a simple monk like this restores them to their liberty. They will laugh at us, mock at us, and cry after us in the streets; and there will not be an Indian who will do what a Spaniard may command him."*

* "Otros tomavan esto por punta de honra, y reparavan en el 'qué diran los Indios.' Si agora los echamos de nosotros, *dezian*, y dexa-

There was nothing that the Spaniards in Ciudad Real did not say and do to molest the bishop. They called him a "Bachelor by the Tiles;" a phrase of that time, signifying one who had not been a regular student of theology, who had entered by the roof, and not by the door. They made verses upon him of an opprobrious kind, which the children sang in the streets. An arquebus, without ball, was discharged at his window to alarm him. His dean would not obey him, and gave absolution to some persons who notoriously had Indians for slaves. The Dominican monks partook of the unpopularity of the bishop. Finally, Las Casas resolved to seek redress, not for his own wrongs, but for those of his Indian flock, from the Royal *Audiencia* of the Confines, and he made a journey to Honduras for that purpose. There is a letter of his, dated the 22d of October, 1545, addressed to that *Audiencia*, in which he threatened the auditors with excommunication unless they should provide a remedy for the evils which existed in his diocese. When he appeared before them, the president, far from listening favorably to the protestations of Las Casas, poured forth a torrent of abuse upon him: "You are a scoundrel, a bad man, a bad monk, a bad bishop, a shameless fellow; and you deserve to be chastised." "I do deserve all that your lordship says," Las Casas replied. The bishop said this ironically, recollecting how much he had labored to obtain for this judge his place.

Notwithstanding his bad reception in the first in-

mos de comprarlos y venderlos como hasta aqui, diran que fuymos tyranos al principio, y que no podemos hazer con ellos lo que hizimos, pues un solo frayle como este los restituye en su libertad. Reyranse de nosotros, mofarannos y gritarannos por essas calles, y no avrá Indio que quiera házer lo que un Español le mande."—Remesal, *Hist. de Chiapa y Guatemala*, lib. vi., cap. 2.

stance from the Auditors of the Confines, the bishop at last succeeded in persuading them to agree to send an auditor to Ciudad Real who should see to the execution of the new laws. The inhabitants of Ciudad Real were informed by letter of this fact, and they determined to make the most strenuous resistance to the return of their bishop into the city. They prepared a protest, in which they said that he had never shown any bull from the Pope, or mandate from the Emperor, authorizing him to exercise the rights of a bishop. They insisted upon his proceeding like the other bishops of New Spain, and not introducing innovations. If he did not assent to this, they would deprive him of his temporalities, and refuse to admit him as their bishop. They placed a body of Indians on the road that he would have to traverse in returning to their city, having determined that they would not let him enter unless, as they said, he would treat them as Christians, allowing them absolution, and not endeavor to take away their slaves, nor to fix the tribute of their *encomiendas*. Against the bishop, who would come "unguarded and on foot, with only a stick in his hand and a breviary in his girdle," they prepared coats of mail and corslets, arquebuses, lances, and swords. The Indians were posted some way out of the city as sentinels, to give notice of his approach. Meanwhile Las Casas had arrived at Copanabastla, where there was a Dominican monastery, and where he learned what reception was awaiting him in his diocese. The Dominicans counseled him not to proceed; but the bishop's opinion was that he should fearlessly prosecute his journey. "For," he said, "if I do not go to Ciudad Real, I banish myself from my church; and it will be said of me, with much reason, 'The wicked fleeth, and no man pursueth.'" He did not deny that the intelligence was true, and that his flock were prepared to kill him. "But," he said, "the minds of men change from hour to hour, from minute to minute, from moment to moment. Is it possible that God has been so chary with the men of Ciudad Real as to deny His holy assistance in causing them to abstain from so great a crime as putting me to death? If I do not endeavor to enter my church, of whom shall I have to complain to the king, or to the Pope, as having thrust me out of it? Are my adversaries so bitter against me that the first word will be a deadly thrust through my heart, without giving me the chance of soothing them? In conclusion, reverend fathers, I am resolved, trusting in the mercy of God and in your holy prayers, to set out for my diocese. To tarry here, or to go elsewhere, has all the inconveniences which have just been stated." So saying, he rose from his seat; and, gathering up the folds of his scapulary, he commenced his journey.

Now the Indian sentinels had heard that the bishop's baggage, which had preceded him, had been taken back, and they were consequently quite at their ease. The inhabitants of Ciudad Real had also heard of this, and there was great joy in the city, as they thought that their preparations had daunted the bishop.

Suddenly the bishop in his journey came upon these Indian sentinels. They fell at his feet, and with tears besought his pardon. It was beautiful to hear the harangue which each of them made, clinging to the feet of the bishop, and speaking in the Mexican language, which is very expressive of the affections."* The kind bishop was not angry with

* "Y era donoso el modo de la arenga que cada uno abraçado con los pies del Obispo dezia en lengua Mexicana, que es muy significativa de afectos."—Remesal, *Hist. de Chiapa y Guatemala*, lib. vii., cap. 8.

the Indians, and his only fear was lest they should be scourged or put to death for not having given notice of his approach. He therefore, with his own hands, assisted by a certain Father Vicente who was with him, tied these Indians to one another, and made them follow behind him, as if they were his prisoners. He did this partly with his own hands, in order that two or three Spaniards who were with him, and a negro, who always accompanied him because he was very tall and could carry the bishop across the rivers, might not be subject to the charge of having bound the Indians. That same night, as the bishop journeyed, there was an earthquake at Ciudad Real, and the citizens said, "The bishop must be coming, and those dogs of Indians have not told us of it; this earthquake is a sign of the destruction that is to come upon the city when he arrives in it."

The bishop traveled all night, and reached Ciudad Real at daybreak. He went straight to the church; and thither he summoned the alcaldes and regidors to meet him. They came, followed by all the inhabitants of the city, and seated themselves, as if to hear a sermon. When the bishop advanced from the sacristy, no man asked his benediction, or spoke a word to him, or made any sign of courtesy. Then the notary to the Town Council rose, and read a paper containing the requisitions which had been agreed upon. To this the bishop replied in a speech of much gentleness and modesty, and his words were producing a considerable effect on his hearers, when one of the regidors, without rising or taking off his cap, commenced a speech, blaming the bishop, whom he described as a private individual, for presuming to summon them there instead of coming to the Town Council.

"Look you, sir," the bishop replied, "when I have to ask you any thing from your estates, I will go to your houses to speak to you; but when the things which I have to speak about relate to the service of God and the good of your souls, I have to send and summon you, and to command that you should come wherever I may be; and if you are Christians, you have to come trooping there in haste, lest evil fall upon you." These words, spoken with great animation, had the effect of dismaying and silencing the bishop's opponents.

He rose and prepared to go into the sacristy, when the secretary of the Town Council went up to him, and presented a petition that he would name confessors. "I shall willingly do so," said the bishop; and with a loud voice he named two confessors. They were, however, well known to be of his own way of thinking. The people, therefore, were not satisfied. The bishop then named two others, of whose good disposition he was well aware, but who were not so well known as his partisans. The monk who had accompanied him on his journey, Fray Vicente de Ferrer, laid hold of the bishop's vestments, and exclaimed, "Let your lordship die rather than do this," for he was not aware of the character of these men whom the bishop had named, and thought he was giving way to clamor. Immediately a great tumult arose in the church; and at that juncture, two monks of the Order of Mercy entered it, who persuaded the bishop and his companion to withdraw from the crowd, and to accompany them to their convent.

Las Casas, having journeyed on foot all night, was exceedingly exhausted; and the monks were giving him some bread, when they heard a great noise, and found that an armed populace had surrounded the convent. Some of the armed men forced their way even to the cell where the bishop was. A new grievance, which had infuriated them, was that their Indian sentinels had been bound and treated as prisoners. The bishop said that he alone was to blame in the matter; that he had come upon these Indians suddenly, and had bound them with his own hands, lest they should be suspected of having voluntarily favored him, and be accordingly maltreated. One of the rioters, a certain Pedro de Pando, said, "You see here the way of the world. He is the savior of the Indians, and look, he it is who binds them. Yet this same man will send memorials against us to Spain, declaring that we maltreat them." After this, another of the inhabitants of Ciudad Real poured out most foul language against the bishop. Las Casas only said, "I do not choose, sir, to answer you, in order not to take out of God's hands your chastisement; for these insults are not addressed to me, but to Him."

While this was going on in the cell of the bishop, one of the mob in the court-yard had been quarreling with Juanillo, the bishop's negro, saying that it was he who had tied the Indians, and he gave the negro a thrust with a pike which stretched him on the ground. The monks rushed forward to assist the negro; and two of them, who were youths, showed such courage that the Fathers of Mercy succeeded in clearing, by main force, their convent from its invaders. It was now nine o'clock in the morning. But by midday so great a change had been wrought in the minds of the inhabitants of Ciudad Real, so completely had they come to a sense of the turbulence and shamefulness of their conduct, that nearly all of them proceeded to the convent, and on their knees besought the bishop's pardon, kissed his hands, and said that they were his children. The alcaldes, as a sign of submission, would not carry their wands of office in his presence; others took off their swords; and, in festal procession, they brought the bishop out of the convent, carried him to the house of one of the principal inhabitants, and sent him various costly presents. Nay, more, they resolved to hold a tournament in honor of their bishop, a mark of their favor and esteem he could, perhaps, have dispensed with.* Certainly few men have ever experienced stranger turns of fortune than Las Casas did in the course of this memorable day of his return to his diocese. The very suddenness of the change of feeling in his flock was a circumstance that might well have engendered in his mind misgivings as to the future, and have disgusted him with the office of ruling as bishop over the turbulent and versatile citizens of Ciudad Real, the chief city of Chiapa.

But, indeed, in no part of the New World would Las Casas have had an easy life. It was at this time that Gonzalo Pizarro's rebellion in Peru was at its height, and that the resistance to the new laws was so great that Charles the Fifth was obliged to revoke them. What anguish must have been caused to Las Casas by the revocation of these laws is known to no man. Notwithstanding the disasters he experienced, which would have crushed the spirit of almost any other person, his zeal never slackened, and his practical sagacity taught him not to reproach Charles the Fifth or his ministers for a backward course of legislation, which he knew had been forced upon them by

* "Puestos en paz los vezinos de Ciudad Real con su Obispo, y visitandole y regolandole como se ha dichó, determinaron de festejarle segundo dia de Pasqua de Navidad con un solemne juego de cañas." —Remesal, *Hist. de Chiapa y Guatemala*, lib. vii., cap. 9.

calamity. For himself, he maintained his ground that the granting of *encomiendas* to private persons was a great injustice to the native Indians; but he seems to have accepted the new position of affairs, and to have bent his efforts to improving that system which he must have felt could not now be destroyed by a mere mandate from the court of Spain. At any rate, he did not protest against the revocation of the new laws as an act of folly or weakness on the part of the Spanish authorities at home. This revocation could not have been known at this time to the *Audiencia* of the Confines, for they fulfilled their promise of sending one of their body to Chiapa.

This auditor heard, with attention and respect, the representations that Las Casas made to him on behalf of the Indians. But one day he thus replied: "Your lordship well knows that although these new laws were framed at Valladolid, with the accordance of sundry grave personages (as your lordship and I saw), one of the reasons that has made these laws hateful in the Indies has been the fact of your having had a hand in them. The conquerors consider your lordship as so prejudiced against them, that they believe that what you do in favor of the natives is not so much from love of the Indians as from hatred of the Spaniards. As they entertain this opinion, if I have to deprive any of them of their slaves or estates, they will feel more its being done in your presence than they will the loss itself. Don Tello de Sandoval (the President of the *Audiencia* at Mexico) has summoned your lordship for a synod of prelates, and I shall be glad if you will hasten your departure, for, until you have gone, I can do nothing."

The bishop had been preparing to attend this synod, and he now took his departure. He never beheld his diocese again.

When he approached the city of Mexico there was a tumult as if a hostile army were about to occupy the city. The authorities were obliged to write to him, begging him to defer his entry until the minds of men should be somewhat quieted.* He afterward entered in the daytime without receiving any insult. He took up his abode in the Dominican monastery, and on the first day of his arrival the viceroy and the auditors sent word that they were ready to receive a visit from him. His reply evinced his habitual boldness, but, at the same time, betrayed the want of worldly wisdom that was occasionally manifest in him. There was quite enough difficulty in the affairs which he had to manage on his own account, but he felt it his duty to inform the king's officers that they must excuse his visiting them, as they were excommunicated, since they had given orders for cutting off the head of a priest at Antequera. This answer was soon made known throughout the city of Mexico, and increased the odium under which Las Casas labored.

The synod of prelates and other learned men commenced its proceedings, and laid down as a basis five principal points. 1st. That all unbelievers, of whatever sect or religion they might be, and whatever sins they might have committed against natural, national, or divine law, have nevertheless a just lordship over

* The hatred to Las Casas throughout the New World amounted to a passion. Letters were written to the residents in Chiapa expressing pity for them as having met the greatest misfortune that could occur to them in being placed under such a bishop. They did not name him, but spoke of him as "that devil who has come to you for a bishop." The following is an extract from one of these letters: "We say here, that very great must be the sins of your country, when God chastises it with such a scourge as sending that anti-Christ for a bishop."

their own possessions. 2d. That there are four different kinds of unbelievers. The object of laying down this maxim is not obvious at first, and requires a knowledge of the controversies of that age. The object was to place the Indians in the second class of unbelievers; and more than once, on great occasions, Las Casas placed them in the same division as the ancient British, thus dividing them from those barbarians who had no arts or polity whatever. 3d. That the final and only reason why the Apostolic See had given supreme jurisdiction in the Indies to the kings of Castile and Leon was that the Gospel might be preached and the Indians be converted. It was not to make those kings greater lords and richer princes than they were. 4th. That the Apostolic See, in granting this supremacy to the kings of Castile and Leon, did not mean thereby to deprive the lords of the Indians of their estates, lordships, jurisdictions, or dignities. 5th. That the kings of Castile and Leon were bound to provide the requisite expenses for the conversion of the Indians to the true faith.

Taking the foregoing as their main principles, the synod made many deductions very unfavorable to the claims of the conquerors; and especially they pronounced what were the conditions upon which absolution should be granted by confessors to the Spanish colonists, into which conditions restitution entered.

The proceedings of this synod were very bold, but Las Casas was not satisfied with them, because the particular point of slavery, though much discussed, was not resolved upon. He therefore summoned a Junta, which was attended by all the learned men except the bishops; and this Junta pronounced that the Spaniards who had made slaves were "tyrants;" that the slaves were to be considered as illegally made;

and that all those who possessed them were bound to liberate them. They also pronounced against the personal service of the Indians.

It must not be supposed that the members of this Junta imagined that their decisions would immediately insure the liberation of the Indians. These learned men contented themselves with declaring to their countrymen what they held to be the truth, and informing them of what was necessary for the salvation of their souls. They were not bound to do any thing more.*

Las Casas did not return from Mexico to his bishopric. Ever since his interview with the Auditors of the Confines he had resolved to go back to Spain; and the reason which he gave to one of his reverend brethren was, that when at court, and near the king and his council, he would be able to do more good service, both to his own province and to the whole Indies, than by staying in his diocese, especially as he had now members of his own order stationed there, who could correspond with him, and inform him of whatever evil might require a remedy.

He accordingly prepared to act upon this resolve. He appointed confessors for his diocese, and regulated the conditions of absolution, which were expressed in twelve rules. He nominated a vicar general for his bishopric, and then proceeded from Mexico to Spain, where he resigned the bishopric.† His return was in the year 1547.

* "Contentavanse con dar á entender á los Españoles la verdad, y dezirles lo que les era necessario para su salvacion, que no estavan obligados á mas."—Remesal, *Hist. de Chiapa y Guatemala*, lib. vii., cap. 17.

† In 1555 he was allowed a pension of 200,000 maravedis=£108 6*s*., a sum not inconsiderable in that day.

One of the biographers of Las Casas states that the bishop was obliged to return to Spain to answer certain charges that were made against him, chiefly touching his formulary of confession, and that he went back as a prisoner. I do not find any authority for this statement; but it is certain that on the bishop's return to Spain he did appear before the Council of the Indies, and had to justify this formulary, which he succeeded in doing.

CHAPTER II.

THE CONTROVERSY BETWEEN SEPULVEDA AND LAS CASAS.

THE learned men of Spain were not all of the Bishop of Chiapa's way of thinking as regarded the rights and claims of the Indians. A certain Doctor Juan Ginés Sepulveda,* principal historiographer to Charles the Fifth, a man of great renown for learning in those days, had recently written a treatise entitled *Democrates Secundus, sive de Justis Belli Causis,* in which he maintained, in a very able manner, the right of the Pope and of the kings of Spain to subdue by war the inhabitants of the New World. Sepulveda called his new work *Democrates Secundus,* because he had previously written a book which was entitled *Democrates: a Dialogue on the Honorable Nature of Military Study.* The *Democrätes Secundus* was also written in dialogue; and in it, Leopold, a German, made a formal statement, which probably was sanctioned by the voice of public opinion throughout Europe at that time, that the Spaniards had, without sufficient attention to the laws of justice, piety, and Christianity, waged war against the innocent Indians. Sepulveda, under the name of Democrates, gave a full reply to his friend Leopold's accusation of the Spaniards.

Sepulveda's work met with no favor, even in the

* Sepulveda corresponded with Erasmus, Cardinals Pole and Contarini, and was the author of many learned treatises.

quarter where he might reasonably have expected that it would be sure to be well received. He submitted his treatise to the Council of the Indies in the first instance, but they would not allow him to print it. He then appealed to Charles the Fifth, praying that his work should be laid before the great Council of Castile. The Emperor consented. It was in 1547, when the court and the great Councils of Spain were at Aranda de Duero, that the royal order from Charles arrived. Las Casas had also joined the court at that time, and then learned what was the nature of this treatise written by Sepulveda, upon which there was so much question. As may be imagined, he made the most determined and vigorous opposition to Sepulveda's views—to use his own words, "discovering and bringing to light the poison of which the work was full." The Council submitted the *Democrates Secundus* for examination to the universities of Alcalá and Salamanca. The decision of these learned bodies was unfavorable to Sepulveda, and the permission to print was still refused. Sepulveda turned to Rome, where he had a great friend, who was Auditor of the Rota; and, under his auspices, the work, or rather an Apology for the work, containing the substance of it, was printed at Rome in 1550.* Charles the Fifth forbade its introduction into Spain. The author thereupon drew up a version in Spanish of his *Apology*, and did what he could to put that in circulation. The *Apology* is now to be found in Sepulveda's Works, reprinted from the Roman edition. It does not contain any thing which would at first sight be thought to be displeasing to the monarchs of Spain. Sepulveda declares that to Jesus Christ all power was given in heaven and earth, and that this power de-

* The title is *Apologia pro Libro de Justis Belli Causis.*

volved upon the Pope, who accordingly possessed authority in every land, not only for the preaching of the Gospel, but also for compelling men to obey the law of nature. The author defends his position by references to St. Augustine, St. Ambrose, St. Gregory, and the great authority of the Middle Ages, Thomas Aquinas. He appeals to History, citing the law of capital punishment enacted by "that most pious emperor," Constantine, against those pagans who should persevere in their rites and sacrifices. He maintains that men who are in a grievous state of error are to be recalled to the truth, whether they like it or not. He urges that more can be effected in a month by conquest than in a hundred years by mere preaching. Miracles are not to be asked for when human means, having the sanction of divine authority, can attain the same end. "The preachers of our time," he says, "without miracles, can not effect more than the apostles did, blessed with the co-operation of the Lord, and their words being confirmed by miracles."* War, therefore, was a necessity. If the natives were taught without being terrified, being obdurate in their old ways, they would be much more slowly moved to adopt the true faith.

If Las Casas had been ardent in his opposition to Sepulveda's doctrines when they were not printed, and while they could be read by those only who un-

* "Quæ omnia incommoda et difficultates, debellatis barbaris, facillime tolluntur, et sic plus uno mense in ipsorum conversione proficitur, quam centum annis per solam prædicationem, non pacatis barbaris, proficeretur. Non enim arbitror, nostri temporis prædicatores sine miraculis plus efficerent quam quondam Apostoli, *Domino cooperante, et sermonem confirmante sequentibus signis.* Quæ signa jam non sunt a Deo postulanda, cum nobis liceat præceptum ejus sequentes prudenti consilio barbaros ad convivium evangelicum, qua diximus ratione, compellere."—SEPULVEDÆ *Opera*, tom. iv., p. 343. Madrid, 1780.

derstood Latin, his ardor was redoubled when they were translated into Spanish, and could be joyfully perused by the conquerors in the Indies and their adherents at court, who would pronounce them to be most comfortable doctrines, and readily assign the palm of knowledge and of wisdom to this learned doctor, who justified the ways of his countrymen to themselves. It is true that the government were not remiss. They seized upon whatever copies of Sepulveda's *Apology* they could lay hold of, and strictly forbade its circulation.* But prohibited works are often not the less read on account of the prohibition. It is not likely that any of the numerous band of agents and proctors who thronged the court of Spain, and besieged it with applications on behalf of the conquerors and colonists of the New World, were ignorant of the arguments which Sepulveda had urged, and which might salve the troubled consciences, if troubled they were, of these conquerors and colonists. Las Casas set himself more seriously to work than ever to refute doctrines so fatal to his cause, and which had thus obtained extended publication and currency.

A great ferment arose about the controversy. In times like our own, when there is so much that is exciting and amusing in literature, it is difficult to imagine the interest that was felt in learned controversy in those ages, when controversy was the chief excitement and amusement of learned men. In this case,

* It is worthy of notice that there could have been no personal hostility to Sepulveda on the part of the government. He was not punished for the publication of the *Apology*. Charles the Fifth's friendship was not withdrawn from him; and he was one of the few persons who afterward visited that monarch in his retreat at Yuste, where he was kindly welcomed by Charles. See the graphic account of *The Cloister Life of Charles the Fifth*, written by Mr. STIRLING, p. 124.

moreover, there were many and great interests concerned.

Las Casas was not the only person who had been shocked by the doctrines or the expressions in Sepulveda's work, and who had sought to controvert them. Melchior Cano, a Dominican, renowned in those times for learning, had found passages in the *Democrates Secundus* "which were offensive to pious ears." The Bishop of Segovia had also been an ardent opponent to Sepulveda, and it was to him that the *Apology* for the work was addressed. Cano's objection to the book seems mainly to have turned upon an expression which had been used by the author in reference to St. Paul, Sepulveda having said that St. Paul had borne contumely with impatience, or words to that effect. A long correspondence ensued between the friends, for Cano was a friend of Sepulveda; but the real gist of the question is not touched upon in this correspondence. Las Casas was the opponent whom Sepulveda had most to fear, and he seems to have had somewhat of the same feeling toward him that his friend Erasmus must have had for the impetuous Luther. The refined scholar Sepulveda, "the Livy of Spain" as he has been called, looked upon the earnest Las Casas as a furious and dangerous person, "of better intentions than judgment;" yet (for he seems to have been an amiable man) declared that he bore no enmity to the bishop, and only prayed that God would grant him a calmer mind, that he might learn sometimes to prefer quiet cogitations to turbulent designs.*

* "Sed ne ipsum quidem auctorem odi, qui forsitan meliore animo quam consilio ductus est; quamquam in eo seditiose facta, et sinistros in me satos per injuriam sermones probare non possum, pro quibus tamen ei mali nihil cupio, sed potius Deum precor, ut ipsi meliorem mentem præbeat, quo discat aliquando quietas cogitationes turbulentis

Sepulveda might feel disgust at the uncontrolled temper of his opponent, and might despise his lesser acquisitions of learning, and his comparatively rude Latinity. But he was soon to learn what strength there was in an adversary whose practical knowledge of the subject in dispute was greater than that of any living man; whose eloquence was equal to his vehemence, and not hindered by it; and who brought a fervor to the cause which exceeded even that of an author publicly defending his own work, and one who must have thought himself most ungratefully used by the court and the universities in Spain.

Charles the Fifth convoked at Valladolid, in 1550, a Junta of theologians and other learned men to hear this great cause argued, "Whether war of the kind that is called a war of conquest could be lawfully undertaken against the nations of the New World, if they had not committed any new faults other than those they had committed in the times of their infidelity."* The Council of the Indies was associated with this Junta; and altogether it consisted of fourteen persons. This practice of summoning persons of special knowledge to assist the authorities in the determination of difficult questions was one of the greatest advantages which the government of Spain possessed at that period.

Doctor Sepulveda appeared before the Junta, and

consiliis anteferre."—SEPULVEDÆ *Epistola ad Melchiorem Canum*, Opera, tom. iii., p. 70.

* "Su Magestad mandó, el año passado de mil é quinientos y cincuenta, hazer una Congregacion en la villa de Valladolid de Letrados, Teologos, y Juristas, que se juntassen con el Consejo Real de las Indias, para que platicassen, y determinassen, si contra las gentes de aquellos Reynos se podian licitamente, y salva justicia, sin aver cometido nuevas culpas mas de las en su infidelidad cometidas, mover guerras que llaman conquistas."—*Disputa entre el Obispo* BARTOLOMÉ DE LAS CASAS, *y Dotor* GINES DE SEPULVEDA. Seville, 1552.

delivered a statement of the arguments on his side. The bishop was then summoned for a hearing, and in five consecutive days he read that laborious work of his which is called the *Historia Apologética.* It is rich in facts and arguments of every description, and he had been many years preparing it.

The Junta had deputed Domingo de Soto,* Charles's confessor, to give a summary of the arguments on both sides. This he did in a very masterly manner. The summary was then submitted to Doctor Sepulveda, who made a reply before the Junta, containing twelve objections to the arguments of the bishop. The bishop then gave twelve answers to these objections, and the proceedings terminated. They were afterward published as a work entitled "A Dispute or Controversy between the Bishop Don Fray Bartolomé de las Casas, lately Bishop of Ciudad Real in Chiapa, and Doctor Ginés Sepulveda, Historiographer to our Lord the Emperor."

* Mr. Hallam, speaking of the *Relectiones Theologicæ* of Francis a Victoria, says, "The whole relection, as well as that on the Indians, displays an intrepid spirit of justice and humanity, which seems to have been rather a general characteristic of the Spanish theologians. Dominic Soto, always inflexibly on the side of right, had already sustained by his authority the noble enthusiasm of Las Casas."—*Literature of Europe*, part ii., chap. iv., sect. iii.

Mr. Hallam also describes, in the following words, a work written by Domingo de Soto, *De Justitia et Jure:* "The first original work of any reputation in ethical philosophy since the revival of letters, and which, being apparently designed in great measure for the chair of the confessional, serves as a sort of link between the class of mere casuistry and the philosophical systems of morals which were to follow, is by Dominic Soto, a Spanish Dominican, who played an eminent part in the deliberations of the Council of Trent, in opposition both to the papal court and to the theologians of the Scotist, or, as it was then reckoned by its adversaries, Semi-Pelagian school. . . . . . It appears to be founded on the writings of Thomas Aquinas, the polar star of every true Dominican."—*Literature of Europe*, part ii., chapter iv., sect. i.

It would be impossible, within the limits which this history must occupy, to give a full account of this important controversy between Las Casas and Sepulveda. The work which Las Casas read in five days embodies much of the knowledge and experience which he had been acquiring for fifty years. We can hardly doubt, moreover, that both the controversialists were aided by other learned men, for an astonishing weight of learning is brought to bear upon the disputed points. The skill with which it is summed up by Charles's confessor is marvelous, considering the immense mass of material with which he had to deal, and that Las Casas was a man who sought to exhaust his subject by an appeal to facts and arguments drawn from every conceivable source.

Doctor Sepulveda divided his statement of the case into four heads. It was lawful, he said, to commence war upon the natives in the New World for the four following reasons:

1st. For the gravity of the sins which the Indians had committed, especially their idolatries and their sins against nature.

2d. On account of the rudeness of their natures, which brought upon them the necessity of serving persons of a more refined nature, such as that which the Spaniards possessed.

3d. In order to spread the faith, which would be more readily accomplished by the prior subjugation of the natives.

4th. To protect the weak among the natives themselves, duly considering the cruelties which the Indians exercised upon one another, slaying numbers in sacrifices to false gods, and practicing cannibalism.*

* "La 1. por la gravidad de los delitos de aquella gente, señaladamente por la idolatria, y otros pecados que cometen contra natura.

It would have been difficult to make a better division of the subject than that adopted by Sepulveda. His fourth reason was well thought of, and put with much skill. He adduced in evidence the immense loss of life which had taken place in the sacrifices to idols among the Mexicans, and was enabled to argue that it exceeded the loss of life in war. This was not so; but still the argument was a very plausible one.

The dealings of the Israelites with the neighboring idolaters formed the basis of the controversy upon the first reason, and gave room for elaborate argument. The doctor relied upon the command given to the Israelites, in the 20th chapter of *Deuteronomy*, to destroy the male inhabitants of those cities which should not be delivered up to them upon their demanding a surrender of the cities.* He dwelt especially on the 15th verse of that chapter, which says, "Thus shalt thou do unto all the cities which are very far off from

La segunda, por la rudeza de sus ingenios, que son de su natura gente servil, y barbara, y porende obligada á servir á los de ingenio mas elegantes como son los Españoles. La tercera, por el fin de la Fé, porque aquella sugecion es mas comoda, y expediente para su predicacion, y persuasion. La quarta, por la injuria que unos entre si hazen á otros, matando hombres para sacrificarlos, y algunos para comerlos."—*Disputa entre* BARTOLOMÉ DE LAS CASAS, *y Dotor* SEPULVEDA.

* "When thou comest nigh unto a city to fight against it, then proclaim peace unto it.

"And it shall be, if it make thee answer of peace, and open unto thee, then it shall be that all the people that is found therein shall be tributaries unto thee, and they shall serve thee.

"And if it will make no peace with thee, but will make war against thee, then thou shalt besiege it:

"And when the LORD thy God hath delivered it into thine hands, thou shalt smite every male thereof with the edge of the sword.

"But the women, and the little ones, and the cattle, and all that is in the city, even all the spoil thereof, shalt thou take unto thyself; and thou shalt eat the spoil of thine enemies, which the LORD thy God hath given thee."—*Deuteronomy*, ch. xx., v. 10–14.

thee, which are not of the cities of these nations." Upon this verse there is a gloss which declares that the words "far off" mean "of a different religion." Sepulveda consequently inferred that the Spaniards might make war upon any nation of a different religion from their own; and he supported this view by other passages quoted from *Deuteronomy*.

The bishop replied that the wars commanded by God against certain nations were not commanded in respect of their idolatry, as in that case the whole world, except Judæa, would have had to be conquered and chastised; but it was only against the Canaanites, the Jebusites, and other tribes who possessed the Land of Promise that the Israelites were commanded to make war. The bishop replied upon the 7th verse of the 23d chapter, which says, "Thou shalt not abhor an Edomite, for he is thy brother: thou shalt not abhor an Egyptian, because thou wast a stranger in his land."

With regard to the gloss which gave to the words "far off" the signification "of a different religion," the bishop did not contend that this was a wrong reading, but he argued that the words did not mean that upon that account alone, namely, difference of religion, war might be made upon distant nations by the Jews. The words "far off" served to distinguish other Gentiles from the seven tribes who occupied the Land of Promise, and to whom no terms of peace were to be offered. With them it was to be a war of extermination; but there was nothing to show that a war with other Gentiles could be lawfully undertaken solely on account of their idolatry. Finally, the bishop urged this general argument, that the examples from the Old Testament, as regarded those cruel chastisements, were given us "to marvel at and not to imitate," for which assertion he alleged the authority of certain Decretals.

Upon the second reason, the rudeness of the Indian nature, Las Casas, with his extensive knowledge of Indian life, was easily triumphant; and upon the third reason, namely, the extension of the true faith, Las Casas could appeal to his own successes and those of his brother Dominicans in "the Land of War."

With regard to Doctor Sepulveda's fourth reason, Las Casas alleged the general rule, "Of two evils, choose the least." Human sacrifices were a less evil than indiscriminate warfare. "Thou shalt not kill" is a more positive command than Thou shalt defend the innocent. Moreover, by these wars the true faith was defamed, and had fallen into odium with the natives. Then Las Casas boldly urged what defense can be urged for human sacrifices, namely, that, to the barbarous and Gentile apprehension, they were an offering up to God of the best that the worshipers possessed. He reminded his hearers of the sacrifice that Abraham was ready to make. The bishop also brought forward instances of great nations, such as the Romans and the Carthaginians, who had not been free from the guilt of human sacrifice; and he quoted Plutarch to show that when the Romans themselves became more humane and civilized in this respect, and, in their march of conquest, came upon barbarous nations who were addicted to human sacrifices, they did not punish them for this cause, but simply prohibited the commission of such offenses for the future.

I can not more briefly convey some idea of the mode in which this remarkable controversy was conducted than by following out some one branch of the argument as it is stated by Sepulveda, contradicted by Las Casas, reasserted by Sepulveda, and again controverted by Las Casas.

In the 14th chapter of St. Luke there is the parable of the man "who made a great supper, and bade many." After the poor, and the maimed, and the blind, and the halt were brought in to the supper, and there was still room, the Lord said unto the servant, "Go out into the highways and hedges, and compel them to come in, that my house may be filled." Sepulveda maintained that this command justified war against the Indians. Las Casas was obliged to use great skill in answering this argument. If he maintained that force was never to be used in order to promote the faith, what was to be said about the past doings of many emperors and popes? Indeed, throughout this controversy, as well as in many others, Las Casas was in constant danger of bringing down upon himself the anger of the highest ecclesiastical and civil authorities; and it is a matter for surprise that, in the course of his long career of controversy, he did not come within the grasp of the Inquisition.

In reply to the doctor upon this point, the bishop said that the words in St. Luke, "*compelle eos intrare*," have two senses. That, in reference to the Gentiles, the passage does not mean external compulsion by means of war, but internal compulsion by the inspiration of God and by the ministry of his angels. To prove this, he adduced the authority of St. Chrysostom in his forty-first Homily. Moreover, St. Thomas Aquinas, in his *Disputations upon Truth*, had discussed this very parable, and had maintained that the compulsion spoken of in the Gospel is not that of force, but of efficacious persuasion, whether by smooth methods or rough methods (*i. e.*, of arguing).* Such is the compulsion alluded to by ST. PAUL in the 2d Epistle to Timothy, the 4th chapter, where the apostle says, "Reprove, rebuke, exhort, with all long-suffering and doctrine;" and again, in the Epistle to Titus, "These things speak, and exhort, and rebuke with all authority." Again, in Jeremiah, the 23d chapter and 29th verse, "Is not my word like as a fire? saith the Lord; and like a hammer that breaketh the rock in pieces?" So that sometimes by adversities, at others by miracles, at others by inspiration, at others by his word, God compels even the obstinate to listen to Him. Nor was Las Casas contented with these authorities, but supported his views by a large body of other evidence. As to what the emperors had done, he maintained that Constantine had made war upon the Goths, not because they were Gentiles, but because they were dangerous barbarians infesting the empire. In St. Gregory's time there had been many powerful Christian emperors, but the saint did not counsel them to make war upon nations on account of their idolatry. To England he did not send armed men, but only St. Augustine, with forty other monks, "like sheep among wolves," as appears from the *History of England*, written by the Venerable BEDE.

Sepulveda replied that the construction he put upon the words "compel them to come in" was not his own, but that of St. Augustine in his letters concerning the Donatists, and also that of St. Gregory, and also of the whole Church, which had not only

* "Y por Santo Thomas en las disputadas *de Veritate*, question: 22, art. 9, donde dize, que en aquella parabola, Fit mentio de compulsione non quæ est coactionis, sed efficacis persuasionis, vel per aspera vel per lenia."—*Disputa entre* BARTOLOMÉ DE LAS CASAS *y Dotor* SEPULVEDA.

maintained this to be the true sense of the parable, but had acted upon it. He said that St. Augustine had maintained that the force which the emperors had used toward heretics and pagans had been the force of the Church; that the saint had cited these words in the *Psalms*, "*Adorabunt eum omnes reges terræ*," and he added that the greater the Church becomes, the more power it uses, so that it may not only invite, but compel to good—the saint greatly relying upon these words, *compelle eos intrare.*

Las Casas, in reply, affirmed that all the doctor had said about St. Augustine was frivolous and false. He had before shown that St. Augustine was speaking only of heretics, and had cited the following passage from the saint: "Does it not belong to pastoral diligence, when the sheep have been seduced away from the flock, to bring them back, when found, by the terrors of the scourge, if they should seek to resist?" This shows that they were heretics "seduced from the flock," not pagans who had never belonged to the flock, that the saint had in his mind; and Las Casas maintained that St. Augustine concludes, in respect to that parable of St. Luke, that those who were first called and were mildly treated were the Gentiles, while those who were compelled to come in from the highways and hedges were heretics.

There is another point in the controversy between Sepulveda and Las Casas which deserves especial mention, because it illustrates the nature of the bishop's course of argument, gives a remarkable instance of the clear and uncompromising decisiveness which pervaded his advocacy of the Indian cause, and also records an interesting historical fact.

Father Luis Cancér had been one of the Dominicans engaged with Las Casas in his peaceful conquest of the "Land of War." Indeed, he was the first monk who had entered that territory, and it was upon his report that the others had been emboldened to persevere in their attempt. Father Luis had hoped to convert the natives of Florida in the same manner that he had converted the inhabitants of Coban.* Unfortunately, however, he landed in Florida at a spot where the natives had suffered from the incursions of hostile Spaniards, and the devoted monk was put to death by the Indians almost immediately after he had disembarked. This was a valuable fact for Sepulveda, who accordingly made use of it in the controversy.

The dignity and greatness of his cause were so predominant in the mind of Las Casas as to leave no room for influences merely personal. It does not appear that he ever expected gratitude from the Indians; nor did the terrible disaster which he suffered at Cumaná from the treachery of the natives leave, apparently, the slightest rancor in his mind. His reply to Sepulveda respecting Luis Cancér's death was as follows: "The first person who entered into those territories [the "Land of War"], and pacified them, was brother Luis, of happy memory, who was afterward slain in Florida, and of whose death the Reverend Doctor Sepulveda desires to avail himself in argument. But it avails him little; for if they had slain all the brotherhood of St. Dominic, and St. Paul with them, not a point of right would have been attained more than there had been before (which was none) against the Indians. The cause of his death was, that in that port where he was taken by those sinners of mariners (who ought to have landed else-

* See vol. iii., p. 332.

where, as they had been instructed), there had entered, and disembarked, four armadas of cruel tyrants, who had perpetrated extraordinary cruelties among the Indians of those lands, and had alarmed, scandalized, and devastated a thousand leagues of the country. On this account they will have a most just cause of war against the Spaniards, and indeed against all Christians, even to the day of judgment. And as these Floridians had no knowledge of monks, and had never seen them, they could not divine that they were missionaries, especially as they were in the company of those who were exactly like in manners, dress, beards, and language to the persons who had done them so much mischief—and the natives saw them eat, drink, and laugh together as friends."*

Las Casas also maintained that even if Father Luis had landed at another part of Florida, and had been slain there, it would not have made any difference. "For," as he says, "it is a divine and most becoming law that some of the servants of the Gospel should die for the Gospel, since by their precious death they may aid more in the conversion of infidels than they

* "Pero aprovechale poco, porque aunque mataran á todos los frayles de Santo Domingo, y á San Pablo con ellos, no se adquiriera un punto de derecho mas del que de antes avia, que era ninguno contra los Indios. La razon es, porque en el puerto donde lo llevaron los pecadores marineros, que devieran desviallos de alli como yvan avisados, han entrado, y desembarcado quatro armadas de crueles tiranos, que han perpetrado crueldades estrañas en los Indios de aquellas tierras, y assombrado, escandalizado, é inficionado mil leguas de tierra. Por lo qual tienen justissima guerra hasta el dia del juyzio contra los de España, y aun contra todos Christianos. Y no conociendo los Religiosos, ni aviendolos jamas visto, no avian de adevinar que eran Evangelistas, mayormente yendo en compañia de aquellos que á los que tantos males, é jacturas les han hecho, eran en gestos, y en vestidos, y en las barbas, y en la lengua semejantes, y vian comer, y bever, y reyr como naturales amigos juntos."—*Disputa entre* BARTOLOMÉ DE LAS CASAS, *y el Dotor* SEPULVEDA.

could have done by toiling and sweating here upon the earth. And so we trust in God that Brother Luis Cancér, who was a renowned servant of God, does help, and will help, in the conversion of those who slew him. For, as they do not know what they do, and, according to their way of thinking, are not slaying monks and servants of God, but deadly enemies from whom they have received great injuries, God our Lord will look upon them with eyes of pity, for the merits of that most blessed Brother Luis. And this is the true divine way and real mode of preaching the Gospel and converting souls, established and approved by God himself, and not that which the doctor advocates, which is contradicted by every law, of God, of man, of nature, and of reason."*

The whole controversy was carried on with an exhibition of skill and learning similar to that which has been shown in the arguments used with respect to the parable in St. Luke.

At the conclusion of his address to the Junta, Las Casas made a fierce onslaught upon Doctor Sepulveda's mode of maintaining the rights of the kings of Spain. The following is the substance of what the bishop said upon this important branch of the controversy. "The doctor founds these rights upon our superiority in arms, and upon our having more bodily

* "Y assi esperamos en Dios, que fray Luys Cancér, que era gran siervo de Dios, aÿuda, é ayadara para la conversion é salud de aquellos que la muerte le dieron. Porque como no sepan lo que hazen é segun su estimaçion no matan frayles, ni siervos de Dios, sino á sus enemigos capitales, de quien tantos males recibieron, Dios nuestro Señor los ha de mirar con ojos de misericordia, por los merecimientos del felicissimo fray Luys. Y esta es la recta via divina, é forma real de predicar el Evangelio, y convertir las animas, por el mismo Dios establecida, é aprovada, no la que el Dotor persuade contraria, por toda ley divina, natural, razonable, y humana reprovada."—*Disputa entre* BARTOLOMÉ DE LAS CASAS, *y el Dotor* SEPULVEDA.

strength than the Indians. This is simply to place our kings in the position of tyrants. The right of those kings rests upon their extension of the Gospel in the New World, and their good government of the Indian nations. These duties they would be bound to fulfill even at their own expense, much more so considering the treasures they have received from the Indies. To deny this doctrine is to flatter and deceive our monarchs, and to put their salvation in peril. The doctor perverts the natural order of things, making the means the end, and what is accessory the principal. The accessory is temporal advantage; the principal, the preaching of the true faith. He who is ignorant of this, small is his knowledge; and he who denies it is no more of a Christian than Mohammed was."

Then, after a not unbecoming allusion to his own prolonged labors, the bishop says: "To this end [that is, to prevent the total perdition of the Indies] I direct all my efforts; not, as the doctor would make out, to shut the gates of justification, and disannul the sovereignty of the kings of Castile; but I shut the gates upon false claims made on their behalf, of no reality, altogether vain; and I open the gates to those claims of sovereignty which are founded upon law, which are solid, strong, truly catholic, and truly Christian."

Thus the controversy ended. The result seems to have been, substantially, a drawn battle. At first, according to Sepulveda, the jurists had to give way to the theologians.* But a timely re-enforcement came

* "Hujus enim artificio, et quorumdam amicorum pertinacia, haud procul ab eo fuimus, ut periculo nostro judices abstraherentur, suumque judicium jureperiti suspectorum theologorum auctoritati post ha-

to Sepulveda's aid in the person of a learned Franciscan monk named Bernardino Arevalo. At the beginning of the controversy he had been unable, from illness, to attend the Junta; but, afterward recovering, he brought such weight to Sepulveda's side of the argument that the Junta ultimately pronounced a sentence* (one theologian alone protesting against it) concurring with the opinions expressed in Sepulveda's treatise *De Justis Belli Causis.* His victory, however, was a fruitless one. The government must have been convinced the other way, or at least must have thought that the promulgation of Sepulveda's views would be dangerous; for Prince Philip, then governing in the name of his father, gave directions that Sepulveda's work should not be allowed to enter the Indies. In Royal Orders dated from Valladolid in October and November of that same year, 1550, the prince commanded the Viceroy of Mexico and the Governor of Terra-firma to seize upon any copy they could find of Sepulveda's work, and to send it back to Spain.†

Sepulveda seems to have felt that Las Casas had conducted the cause with exceeding vigor, and had

berent, ut aliqui fecerant in eadem causa eisdem præstigiis ludificati."—SEPULVEDÆ *Opera*, tom. iii., lib. v., p. 241.

* "Ita brevi factum est, ut judicibus iis, quos error abstulerat, in viam redeuntibus, omnes eam sententiam probarent, in qua ipse tuenda jam multos annos fueram occupatus, ut barbaros Novi Orbis, quos Indos vocamus, in Christianorum ditionem redigi jus et fas esse censerent, uno dumtaxat theologo contradicente."—SEPULVEDÆ *Opera*, tom. iii., lib. v., p. 244.

† "Y por si acaso contra este orden, alguno se tragesse á estas partes, por una su Real Cedula, despachada en Valladolid á tres de Noviembre de mil y quinientos y cinquenta, manda al Governador de Castilla del Oro, que aora se llama Tierra Firme, le recogiesse y le bolviese á España. Y lo mismo escrive su Alteza al Virrey de México firmando la carta en San Martin á los 19 de Octubre del mismo año de 1550."—REMESAL, *Hist. de Chiapa y Guatemala*, lib. x., cap. 24.

proved himself a terrible opponent; for, in a private letter describing the controversy, Sepulveda speaks of him as "most crafty, most vigilant, and most loquacious, compared with whom the Ulysses of Homer was inert and stuttering."* Las Casas, at the time of the controversy, was seventy-six years of age.

* "Quod quæris de judicio doctissimorum gravissimorumque virorum, quos ex omnibus regiis consiliis delectos cum quatuor theologis eruditissimis Carolus Cæsar causam de bello barbarico cognoscere voluit, quam ego causam libello persecutus eram, cui titulus est *Democrates Secundus, sive de Justis Belli Causis:* longum esset præstigias, artes et machinamenta commemorare, quibus me deprimere, et veritatem atque justitiam obscurare conatus est artifex ille versutissimus, et idem vigilantissimus et loquacissimus, cui Ulysses Homericus collatus iners erat et balbus."—SEPULVEDÆ *Opera*, tom. iii., lib. v., p. 241.

CHAPTER III.

FINAL LABORS AND DEATH OF LAS CASAS.

THE controversy with Sepulveda was but one of many of the labors of Las Casas, and he continued to exercise his self-imposed functions of Protector of the Indians with his accustomed zeal. He resided in the Dominican college of St. Gregory at Valladolid, with his faithful friend and spiritual brother Ladrada, who seems to have spurred him to exertion in behalf of the Indians, as may be gathered from the following anecdote: Ladrada, being deaf, was in the habit of speaking loudly; and the collegiate fathers could hear him, when he was confessing Las Casas, exclaim, "Bishop, beware lest you go to hell if you do not labor for a remedy for those poor Indians, as you are in duty bound to do." But this was more an admonition than a correction, as REMESAL observes, for never was there known in Las Casas the slightest carelessness in this respect, especially in those days.*

In the year 1555 there occurred a great occasion for all the efforts that Las Casas could make on behalf of the Indians. Philip the Second had succeeded to the throne of Spain. He ruled over immense possessions, such as might well make him a terror to the European family of nations. But his finances

* "Obispo, mirad que os vays al infierno, que no bolveys por estos pobres Indios como estays obligado. Era mas amonestacion que correccion, porque nunca se le sintió el menor descuydo del mundo en esta parte, principalmente en aquellos dias."—REMESAL, *Hist. de Chiapa y Guatemala*, lib. x., cap. 24.

were in a most deplorable state,* and any project for improving them must have been very welcome to the king and his councilors.

Now there was one easy mode by which, with a few strokes of the pen, Philip could raise a very large sum of money. All the Spanish colonists in the New World held their possessions upon a most uncertain tenure. Philip had only to give up the claims of the crown to the reversion of the *encomiendas*, and he would be sure to receive an ample and immediate recompense. Neither had the monarch to begin the negotiation. There was already in England, attending Philip's court, "a sinner," as Las Casas calls him, from Peru, who was urging some such measure on the monarch.† Never was the fate of the Indians in greater peril. There were, how-

* A modern historian has thus briefly described his condition: "Hardly ever did monarch ascend his throne under more disadvantageous circumstances than Philip II. While his old enemies were re-enforced by the accession of a new one whose hostility he most deprecated, by a pope who deemed himself born to annihilate the Spanish power; while he was threatened with formidable wars simultaneously on the Flemish, the Milanese, and the Neapolitan frontiers, he found all the resources of the state exhausted, the fountains of the regular revenue dried up, the land laden with debt, the rate of interest crushing, credit tottering. Might he hope to retrieve his desperate circumstances? Might he even hope to rally the energies of his state to a vigorous defense?"—RANKE, *Fürsten und Völker von Sud-Europa, etc.*, Kelly's translation, p. 90.

† "Los dias passados, padres mios, embié á vuestras Reverencias una carta grande que quando en Yngalaterra un pecador de los tyrannos del Perú, llamado Don Antonio de Ribera, comencó á engolosinar al Rey nuestro Señor, viendole necessitado de dineros, offreciendole muchos millones de castellanos ó ducados porque les vendiese los repartimientos ó encomiendas de las gentes de aquellos reynos (la qual venta si passara no quedara Yndio en todas esas Yndias que no fuera enagenado y vendido si Dios no lo impidiera por medio del maestro Miranda su Ministro) una carta digo que escriví al dicho maestro respondiendo á ciertas preguntas sobre las objeciones que allá le ponian los que la venta procuravan."—*Extract from a letter of* LAS

ever, two persons, both of whom had laid down their high offices, and had retired into monasteries, who were towers of strength to the poor Indians. These were Charles the Fifth and Las Casas. The latter had shown great boldness on many occasions of his life, but on this his daring verged upon audacity. His appeal to Philip was made through the king's confessor, Bartolomé Carranza de Miranda. Through him he dares to tell the monarch that any conclusion he may come to in England will be rash, because he is surrounded by few advisers, and those having no especial knowledge of the New World, and not being in communication with the Council of the Indies. If the king commits an error on this great occasion, can he allege the pretext of invincible ignorance? Las Casas boldly tells Carranza that in England and Flanders our sovereigns seem to have forgotten that they have a kingdom of Spain to govern. What right have they to impose upon the miserable Indians tributes of money, watered with tears, to pay the debts of their crown? What an overthrowal of all just ideas, and what an atrocity it is, to wish to promote the interests of the king, without thinking even of God! If such a system is persisted in, will they in England and Flanders look with a favorable eye at this maxim, that the means may become the end, and the end the means? As to the *encomenderos* possessing any claim, they have not merited a single *maravedi*. "On the contrary, I maintain," adds Las Casas, "that the king will be rigorously punished for not having chastised these assassins as they have deserved.* The kings of Castile owe a

CASAS, *printed by* MR. STEVENS. I do not know who the reverend fathers were to whom Las Casas addresses this letter.

* "Je dirai, au contraire, que le roi sera rigoureusement puni pour

great debt to him who discovered the New World. They are also under obligation to those who have restored the royal authority in Peru. But they are not, on that account, to deliver up the wretched inhabitants as one gives up to the butcher the most stupid animals to be slaughtered. If your paternity thinks it right to read this clause to his highness, or indeed the whole of my memorial, I beg you to believe that I shall feel the greatest satisfaction."

To show that he was not the only person entirely opposed to the sale of the reversions of the *encomiendas*, Las Casas, in the course of this letter, makes the following statement: "It is about fifteen days ago that a member of the Council of the Indies, horrified at what is now known of the situation of America, and at the proposition which is now mooted, made me fear the judgments of God, reproaching me with not doing half my duty in that I did not summon, twenty times a day, the whole earth to my aid, and that I did not go, with a stick in my hand and a beggar's wallet on my back, even into England, to protest against these tyrants; for it was to me that God had intrusted this charitable and difficult undertaking. What would he have said if he had seen all that I have seen for the last sixty years?"

It is impossible to tell what effect this letter had upon Carranza and upon Philip; but it is probable that it was considerable, for it is evident, in the course of the letter, that they had written to consult Las Casas upon the subject.*

Charles the Fifth was as decided as Las Casas upon

n'avoir pas châtié ces assassins comme ils l'ont mérité."—LLORENTE, *Œuvres de Don Barthélemi de Las Casas*, tom. ii., p. 135. Paris, 1822.

* "Je répondrai un peu plus loin à ce qu'elle" (son Altesse) "a dit de la nécessité de pourvoir à l'entretien des Espagnols qui sont em-

the point at issue. If we may trust the report of the Venetian embassador, this was almost the only public matter that Charles had influenced, up to that time, since his retirement into the monastery of Yuste.* The scheme, therefore, of selling the reversion of the *encomiendas*, which would have led to the total slavery of the Indians, was abandoned.

Las Casas continued to occupy himself in the affairs of the Indies, corresponding with persons in America, and being referred to for advice and information by the council at home.

He also continued to labor at his greatest literary work, the *History of the Indies*. This work is said to have been commenced in 1527, when he first became a Dominican monk; but it is clear from the last sentence but one in this History that he was still engaged upon it in the year 1561, the eighty-seventh year of his own age.†

In 1564 he had reached his ninetieth year, and in that year he wrote a treatise on the subject of Peru, which is, perhaps, one of the best that his fertile pen ever produced. As if he were aware that whatever he should do now must be done speedily, this paper

ployés dans les Indes."—LLORENTE, *Œuvres de Don Barthélemi de Las Casas*, tom. ii., p. 135.

* "SORIANO: Benche molti delli principali per el bisogno grande che si havea de denari per la guerra, lodassero questo partito, S. M. Cesarea non ha mai voluto accettarlo, per non far torto all' Indiani di sottometterli a tanti tiranni et per non mettersi in pericolo d' una rebellione universale. Questa è una delle cose (forse sola) che sia stata regolata secondo il parere d' imperatore dappoi che questo re è al governo."—RANKE, *Fürsten und Völker von Sud-Europa, etc.*, Kelly's translation, p. 90.

† "Pero esta ignorancia y cequedad del Consejo del Rey tubo su origen primero, lo qual fué causa de proveer que se hiciesen aquellos requerimientos, y plega á Dios que hoy, que es el año que pasa de sesenta y uno, el consejo esté libre della."—LAS CASAS, *Hist. de las Indias*, MS., lib. iii., cap. 166.

is composed with more brevity, though not with less force, than almost any of his productions. In it there is a statement which the student may look for in vain among the most elaborate histories that were written at that period, or have been written since, of the Spanish conquest in America. It is constantly mentioned that the tribute to be raised from *encomiendas* in this or that district was settled by this or that governor or royal auditor, but no accurate account is given of what the tribute was. In this treatise of Las Casas is set forth the tribute to be paid annually by five hundred Indian families in Arequipa. They are to furnish, (1), 180 Peruvian sheep. An additional hardship was, that these sheep could not be procured in that district, but had to be sought for in a neighboring province. (2), 300 pieces of cotton goods, each sufficient for the dress of an Indian; (3), 1000 bushels of maize; (4), 850 bushels of wheat; (5), 1000 fowls; (6), 1000 sacks, with cords to them; (7), 60 baskets of *coca;* (8), 100 cotton napkins; (9), 30 swine; (10), 50 *arrobas* of *camaron* (a kind of fish); (11), 500 *arrobas* of another kind of fish; (12), 5 *arrobas* of wool; (13), 40 skins of sea-wolves, dressed, and 40 others undressed; (14), 2 *arrobas* of cord; (15), 3 tents; (16), 8 table-cloths; (17), 2000 baskets of pepper; (18), 2 *arrobas* of balls of cotton; (19), 9 house-cloths; (20), 3 *arrobas* of fat, to make candles; (21), 15 Indians for the domestic service of the Spanish *encomendero;* (22), 8 Indians for the cultivation of his garden; (23), 8 others, to have charge of his flocks and cattle.

This monstrous tribute* might well call forth in-

* It was in reference to immoderate assessments of the kind mentioned in the text that the Spanish government were constantly providing a remedy. Many proofs of their assiduity on this point might be adduced. That the Spanish government ultimately succeeded in

dignation even from a man of ninety years of age. Upon such a tribute Las Casas rests his assertion that the Indians are deprived of their goods and of their liberty, and that it is impossible not to apply the epithet of tyrannical to the government under which they live; for, according to Aristotle, every government of a free people ought to have for its object the temporal and the spiritual good of the members of the body politic. Such was the intrepid writing, skillfully interwoven with the most important facts, which Las Casas had the energy to produce at this advanced period of his life.

Of all that is done in any great transaction, so small a part can be told, that the historian is often most unwillingly compelled to commit an act of seeming injustice when he carefully commemorates the deeds of the chief of a party, to the exclusion of those of many of his associates. Las Casas was but one, though immeasurably the first, of a numerous

effecting something like moderation in the tribute paid by the Indians may be seen from the following passage: "En una cedula de Valladolid, de dos de Febrero del año de 1549, í otros de los años de 1551, 1552, 1576, que estan en el dicho segondo tomo, í se han renovado por la del servicio personal del año de 1601, cap. 3, mandan, que para que se execute mejor lo referido, í en mayor alivio de los Indios, los tributos se les carguen, í tassen en lo que mas acomodamente pudieren pagar, avida consideracion á los frutos í cosas que lleva cada provincia ó á lo que ellos saben obrar por sus manos, por que no pudiessen ser molestados, pidiendoles lo que no pudiessen aver í pagar facilmente. Í esta moderacion, í tassa, se encargó ultimamente en las provincias del Perú, al Virrey don Francisco de Toledo, que las anduvo, *í visitó todas personalmente para el efeto, í las dexó hechas con gran suavidad, equidad, í destreza*, como lo refieren Acosta, í Agia, í el Licenciado Marienzo, que le acompaño í ayudó en lo mas de ellas; í en la Nueva-Éspagna á la Audiencia de Mexico, í al Virrey don Antonio de Mendoza, que tambien lo ajustaron, í suavizaron quanto pudieron, como lo testifica Fr. Juan de Torquemada."—SOLORZANO, *Politica Indiana*, lib. ii., cap. 19.

body of men who may rightly be called the Protectors of the Indians. Among these protectors was an ex-auditor of the *Audiencias* of Guatemala and Mexico named Zurita. He also informed the Emperor of the excessive nature of the imposts levied upon the Indians, and declared that it was one of the causes which led to the depopulation of the New World.* Another cause of the destruction of the Indians, according to Zurita, was their being compelled to work at the great edifices erected in the Spanish towns. They were forced, he says, to labor from the point of day until late in the evening. "I have seen," he adds, "after the *Angelus*, a great number of Indians cruelly conducted from their work by a very powerful personage. They bore along an enormous piece of wood, as large as a royal pine-tree, and when they stopped to rest, a negro who followed them, armed with a whip, forced them to continue their march, striking them with this whip, from the first man to the last, not that they should gain time and undertake other labors, for the day's work was finished, but to prevent them from resting, and to keep up the bad habit, so common, of beating them incessantly, and maltreating them. As they were all naked, except that they wore a piece of linen round their loins, and as the negro struck as hard as he could, all the strokes of the whip

* "En général, dans toutes les Indes, quoiqu'on ait cherché à dire le contraire, les races indigènes diminuent et disparaissent, par suite du désespoir que causent aux Indiens les impôts, la manière de les percevoir, l'impossibilité où ils sont de se nourrir et d'élever leurs enfants, ce qui les force de les abandonner malgré toute la tendresse qu'ils leur portent. Ils quittent leurs maisons, leurs champs qui, à la vérite, sont de peu de valeur, et passent dans d'autres pays, rôdant sans cesse d'une contrée dans une autre, où bien ils se cachent dans les forêts où les tigres et les autres bêtes féroces les dévorent."—ALONZO ZURITA, *Rapport sur les Chefs de la Nouvelle Espagne*, TERNAUX-COMPANS, *Voyages*.

had their full effect. Not one of the Indians said a word or turned his head, for they were all broken down by misery. It is the custom to urge them constantly in their work, not to allow them to take any rest, and to chastise them if they attempt to do so. This ill treatment of the Indians is the cause of my having, with the permission of your majesty, resigned my place of auditor." Such testimony as the above, confirmed by the resignation of office on the part of the witness, is most important in support of the statements and the conduct of Las Casas, the chief Protector of the Indians.

The memorial on Peru, written by Las Casas in his ninetieth year, appears to have been the last effort of his fertile pen. Two years later, however, in 1566, he came forward, not to write, but to act on behalf of his Indians. In that year a grievance that was suffered by the province of Guatemala was made known to him. The Guatemalans had been deprived of their *Audiencia*. The Dominicans in that province wrote to Las Casas, telling him that the country suffered very much for the want of an *Audiencia*. The natives had no chance of justice, as they had to make a journey to Mexico in order to prosecute any appeal. Las Casas well knew the importance of this matter. He accordingly left his collegiate monastery at Valladolid and went to Madrid. There he put the case of the Guatemalans so strongly to the king and to the Council of the Indies that the *Audiencia* was restored to Guatemala. This was the last work of Las Casas. He fell ill at Madrid, and died there in July, 1566, being ninety-two years of age. His obsequies were attended by a large concourse of the inhabitants of that city; and he was buried with all due solemnity in the convent chapel of "Our Lady of Atocha."

In parting from Las Casas, it must be felt that all ordinary eulogies would be feeble and inadequate. His was one of those few lives that are beyond biography, and require a history to be written in order to illustrate them. His career affords, perhaps, a solitary instance of a man who, being neither a conqueror, a discoverer, nor an inventor, has, by the pure force of benevolence, become so notable a figure that large portions of history can not be written, or at least can not be understood, without the narrative of his deeds and efforts being made one of the principal threads upon which the history is strung. Other men have undertaken great projects of benevolence, and have partially succeeded in them; but there is not any man whose success or failure in such endeavors has led to the great civil and military events which ensued upon the successes and failures of Las Casas. Take away all he said, and did, and preached, and wrote, and preserved (for the early historians of the New World owe the records of many of their most valuable facts to him), and the history of the Conquest would lose a considerable portion of its most precious materials.

It may be fearlessly asserted that Las Casas had a greater number of bitter enemies than any man who lived in his time, and many were the accusations they brought against him. But these were, for the most part, frivolous in the extreme, or were pointed at such failings as are manifest to every reader of his life. There is nothing unexpected in them. That he was hasty, vehement, uncompromising, and occasionally, though rarely, indiscreet, must be very clear to every one. But such a man was needed. It was for others to suggest expedients and compromises. There was one person always to maintain that strict justice should be done to the Indians, and to uphold the great principle that monarchs were set to rule for the benefit of their subjects. Without him the cause of the natives would at once have descended into a lower level. Then, though vehement, he was eminently persuasive, and few who came near him escaped the influence of his powerful and attractive mind. The one event of his life which his enemies fastened upon for censure, and as regards which their accusations are certainly not frivolous, was his unfortunate attempt at colonization on the coast of Cumaná. To do those enemies justice, it must be admitted that they did not know the motives which had actuated him in obtaining that territory, nor how little blame could be attributed to him for the failure of that romantic enterprise. They could only ridicule his laborers, adorned with crosses, as they said, like the Knights of Calatrava, and declare that, as a colonist, he had made a signal failure. These accusers were not aware that, but for the rapacity of conquerors like themselves, who had previously infuriated the natives, Las Casas might have succeeded in converting and civilizing the inhabitants of the Pearl Coast, as he afterward succeeded in peaceably reducing the inhabitants of "the Land of War."

The event in his life which his contemporaries did not notice, but which has since been much deplored and greatly magnified, was his being concerned in the introduction of negroes into the New World. For this he has himself made a touching and most contrite apology, expressing at the same time a fear lest his small share in the transaction might never be forgiven to him. In the cause of the Indians, whether he upheld it in speech, in writing, or in action, he appears never for one moment to have swerved from the exact path of equity. He has been justly called "The Great Apostle of the Indies."

CHAPTER IV.

LAWS RELATING TO ENCOMIENDAS AND PERSONAL SERVICES.

THE laws respecting *encomiendas* were considered to form the most important branch of legislation in America at the time of the conquest, and the growth of society in the Spanish Indies has ever since been so much influenced by these laws, that a clear understanding of them affords the surest insight into the history of almost all those regions in the New World which have not been colonized by the English or the French.

Moreover, a remarkable circumstance in connection with these laws is, that the modifications of them, which took place from time to time, were not only results, but in their turn became causes of striking civil and military events in Spanish America. It has been seen that royal orders from the court of Spain, affecting Peru, and the injudicious execution of them, were the causes that led to all the rebellions which kept that country for a long period in a state of utter confusion. It is not, therefore, to be wondered at that a Spanish conqueror should have regarded the Protectors of the Indians, with Las Casas at their head, as his especial enemies, and as the chief scourges of the land.

By the aid of some of the great lawyers of Spain, who devoted themselves to this difficult subject (chiefly ANTONIO DE LEON and JUAN DE SOLORZANO), a succinct account may be given of the various laws which regulated the *encomienda* system in Mexico and Peru for a hundred years, dating from the conquests of those countries.

In Peru, the discoverer Pizarro, when he first went to Spain, and while he was in partnership with Almagro and De Luque, received from Charles the Fifth the power of granting *encomiendas*. It was then held that these grants were in recompense to the discoverers and conquerors, and the tenure was for their lives only.

Afterward came the Law of Succession, passed in 1536. By that law Pizarro had the power of granting *encomiendas* for two lives. Then came the new laws, promoted chiefly by Las Casas, which prohibited altogether the granting of *encomiendas*. Blasco Nuñez Vela was sent to execute these laws. It has been seen how he failed in his mission, and how the new laws were abrogated by a royal order of the Emperor Charles the Fifth, given at Malines in 1545. The President De la Gasca possessed the power of granting *encomiendas*, as also did the viceroys of Peru who succeeded him. All the *encomiendas* thus granted fell under the general Law of Succession, and the period of their tenure was for two lives. Afterward they were to be incorporated into the possessions of the crown.

In Mexico the course of events was very different. The first discoverer, Cortez, made a general *repartimiento*, but it was provisional. As he had not been sent out by the court of Spain, he possessed no power to give Indians in *encomienda*, and his repartition was never confirmed. Cortez was superseded by an *Audiencia*. They possessed the power of granting *encomiendas*, but they exercised that power so badly, and with so much favoritism, that their repartition was annulled. They were superseded by a second *Audiencia*, which had for its president the Bishop of St. Domingo, whose wise administration of New Spain has been already recorded. This second *Audiencia* did not possess the power of granting *encomiendas;* that is, if an *encomienda*, by the death of its original possessor, had lapsed to the crown, they did not possess the power of regranting that *encomienda*. The power they did possess was to deal with the grants which had been unjustly made by the former *Audiencia*. The new auditors were to make a new repartition, not of the lapsed, but of the current grants. This they did, but their repartition was never formally confirmed, and the conquerors of New Spain continued to hold their *encomiendas* merely by tacit permission. Then came the Viceroy Mendoza to govern the country; but he never possessed the power of granting *encomiendas*. Not that he was distrusted by the government at home; but the rightfulness of any mode of assigning the Indians to their conquerors was much questioned and debated at that period. Then came the celebrated Law of Succession. This law had its origin in Mexico in the following manner. After the second *Audiencia* had arrived, two of the original conquerors died, leaving widows. It was the duty of the auditors to incorporate the *encomiendas* of the two deceased conquerors into the possessions of the crown, and to place them under a royal corregidor, leaving nothing for the widows. This appeared to the auditors a great hardship; and they ventured to give one of these Spanish ladies an Indian village in *encomienda* which had belonged to her late husband, and to the other lady they assigned the tribute arising from her deceased husband's *encomienda*. They then informed the Emperor of the decisions they had come to, which naturally had given great satisfaction to the conquerors, and had encouraged them to marry. Charles the Fifth and his ministers approved of these grants to the widows; and the practice that began thus was extended, in a year or two afterward, and made universal in the Indies by the passing of the Law of Succession. It was still a strictly feudal tenure. The *encomendero* was bound to provide for the instruction of his Indians in the true faith, and he was liable to military service. If the son to whom the *encomienda* descended was a minor, he had to provide an esquire to serve for him. Moreover, the maintenance of the family fell upon him. If it was a daughter to whom the *encomienda* descended, she was bound to marry within a year after her arriving at marriageable age—doubtless with a view to there being some person who could fulfill the feudal duties incumbent on the owner of an *encomienda*.

An *encomienda* could not be divided; might not be pledged; and, without express permission from the court of Spain, no person was to have more than one *encomienda*.

Such was the state of the law until 1542, when the new laws were passed; and Don Tello de Sandoval was sent, as visitor, to superintend the execution of these laws in Mexico. It has been seen that Sandoval, acting in concert with the viceroy, Mendoza, postponed the execution of the new laws in Mexico, and suffered an appeal to be made against them to the Emperor by the conquerors of New Spain. The new laws were partially revoked, and these conquerors were left with the same holding of their *encomi-*

endas, namely, by "tacit permission," that they had before—the duration of which, according to the Law of Succession, was to be for two lives. But these *encomiendas*, both in Mexico and Peru, have remained in full force to modern times, a circumstance which has now to be accounted for.

As might have been expected, the colonists made great efforts to have these grants (which were their chief possessions) continued to them; and in New Spain they succeeded so far that in 1559 a third life was granted, which Antonio de Leon well describes as the life granted by "connivance" (*disimulacion*). There is a letter, addressed by the court of Spain to the Viceroy of New Spain, who had evidently submitted his doubts and difficulties on the subject to the government at home, in which occurs the following passage: "And as regards the son or daughter that may survive as heirs, you will merely allow them the possession, without, however, giving them a title; and you will bear in mind that all that is said above is to remain in force until it is decided by Us as to what is to be done in the whole matter."*

Soon afterward there arose a discussion about the fourth life. The viceroy of that day was inclined to let this pass by a kind of connivance; but the government at home sent word to him that he was to take heed that the "tacit permission" applied only to the third life, and that the rest of the royal ordinances must be carried into execution (*i. e.*, that the *encomi-*

* "Mas expressamente se aprovó despues; que resolviendo en otra carta acordada, algunas dudas propuestas por el Virrey, í llegando á la referida, se le dixo: *I al hijo, ó hija que huviere de suceder, dissimulareis con ellos, sin dar les titulo, í estareis advertido que todo lo susodicho se estienda, hasta tanto que par Nos se tome resolucion de lo que en todo ello se ha de hazer.*"—ANTONIO DE LEON, *Confirmaciones Reales*, parte i., cap. 4.

endas, when they fell vacant, should be incorporated in the possessions of the crown) until some other arrangement should be made, which the government were at that time discussing. This was in the year 1576. The discussion seems to have lasted for more than a quarter of a century, for it was not until the year 1607 that the matter was settled. At that period the court of Spain was not strong enough to resist the importunity of the claimants; and not only was the fourth life granted, but the third life, which had hitherto been tacitly allowed, as it were, was at last formally conceded to the colonists of New Spain. Each *encomienda*, therefore, had now legally been granted by the crown for four lives.

Twenty-one years afterward a similar question arose about the grant of a fifth life. The court of Spain now probably perceived that it would be obliged to grant this life, and resolved to gain some profit by the concession. It accordingly fixed a rate of composition, the terms of which were settled by a royal order from Madrid, dated April, 1629.* This grant of a fifth life in New Spain corresponded to the grant of a third life in Peru, where the *encomiendas* had been originally granted at a much later period than in New Spain, by the President Gasca after the defeat of Gonzalo Pizarro, and by the Marquis de Cañete after the minor rebellions in Peru. It is not necessary to trace the granting of *encomiendas* in the other American colonies of Spain, as these various colonies partook the fortunes either of

* The Law of Succession was on this occasion broken through, and composition was allowed upon the *encomienda* passing to a stranger.

"Si los tales Encomenderos no tuvieren hijos, í quisieren que passe la sucession á algun estraño, pagarán la vida, í acudirán al Consejo á componerse por esta gracia."—ANTONIO DE LEON, parte i., cap. 4.

Mexico or Peru, and the grant of that life which was the fifth in New Spain, was a general grant for the whole Indies.

The possession of *encomiendas* in the Spanish colonies has thus been traced for more than a hundred years: in Peru, for example, from the beginning of the Conquest, which may be said to have commenced about the year 1529, to the grant of the third life in 1629, and in Mexico for a longer period.

The *encomienda* system remained in full force until the reign of Charles the Third of Spain, at which period, it appears, it was annulled,* and a new system of government was adopted, under the administration of the Count de Galvez.†

The laws with respect to personal service were much more clearly defined than those respecting *encomiendas*. There was no connivance allowed in this case; but more than a hundred years elapsed before the court of Spain succeeded in abolishing these personal services of the Indians, although monarch after monarch made the greatest effort to do away with them. The necessity for the employment of In-

* "C'est le roi Charles III. surtout, qui, par des mesures aussi sages qu'énergiques, est devenu le bienfaiteur des indigènes: il a annulé les *encomiendas;* il a défendu les *repartimientos*, par lesquels les *corregidors* se constituoient arbitrairement les créanciers, et par conséquent les maîtres du travail des natifs, en les pourvoyant, à des prix exagérés, de chevaux, de mulets et de vêtemens (*ropa*). L'établissement des intendances, que l'on doit au ministère du Comte de Galvez, est devenu surtout une époque mémorable pour le bien-être des Indiens."—HUMBOLDT, *Essai sur la Nouvelle-Espagne*, tom. i., liv. ii., chap. 6.

† The Count de Galvez, better known, perhaps, in Spanish history as the Marquis of Sonora, served under the Count of Florida Blanca, who much approved his services.—See FLORIDA BLANCA'S account of his own administration, in the Appendix to COXE'S *History of the House of Bourbon.*

dians was so urgent that it defied or eluded the vigilance of the Spanish sovereigns.

The last time that the personal services of the Indians were mentioned in this history was when the publication by the auditors of Lima of Charles the Fifth's edict of 1549, prohibiting such services, led to the rebellions of Sebastian de Castilla and Hernandez de Giron. In 1563 the same prohibition that had been given in 1549 was re-enacted at Monçon, in Aragon, against personal services. The main object of this law was, that the Indians held in *encomienda* should not compound for the tribute which they had to pay to their lords by rendering personal services. If any Indians should serve the Spaniards, it must be of their own free will, and in no other manner.* Similar orders were issued to the several viceroyalties of the Indies in the years 1568, 1581, 1595, and 1601. There is no doubt, however, that the evil of personal services continued. It was nearly impossible that it should have been otherwise; and, in justice to the Spanish colonists, it can not but be admitted that it would have been excessively difficult for them to provide the requisite labor if the laborers were to be perpetually changed. Even the employment, in personal services, of the Indians who were called *Mitayos*, was, except in special instances, forbidden. When the Indians of an *encomienda* could pay their tribute either in coin, or in some grain, or other product of the land, they were to do so.

The royal order of 1601, which entered into minute detail, was doubtless framed in consequence of a perception on the part of the home government that

* "Que si algunos sirvieren à los Españoles, sea de su propia voluntad, í no de otra manera alguna."—SOLORZANO, *Politica Indiana*, lib. ii., cap. 2.

they should not be able to control the practice of personal service unless by declaring the special cases in which, as a matter of necessity, the Indians might be employed. And this employment was not "personal service" in the original meaning of the term, for it was not necessarily rendered to the Spanish lord. His demand for tribute being satisfied, he had no more claim upon the services of his Indians than any other person had. The effort of the government was steadily directed to the object of keeping the Indians within the locality of their *encomiendas.* In Peru, for instance, it was only the seventh part of the adult male Indians in any *encomienda* that might be employed as *Mitayos;* and in New Spain, only four* in each hundred. When the time of their *Mita* had expired they must return to their villages; and the same set of men were not allowed to be sent immediately again. If there were spare laborers in an *encomienda,* they might hire themselves out to the Spaniards as freemen; and, in that case, every possible precaution was taken to secure them the payment of fair wages. No Indian, for instance, might be paid his wages in wine.

Again, the Spaniards were absolutely forbidden to employ the Indians in pearl fisheries, in sugar-mills, in woolen manufactories, in vineyards, or in the cultivation or gathering of woad. The cultivation of *coca*† was allowed, because its leaves were very ser-

* This was for work in the mines. When employed in agricultural labor, ten in each hundred of the Indians in New Spain were employed as *Mitayos* for twenty weeks of the year, and for the remaining weeks two in each hundred.

† "Los Indios la precian sobre manera, y en tiempo de los Reyes Ingas no era licito á los plebeyos, usar la Coca sin licencia del Inga, ó su Governador. El uso es traerla en la boca, y mascarla chupandola, no la tragan: dizen que les da grande esfuerço, y es singular re-

viceable to those employed in mining. But so tender was the Spanish court of its Indians, that, in the ordinance concerning the cultivation of *coca*, there is special provision made for their protection against the danger to their health from working in a humid district.

The words of the law are the following: "As the country where *coca* is grown is humid and subject to rain, and the Indians, in their work, generally get wet, and then fall ill from not changing their wet clothes, We command that no Indian shall commence working that land without being provided with a change of clothes. And the master of the *coca* plantation must take especial care that this be done, under a penalty of paying twenty baskets of *coca* for each time that he may be found to bring any Indian to this work without complying with the regulations herein set forth."*

The Indians were allowed to work at the mines, but under strict regulations.

Among other provisos, there was a general order that no Indian should be allowed to carry a burden that weighed more than two *arrobas* (half a hundred weight).

galo para ellos. Muchos hombres graves lo tienen por supersticion, y cosa de pura imaginacion. Yo, por dezir verdad, no me persuado, que sea pura imaginacion, antes entiendo que en efecto obra fuerças y aliento en los Indios, porque se veen efectos, que no se pueden atribuyr á imaginacion, como es con un puño de coca caminar doblando jornadas sin comer á las vezes otra cosa, y otras semejantes obras."—Acosta, *Hist. Nat. de Indias*, lib. iv., cap. 22.

* "Porque la tierra donde la Coca se cria es húmeda y lluviosa, y los Indios de su beneficio ordinariamente se mojan, y enferman de no mudar el vestido mojado: Ordenamos que ningun Indio entre á beneficiarla, sin que lleve el vestido duplicado para remudar, y el dueño de la Coca tenga especial cuidado que esto se cumpla, pena de pagar veinte cestos de Coca, por cada vez que se hallare traer algun Indio contra lo susodicho, aplicados en la forma referida."—*Recopilacion de las Indias*, tom. ii., lib. vi., tit. 14, ley 2.

There was also a law that the Indians of *Mita* or repartition should not be employed, if it could possibly be avoided, in climates which differed from their native ones.*

The efforts which were made by the court of Spain in behalf of the Indians may be well exemplified by an order which went out in 1609, declaratory of the great law of 1601 respecting personal service, of which the celebrated lawyer, Solorzano, was himself sent to supervise the execution. He mentions that the Conde de Lemos especially charged him to see to the execution of the royal orders respecting personal service; and in this declaratory law it is ordained that no Indian should, even for a crime, be condemned to give personal service to an individual colonist.† This same lawyer was also intrusted with the drawing up of a law in 1634, in which the former prohibitions were repeated, and he declares that the Spaniards who should violate these edicts were to be liable to excommunication; this, moreover, being one of those special cases reserved for the See of Rome.‡

* See ley 29, lib. vi., tit. 12. Del Servicio Personal: *Recopilacion de Leyes de las Indias.* "Que no se repartan Indios, para sementeras ni otras cosas, á diferentes temples."

† "I finalmente, por otra cedula declaratoria de la passada, dada en Aranjuez á 26 de Mayo de 1609 dirigida al Marques de Montesclaros Virrey del Perú, í mirada, í despachada con grande acuerdo, siendo Presidente del Consejo el Excelentissimo Conde de Lemos don Pedro Fernandez de Castro, que fué quien me propuso, í consultó para la Plaça de Oidor de Lima, alentandome á que la acetasse, í encargandome con particular cuidado, al tiempo de la partida, que por lo que en mi fuesse procurasse la execucion de la dicha cedula. En el capitulo 27 della, expressamente se manda: *Que no puedan los Indios por sus delitos ser condenados á ningun servicio personal de particulares.* Í en el siguiente, se renueva el que vá referido, de la cedula de 1601, agravando las penas contra los juezes que tuvieren omission en executarlo."—SOLORZANO, *Politica Indiana*, lib. ii., cap. 2.

‡ "En tanto grado, que están descomulgados los que usan dellas, í

The Spanish Conquest brought about so many forms of Indian servitude, that it is very difficult to master the nature of them all, and to follow them into all their minute details, especially as the name under which the Indians served sometimes remains unaltered, although the service itself had changed its character. This was the case with the *Mitayos.* Originally their service was entirely connected with the system of *encomiendas.* If they gave personal service, it was a means by which the lord gained something more than tribute from his *encomienda,* or, rather, took a part of his tribute in a form which was especially beneficial to him and oppressive to his Indians. The abolition, however, of any claim to personal service on the part of the Spanish lord of the *encomienda* did not cause a discontinuance of the system of employing *Mitayos.* It is true that the *Mitayos* were no longer a necessary part of an *encomienda.* If the tribute could be paid without a certain number of the Indians being sent out from the community to labor for the rest, there was no need for the appointment of a *mita* in that community. Still, in practice it would have been found that *Mitayos* were sent out from every Indian village long after the laws entirely abrogating personal service had been passed, and were substantially obeyed. These *Mitayos,* however, were merely Indian laborers, sent by their native caciques to the market-place of the adjacent Spanish town, to be hired by any one who chose to pay a certain fixed sum for

es este uno de los casos reservados á la Sede Apostolica, por la Bula de la Cena del Señor, como lo enseñan Silvestro, Navarro, í en nuestros terminos el Padre Joseph de Acosta."—SOLORZANO, *Política Indiana,* lib. ii., cap. 2.

their hire. That the caciques were in many instances compelled to send *Mitayos* is certain; but this compulsion was held to be for the public service and for the good of the Indians, not for the benefit of the Spanish owner of the *encomienda.* It appears, moreover, that these *Mitayos* were not bound by law to work for any particular master unless they were satisfied with his service. There is no doubt that great injustice may have occurred in the choice made by the native cacique of the persons under his authority whom he selected to serve as *Mitayos;* but, so far as the Spaniards were concerned, it does not appear that the *Mitayos* were left without considerable protection from the law; and the overpowering indolence of the Indians after the Spanish Conquest doubtless induced the government to allow this modified system of compulsory labor to continue.

Lastly, there were, in Peru, the *Yanaconas.* The meaning of this word *Yanacona,* in the Peruvian language, is "Slave;" and there had been a class of men bearing this name when the Peruvian dynasty flourished. Some of these *Yanaconas* had, no doubt, fled from their masters to the Spaniards. Other Indians had gathered round the Spanish habitations, as cattle choose any particular spot for pasture. At least such was the account which the Spaniards gave of the matter. The Spanish conquerors also alleged that certain vagabond Indians, belonging to no particular tribe, had been made over to them by the caciques of different districts. It may readily be conjectured that, in whatever manner the Spaniards contrived to get hold of individual Indians, they would call them *Yanaconas,* wishing them to be considered as persons not partaking of the full claim to liberty which was declared by the court of Spain to belong to the Indians generally.

These Yanaconas, therefore, were treated as vassals *adscripti glebæ.* They worked on the lands of the Spaniards, having their own small portions of land, and were held to be inalienable from the property. They were not very numerous: there might have been fifty thousand in Peru in the middle of the sixteenth century; but the government did not omit to watch over their rights and interests. And, eventually, in 1618, under Philip the Third, a law was passed having for its object to bring those *Yanaconas* into separate settlements, with lands of their own, allowing them at the same time the option of working where they had been accustomed to work, and, in that case, forming the settlement as close as might be to the Spanish planter's estate where the *Yanaconas* had hitherto resided.* It would have been difficult to make a more kindly or thoughtful provision for the welfare of this particular class of Indians, and for extinguishing whatever remnant of slavery was to be found in the system by which the *Yanaconas* had been attached to the lands of their Spanish masters.

An account has now been given of the laws affecting *encomiendas* and personal services, which legislation makes manifest the long-continued contest that existed between the conquerors and the Protectors of the Indians. There is, however, one general law, which may be considered as expressing in itself all the tenderness with which the court of Spain sought to treat its new subjects, the Indians. From a fear lest they should be imposed upon in their dealings with the Spaniards, they were considered by the law as minors.† It is hardly possible to carry legislation

* See ley 12, lib. vi., tit. 3.

† "Otro Privilegio tienen assimismo los Indios, que no se puede

farther in favor of any race or class. This provision existed as late as the beginning of the present century. In the travels of a most intelligent Frenchman, M. DEPONS, an agent to the French government at Caraccas, it is stated that "one of the most advantageous privileges of the Indians is that of being considered as minors in all their civil transactions. It is left to their discretion to execute, or not to execute, whatever contracts they make with the Spaniards without the interposition of the judges. They can insist on canceling them in every stage of any business. Their fixed property can not legally be purchased but at a judiciary auction, or sheriff's sale. If the article to be sold is of little value, the permission of the judge is sufficient; but that is not granted till it appears by the most satisfactory vouchers that the bargain is advantageous to the Indian."*

passar en silencio, í usan, í gozan del en los contratos, especialmente quando disponen de bienes raizes, ó de otras cosas de precio, í estimacion. Í es, que aunque sean mayores de edad, se pueden restituir, í aun dezir de nulidad contra los tales contratos, sino se hallaren hechos con autoridad de justicia, í especial intervencion í consentimiento de su Protector General, ó del particular que se les suele señalar en semejantes casos."—SOLORZANO, *Política Indiana*, lib. ii., cap. 28.

* See *Travels in South America*, by F. DEPONS, vol. i., p. 233. London, 1807.

CHAPTER V.

LAWS REGULATING NEGRO SLAVERY, AND PREVENTING THE SLAVERY OF THE INDIANS.

THE foregoing laws and the privileges of the Indians must have rendered labor scarce in the Spanish Indies. The fatal consequence naturally ensued of an increased demand for negro labor; and, accordingly, licenses for importing seventeen thousand negro slaves were offered for sale in the year 1551.* In the following year Philip the Second concluded a bargain for the grant of a monopoly to import twenty-three thousand negroes into the Indies;† and so this traffic went on until the great *assiento* of 1713,‡ between the English and the Spanish govern-

* "La venta de las 17,000 licencias de esclavos, por las quales en esa corte se han ofrecido 102,000 ducados á luego pagar, hemos tratado con mercaderes, í dicen no poder dar el dinero luego."—*Coleccion de* MUÑOZ, MS., tom. 86.

† "Capitulacion del Principe con Fernando Ochoa de Ochandiano, cambio en corte en que Su Alteza en nombre de Su Magestad le dá 23,000 licencias de esclavos para pasar á Indias á ocho ducados cada uno, í se obliga á que dentro de 7 años no dará otro licencia alguna." —*Coleccion de* MUÑOZ, MS., tom. 86.

‡ "It was at this time that a memorable arrangement with Spain, known by the name of the *Assiento*, or Contract, gave the British an exclusive right of carrying on the most nefarious of all trades to the Plata—a trade which was then as universally thought lawful and just as it is now acknowledged to be impious and inhuman. The British engaged to transport annually to the Spanish Indies, during a term of thirty years, four thousand eight hundred of what were called, in trade language, Indian pieces, that is to say, negro slaves, paying a duty per head of thirty-three escudos and one third."—SOUTHEY, *Hist. of Brazil*, vol. iii., chap. xxxiii.

ments, was concluded, respecting the importation of negroes into Spanish America. The number of negroes imported into America from the year 1517, when the trade was first permitted by Charles the Fifth, to 1807, the year in which the British Parliament passed the act abolishing the slave-trade,* can not be estimated at less than five or six millions.†

The court of Spain was not inattentive to the treatment of the negroes any more than to that of the Indians. As early as 1537, there is a letter from Cuba, addressed by some official person to the Empress, informing her majesty that the negroes are stronger than the Indians; that they are well fed; and that, in accordance with the royal orders, they have a holiday of four months' duration—an indulgence which he very naturally objects to, saying that tumults and murders take place during this holiday.‡

* The contest about the slave-trade, the greatest, perhaps, that has ever occurred in England upon a matter of principle—certainly the greatest if we except the contest for Parliamentary government—was commenced as far back as 1759, and was carried on with vigor for thirty years previous to 1807. The chief men of the nation entered warmly into the dispute. Adam Smith, Bishop Warburton, Bishop Horsley, Bishop Porteus, Paley, Robertson the historian, John Wesley, Cowper the poet, Granville Sharp, Wilberforce, Clarkson, Zachary Macaulay, Pitt, Fox, Burke, Windham, Sheridan, Lord Grey, Grenville, Canning, Brougham, were all abolitionists. The Quakers, the Wesleyans, and the City of London supported the negro cause.

According to a petition to the House of Commons from certain Liverpool merchants, "the Middle Passage was one of the happiest periods of a negro's life." On the other hand, Fox, when dying, said, "Two things I earnestly wish to see accomplished—peace with Europe, and the abolition of the slave-trade. But of the two I wish the latter."—Bandinel *On Slavery*, p. 119.

† A much higher estimate has been made; but I wish to keep within due bounds in a calculation which it is almost impossible to render accurate. It appears that in one year, 1768, the importation was 97,000.—See Bandinel *On Slavery*, p. 63.

‡ "Los negros son en manera de mas calidad que los Indios. Por

It is true that in the collection of laws which was afterward drawn up in Spain for the government of the Indies, the greater part of the laws that refer to the negroes are those which were framed to guard against their revolting, and to provide what should be done with the *Cimarones*, or *Maroons*, the name given to fugitive negroes in a state of revolt. The negroes were not docile like the Indians, and were evidently considered as most dangerous people.* It was therefore enacted that the negroes should not bear arms, and that they should not go out at night in the cities.† Great care was also taken that the negroes should not oppress the Indians; and the Indian villages were not to be molested by negroes any more than by the Spanish colonists.

There is one law, however, of high importance in favor of the negroes, which law runs thus: "We command our royal *Audiencias* that if any negro, or negress, or any other persons reputed slaves, should publicly demand their liberty, they should be heard, and justice be done to them, and care be taken that they should not, on that account (*i. e.*, on account of their having demanded their liberty), be maltreated by their masters.‡

lo comun se les da de comer bien. La comida era cacabi, boniatos y carne. Les dan su huelga de 4 meses segun las ordenes, 'y de mi parecer esto no se les debia dar, porque si desvarios y muertes desamparadas suyas acaescen, es mediante este tiempo.'"—*Col. de* Muñoz, MS., tom. 81.

* Ley 13. "Que las Justicias tengan cuidado sobre procedimientos de los Esclavos Negros, y personas inquietas."

† Ley 17. "Que en Cartagena no trayga armas ningun esclavo, aunque sea accompañando á su amo."

Ley 18. "Que los Ministros de las Indias no den licencia para traer Negros con armas."—*Recopilacion de Indias*, tom. ii., lib. vii., tit. 5.

‡ "Ordenamos á nuestras Reales Audiencias, que si algun Negro, ó Negra, ú otros qualesquiera tenidos por esclavos, proclamaren á la

The earliest law that declares the grounds on which the negroes could demand their liberty dates from the year 1528, in which it is provided that a negro, having served a certain time, should be entitled to his liberty upon the payment of a certain sum, not to be less than 20 marks of gold—the exact amount, however, to be settled by the royal authorities.* That many of the negroes did obtain their liberty may be inferred from the fact of there being several laws having reference to free negroes—enacting, for instance, what tribute they should pay, and with whom they should live; and commanding that free negresses, unless married to Spaniards, should not wear gold ornaments, pearls, or silk.†

Provision was also made that in the sale of the children of Spaniards and negresses, their parents should have a right of pre-emption.‡

In later times, under the admirable administration of Count Florida Blanca, during the reign of Charles

libertad, los oygan, y hagan justicia, y provean que por esto no sean maltratados de sus amos."—*El* EMPERADOR D. CARLOS, *y el* CARDINAL GOVERNADOR, *en Madrid, á* 15 *de April*, 1540. *Recopilacion de las Indias*, ley 8, tom. ii., lib. vii., tit. 5.

* "Assimismo soy informado, que para que los negros, que se passan á essas partes se asseguressen, y no se alçassen ni se ausentassen, y se animassen á trabajar y servir á sus dueños, con mas voluntad demas de casallos, seria bien que serviendo cierto tempo, y dando cadauno á su dueño hasta veynte marcos de oro, por lo menos, y dende arriba lo que á vosotros os pareciere, segun la calidad y condicion y hedad de cada uno, y á este respeto subiendo ó abaxando en le tiempo y precio, sus mugeres y hijos, de los que fuessen casados, quedassen libres y estuviessen dello certinidad: será bien, que entre vosotros platiqueys en ello, dando parte á las personas que vos pareciere que convenga, y de quien se puede fiar y me embieys vuestro parecer."—PUGA, *Provisiones*.

† "Que las Negras, y Mulatas horras, no traygan oro, seda, mantos, ni perlas."—*Recopilacion de Indias*, ley 28, lib. vii., tit. 5.

‡ "Que vendiéndose hijos de Españoles y Negras, si sus padres los quisieren comprar, sean preferidos."—*Ibid.*, ley 6, lib. vii., tit. 4.

the Third of Spain, it is evident that the negroes were humanely cared for by the government, being taught to read and write, having the privilege of purchasing their freedom, and also the power of getting themselves transferred to another master if their own had been guilty of cruelty to them.*

Whatever care might have been taken by the Spanish government for the welfare of the negroes when they had become inmates of the colonies, it does not appear that any provisions were made for diminishing their sufferings during "the Middle Passage." Thrown pell-mell into the hold of the vessel, without beds, without clothes, loaded with chains, and scantily fed, the miserable survivors arrived at the end of their voyage half dead, and covered with sores and ulcers. The great port for the reception of negroes in America was Carthagena. The hideous state of this traffic is learned from the life of a certain Jesuit father named Pedro Claver, who was called the Apostle of Carthagena. For forty years he devoted himself to mitigate the sufferings of the negroes, and was always present at the debarkation from any slave vessel, accompanied by interpreters, and bringing with him food and restoratives of various kinds. Many of the slaves died immediately after they had received

* "While treating on a subject so important to the colonial system of Spain, it is satisfactory to advert to the humanity shown by the Spaniards toward their slaves. Household negroes were taught to read and write, and instructed in the principles of the Christian religion. Any slave, on producing to the governor proofs of ill treatment by his owner, might insist on being transferred to another master, at a price fixed by arbitration, which the master was not permitted to refuse. Should a slave by industry and economy have acquired sufficient to purchase his freedom, he was entitled to demand it on the payment of an equitable price, which, if necessary, was to be settled by arbitrators named by the governor."—COXE'S *Bourbon Kings of Spain*, vol. v., chap. lxxix.

the rite of baptism from the hands of the good father.* This benevolent man was not, like Las Casas, a great reformer. He does not seem ever to have protested against the horrors of negro traffic, but to have devoted himself to succoring the miserable creatures on their arrival, and to instructing and protecting them while they remained at Carthagena. At the end of his ministration he was succeeded in his pious office by another monk, who was sent out by the King of Spain to have the charge of baptizing the negroes. It is extraordinary that neither the humanity of the Spanish government, so prompt on many occasions, nor the pecuniary loss occasioned by the cruelty of the traders, ever caused wise and humane regulations to be issued with respect to the treatment of the negroes during "the Middle Passage," which remained one of the greatest scandals on the earth from that day down to this day.

In considering the whole subject of the dealings of the Spanish government with the New World, the difficulties that the Spanish monarchs found in settling the *encomiendas* and in restricting the personal services of the Indians have been treated. There is, however, a third branch of the subject, which has been but little dwelt upon, and which, for the honor of the Spanish government, deserves to be made clear. If it

* "Il s'informait d'abord de tous ceux qui étaient nés pendant le voyage, pour leur conférer le baptême, il visitait ensuite ceux qui étaient dangereusement malades, pour les disposer, ou au baptême, ou au sacrement de pénitence, solon qu'ils étaient, ou n'étaient pas encore chrétiens. Comme il arrivait que plusieurs mouraient immédiatement après cette grâce, il semblait que la divine Providence ne les eût conservés jusque là que pour donner à son serviteur la consolation de les sauver."—B. G. Fleuriau, *La Vie du Ven. Pierre Claver, Apôtre de Carthagène et des Indes Occidentales*, p. 74; ed. Liége, 1851.

had not been for the most vigorous efforts on the part of the kings of Spain, their ministers, and the other protectors of the Indians, the natives of America would have been just as much enslaved as the negroes. For the first fifty or sixty years after the Conquest, Spanish statesmen had to make constant resistance to the insidious growth of an Indian slave-trade. On this point Ferdinand and Isabella had to censure Columbus. The authority of Pope Paul the Third, and afterward that of Pope Clement the Eighth, were brought to bear upon this subject; and many Spanish ecclesiastics besides Las Casas maintained a continuous protest against the existence of a slavery among the Indians, which had shown itself in the most unmitigated form.

Occasionally even the Spanish kings and statesmen had to give way in particular cases, and slave-owning and slave-dealing were allowed when Caribs, Cannibals, and a certain tribe called Chichimecas were concerned, these Indians being held to be especially barbarous and deserving of castigation. General orders, however, were issued in the year 1526, insisting upon the freedom of the Indians,* which made no exception even as regards Cannibals or Caribs.

As might be expected, this question of slavery was settled in the most distinct manner in the new laws.

* "Que las Justicias procurasen de saber quienes tenian Indios esclavos, traidos de sus Tierras; í queriendo ellos, los hiciesen bolver á ellas, si buenamente, í sin incomodidad se pudiese hacer; í, no se pudiendo, los pusiesen en su libertad, segun que para ello le diese lugar la capacidad de sus Personas, teniendo consideracion al provecho de los Indios, para que fuesen tratados como libres, bien mantenidos, í governados, sin darles demasiado trabajo; í que si los dichos Indios fuesen Christianos, no se dexasen bolver á sus Tierras, por el peligro que á sus Animas se les seguia."—Herrera, *Hist. de las Indias*, dec. iii., lib. ix., cap. 2.

The words are the following: "Item. We order and command that henceforward, for no cause whatever, whether of war, rebellion, ransom, or in any other manner, can any Indian be made a slave." The new laws are always said to have been abrogated. Such was the language of the time. But this was not so. The Spanish colonists and conquerors, in speaking of the new laws, always had in their minds the six principal clauses which most affected them. But the new laws consisted of forty clauses, and many of them were not revoked. The foregoing clause, for instance, about slavery, was never revoked, but, on the contrary, was enforced in the most emphatic manner in the year 1553.* From official correspondence that passed between the king's officers in the Indies and the court of Spain may be learned the immense difficulty which was experienced in carrying these provisions into effect. The Licentiate Cerrato, to whom was intrusted the execution of the new laws in Venezuela and the Pearl Coast, at the same time that Blasco Nuñez Vela was sent as Viceroy to Peru, writes thus to the Emperor from St. Domingo in the year 1545, pointing out the extreme perplexity of his duties. He says, "It is a very laborious and odious business. To examine whence they (the Indian slaves) come, and how they came to be slaves, is impossible. There is no account of them, or any other title than that they are branded, and have been sold

* "Si las personas que los tienen por esclavos, no mostraren in continenti titulo de como los tienen í posseen legitimamente, sin esperar mas probanca, ni á ver otro mas titulo, í sin embargo de qualquier posesion que aya de servidumbre, ni que esten herrados, aunque no se pruebe por los Indios cosa alguna, í tengan carta de compra, ó otros titulos de posseedores dellos; porque estos tales por la presuncion que tienen de libertad en su favor, son libres como vassallos nuestros."—SOLORZANO, *Política Indiana*, lib. ii., cap. 1.

and bought."* It appears from this letter that there were at that time no less than five thousand Indian slaves in St. Domingo.† The reply to this letter was given by Prince Philip, who was governing in Spain for his father; and the substance of it was as follows: The prince commanded that with respect to these so-called slaves, all the women and all the children under fourteen years of age should at once be set at liberty. Touching the rest, as many of them as the possessor should not prove to have been taken in just war were to be considered as free men, although they might have been marked with the brand. Restitution was ordered of the king's fifths in any case where it should be proved that the fifths had been paid upon these slaves. Finally, proclamation was ordered to be made of the last royal order in the matter, which was either that contained in the new laws, or one of the same tenor.‡

It may be observed that even this rescript of the prince still left some Indians in slavery. Three years later, in 1548, the same Licentiate Cerrato, who was a most vigorous protector of the Indians, writing from Honduras, informs the Emperor that no less than six

* "Es negocio este muy travajoso i odioso. Examinar de donde í como vinieron imposible. No hay mas razon, ni titulos que estar herrados, í la compra í posesion."—*Coleccion de* Muñoz, MS., tom. 84.

† This may appear inconsistent with foregoing statements made in this history, that Hispaniola was depopulated of Indians. But these slaves were all, I believe, imported; and St. Domingo was a sort of dépôt for them. Some came from Cubagua while the cause alluded to in the text was pending.

‡ "En respuesta adjunta del Principe se les manda poner desde luego en libertad todas las mugeres í los niños minores de 14 años. Cuanto á los demas, á quantos el poseedor no probare ser havidos en justa guerra í en que precedieron los requisitos í diligencias mandados, dense por libres aunque esten herrados í tengan cartas de compra. En los tales libertados de los que conste haverse pagado un quinto, abonese de la Real Hacienda. Tambien se pregonaron la provision."—*Coleccion de* Muñoz, MS., tom. 84.

thousand Indians have been made slaves on that coast and taken to Peru. The coast, he adds, is depopulated. Cerrato was thoroughly supported by the home government. The royal order on the letter is, "Let him chastise it [the slave traffic] with all the rigor of justice."* And so the evil was gradually suppressed. The Spanish jurists, ecclesiastics, and statesmen, with rare exceptions, were firm opponents to this slavery, and ultimately their views prevailed.

It naturally occurs to ask how it was that the same principles which were applied in favor of the Indians were not adduced in favor of the negroes. One of these principles was, that the law of Christ could not be an enslaving law. How, then, did men reconcile their consciences to negro slavery? No better answer can be given than the very words of the most elaborate Spanish writer on these subjects. The Portuguese had sought to introduce into the Spanish possessions slaves which had come from Java or Malacca. But this traffic was pronounced illegal by the *Audiencia* of Lima, who founded their decision upon the general opinion of the jurists of Spain. After narrating this fact, SOLERZANO proceeds in these words: "To which [*i. e.*, to the fact of the laws of Spain not allowing of this Portuguese traffic] the practice of introducing negro slaves is not a contradiction. For, as regards these negroes, we proceed in good faith, that they are either sold by their own desire, or that there are just wars among themselves in which they capture one another, and the captives are afterward sold to the Portuguese, who bring them to us (being called *Pombeiros* or *Tangomangos*), as Navarro, Molina, Rebelo, Mercado, and other authors say, concluding, however, finally, that they hold this traffic to be of a sufficiently perilous, delicate, and miry character,

* Cerrato's letter, *Coleccion de* MUÑOZ, MS., tom. 85.

by reason of the frauds which in it, ordinarily, the Portuguese are accustomed to commit, and do commit; but that it does not concern individuals to search into these frauds."*

The justification thus propounded by these learned jurists for the introduction of negro slaves is doubtless very shallow; but still it was a great advance in humanity that they should lay down the principle that, in no wars of their own nation with barbarians, could slaves, as a general rule, be righteously made. The almost indomitable natives of Chili gave the Spaniards so much trouble that, even as late as the year 1625, in the reign of Philip the Fourth of Spain, the Chilians might be made slaves in war; but this was the only exception to the general rule in the Spanish dominions throughout the New World—that Indian captives were not to be considered as slaves.

The monarchs of Spain were well aware that the laws to prevent slavery would not be effectual unless officers were specially appointed to see that the laws were obeyed. In every viceroyalty, therefore, and in every district governed by an *Audiencia*, there was appointed an officer, whose business it was to journey through the country, and annul slavery every where; and he was commanded "to restore the Indians to their natural liberty, notwithstanding any title of possession that the master might be able to produce."†

* "Porque en estos vamos con buena fé, de que ellos se venden por su voluntad, ô tienen justas guerras entre si, en que cautivan unos a otros, y á estos cautivos los venden despues á los Portugueses, que nos los traen, que ellos llaman *Pombeiros*, ó *Tangomangos*, como lo dizen Navarro, Molina, Rebelo, Mercado, i otros Autores, concluyendo finalmente, que todavia tienen por harto peligrosa, escrupulosa, í cenagosa esta contratacion, por las fraudes, que en ella de ordinario se suelen cometer, í cometen; pero que estas no les toca á los particulares averiguarlas."—Solorzano, *Politica Indiana*, lib. ii., cap. 1.

† "Que se nombre un ministro, ó persona de satisfaccion, que con-

Many other laws were passed in favor of the Indians. All crimes against them were made by Philip the Second more severely punishable than if these crimes had been committed against the Spaniards themselves.*

The Spanish monarchs were, without exception, eminent protectors of the Indians; and this branch of the subject can not be more fitly brought to a close than by quoting the memorable words of Philip the Fourth of Spain, written with his own hand at the end of a law which was made general for the Indies in 1628, and which had for its object the protection of the Indians when employed in manufactories or in other works. "I desire that you give satisfaction to me, and to the world, respecting the mode of treating these my vassals; and if you do not (in such a manner that in reply to this letter I may see that exemplary punishments are inflicted upon those who shall have committed excesses in this respect), I shall consider myself ill served by you; and I have to assure you that if you do not provide a remedy for these abuses, I must; and I command you to take great heed, even of the slightest omissions in this point of your duty, as being an offense committed against God, against me, and to the total ruin and destruction of those kingdoms, the natives of which I esteem, and desire that they be treated in a manner befitting their merits, as vassals who serve the monarchy so much, and have so largely added to its grandeur and its renown."†

ozca de la libertad de los Indios."—*Recopilacion de las Indias*, ley 9, tom. ii., lib. vi., tit. 2.

* "Que los delitos contra Indios sean castigados con mayor rigor, que contra Españoles."—D. Felipe II. en Madrid á 19 de Diciembre de 1593.—*Recopilacion de Indias*, ley 21, tom. ii., lib. vi., tit. 10.

† Solorzano, *Política Indiana*, p. 58.

CHAPTER VI.

RESULTS OF THE SPANISH LEGISLATION IN FAVOR OF THE INDIANS.

IT remains to be seen whether the foregoing legislation in favor of the Indians was as prosperous in its results as might have been expected. It is to be feared that an answer must be given in the negative. But it is very difficult to determine this question, for there was a disturbing influence of the greatest importance, namely, the depopulation of the Spanish Indies through natural* and other causes. As an example of rapid depopulation in New Spain may be adduced a fact recorded by an official person who addressed the Emperor in a dispatch dated the 3d of December, 1552. He says: "I am in the country about Vera Cruz. In most of the towns nothing is remaining but the sites: where there were two thousand, or ten thousand, or twenty thousand Indians, there have not remained more than forty inhabitants; and sometimes only four, six, seven, or eight. The town that has most numbers only two hundred inhabitants."† This official person attributes the diminution of the Indians to the excessive labors they had undergone from the *encomienda* system before set-

* It is almost impossible to overestimate the effect of such diseases as the small-pox upon the delicate natives of the New World.

† "Estoy en el partido de la Vera Cruz. En los mas pueblos no han quedado mas de los sitios, que de 2, 10, 20 mil í mas indios, no han quedado cuarenta, í muchos á 4, 6, 7, 8 vecinos. El pueblo que mas tiene no llega á 200."—*Coleccion de Muñoz*, MS., tom. 86.

tled tributes had been appointed, and personal service forbidden. But there can be no doubt that the effects of epidemic diseases must also be taken largely into account, a view which nowhere meets with more exact confirmation than in the ample history, written by LOZANO, of the Jesuit missions of Tucuman and Paraguay. Speaking of a certain epidemic, he says: "This epidemic was first noticed in Carthagena, in the Terra-firma, in the year 1588, and it passed over all South America to the Straits of Magellan, not omitting the most remote corner.* It was much more fatal to the natives than to the Spaniards. In a Spanish family where there had been thirty Indian servants, the family was frequently left without a single servant." The Indian children were so struck down by this epidemic that it is stated that not one out of a hundred escaped with life. The poor Indians offered no mental resistance to the ravages of this disease (which seems to have resembled the diphtheria† of modern times). When an Indian father of a family found himself attacked by the epidemic, he chose his burial-place near the church, and then, pointing it out to some missionary, exclaimed, "Here, father, you have to bury me, my wife, and my children." The accounts of the numbers who perish in any epidemic are likely to be considerably exaggerated. The rite of baptism, however, being held to be

* "Principióse la epidemia desde la Ciudad de Cartagena en Tierra-firme, el anno de mil quinientos ochenta y ocho, y fué discurrriendo por toda la America Meridional, hasta el Estrecho de Magallanes, sin perdonar el rincon mas remoto, donde no se sintiessen los efectos de su furor."—LOZANO, *Historia del Paraguay*, tom. i., lib. i., cap. 13. Madrid, 1754.

† "Cerrabanseles las fauces, de manera, que ni daban passo de lo interior al aliento, ni de lo exterior al alimento, feneciendo la misera-ble vida entre las congoxas del ahogo."—LOZANO, *Hist. del Paraguay*, tom. i., lib. i., cap. 13.

so important in the Roman Catholic Church, furnishes some figures which probably are not inaccurate. It is related of a certain Jesuit father that he baptized six thousand five hundred in a town called Villa Rica, and that four thousand and sixty of them died of the epidemic.*

This depopulation of Spanish America must have been very unfavorable to the civilization of the Indians. What would have been desirable would have been that while the *encomienda* system, in its most mitigated form, should have prevailed—the Indians thereby living mostly under the rule of their own caciques, and tilling their own lands—there should have been a surplus population flowing over into the Spanish settlements, and gradually learning various mechanical arts, which the Indians were very skillful in acquiring whenever there was a sufficient pressure upon them to do so.

But, indeed, it may be noticed how few nations have had what appear to us favorable opportunities for growth and development. Sometimes they grow too fast; sometimes too slowly; sometimes there is not enough hardship; often there is too much. Sometimes they are oppressed by the immediate vicinity of powerful nations; at other times they are not sufficiently constrained by potent and vigorous neighbors. The Peruvian Indian had worked well under a despotism which demanded much labor from him, but at the same time provided for all his comforts. Placed under the Spanish dominion, he was subject to a rule which was fitfully severe and self-seeking, also fitfully benevolent, according as the colonists and conquerors prevailed, or as the clergy, the court of

* "Bautiza el Padre Ortega 6500 Infieles in Villarrica, y mueren los 4060."—LOZANO, *Historia del Paraguay*, tom. i., lib. i., cap. 14.

Spain, and the other protectors of the Indians were able to carry out their benevolent aspirations for the good of the Indian population. For a hundred and fifty years, at least, there was a constant struggle between these two great parties of the Spaniards.* And when the clergy and the humane statesmen of Spain at last prevailed, the poor people they had anxiously and benevolently legislated for had dwindled down into a state of feebleness and inanition which deprived this legislation of its chief power of doing good.

A Bishop of Mechoacan, writing to King Charles the Fourth in 1799, evidently takes it for granted that the measures which the government of Spain had up to that period adopted for the protection of the Indians had not proved successful. He says: "The law forbids the mixture of race. It forbids the white man from inhabiting the Indian villages. It prevents the natives from establishing themselves in the midst of the Spaniards. This state of isolation fetters civilization."† The bishop maintains that the Indian caciques who governed in the villages did not protect the communities intrusted to them; and that their interest was to keep their people in a state of ignorance. Hence, he conceives, have arisen the indifference and apathy which are visible among the

* This is broadly stated in a letter addressed by a certain Doctor Vasquez to Philip the Second, in which are the following words: "En casi todas las provincias de las Indias ha havido í hay entre los Españoles dos vandos: uno de los conquistadores í encomenderos, í otra de los religiosos que se han embiado para conversion í doctrina de los Indios."—*Coleccion de* Muñoz, MS., tom. 88.

† "La loi défend le mélange des castes; elle défend aux blancs de se fixer dans les villages Indiens: elle empêche que les natifs ne s'etablissent au milieu des Espagnols. Cet état d'isolement met des entraves à la civilisation."—Humboldt. *Essai sur la Nouvelle-Espagne*, tom. i., liv. ii., cap. 6.

Indians. His remedy would be to pass an agrarian law, and thus to give the stimulus which is always to be found in individual proprietorship. It must not, however, be forgotten that if, in the first instance, the natives had not been protected by the system of *encomiendas*, there might have been no Indians left upon the face of the earth, or, at least, none who were not in a state of slavery, differing in no degree from the slavery of the negro.

While the historian must fully admit the large destruction of Indian life produced by epidemic diseases in Spanish America, that also which was directly occasioned by their conquerors must not be underrated by him, for it was immense. The wars of the Spaniards, whether among themselves or upon Indian nations "not yet reduced," were always conducted with exceeding loss of life to the Indians already in the power of the Spaniards. It was not only that upon them was thrown the burden of transport and of camp labor, but the other consequences of war were largely fatal to these poor people. Their cattle were taken away; their homes were deserted; their lands were left uncultivated. It is evident, from the course of this history, that these sad consequences must have followed; but occasionally there is direct testimony upon the subject. In 1539, when the feuds between the Almagros and the Pizarros were at their height, the Council of the Indies received a letter from Panamá in which the following statement occurs: "The news from Peru is very bad. As our people have carried off the provisions from Cusco and more than fifty leagues round it, and have taken the cattle, more than eighty thousand Indians have died of hunger. All those (journeying from Peru) agree in this. And they say that the Indians, going in procession with crosses through Cusco, asking for food, fall down dead in the streets."*

As an instance of the various ways in which the depopulation of the Indies took place, the evidence of a certain monk is worth citing, who addressed a letter to the Emperor from Santa Fé de Bogotá in the year 1550. After recounting various atrocities of the Spaniards, the monk informs Charles the Fifth that, "in order to people fifty Spanish houses, five hundred Indian dwellings are dispeopled."† It is probable that this violent change of domicile tended greatly to diminish the population so rudely transplanted. In fine, the more this question of the depopulation of the Indies is examined, the less extravagant does the assertion of LAS CASAS appear. He maintained that, in the first forty years after the discovery of America, twelve or fifteen millions of the natives had been destroyed by the Spaniards.‡ If the term were extended to sixty years, by which time the conquest was nearly brought to a conclusion, and if the ravages oc-

* "Las noticias del Perú son mui malas. Por haber tomado los nuestros los mantenimientos del Cuzco, í mas de 50 leguas en largo, í tomado los ganados, han muerto de hambre mas de 80,000 Indios. Convienen todos en esto, í que andando los Indios por el Cuzco en procesion con cruces pidiendo de comer se caen muertos por las calles."—*Á los* SEÑORES CARDENAL DE SIGUENZA, *í del* CONSEJO DE INDIAS—DOCTOR ROBLES; *Panamá* 20 *Setiembre*, 1539.—*Coleccion de* MUÑOZ, MS., tom. 81.

† "Para poblar 50 casas de Españoles se despueblan 500 de Indios."—*Nuevo Reyno.*—*Al* EMPERADOR *en el Consejo.*—*Frai* GERONIMO DE SAN MIGUEL. *Santa Fé*, 20 *de Agosto*, 1550.—*Col. de* MUÑOZ, MS., tom. 85.

‡ "Daremos por cuenta muy cierta, y verdadera, que son muertos en los dichos quarenta años por las dichas tiranias, é infernales obras de los Christianos, injusta y tiranicamente, mas de doze cuentos de animas, hombres, y mugeres, y niños, y en verdad que creo sin pensar engañarme, que son mas de quinze cuentos."—LAS CASAS, *Destruycion de las Indias*, p. 5.

casioned by disease be taken into account, the lower of the two numbers assigned by LAS CASAS, namely, twelve millions, may not unreasonably be accepted as very near the truth. Moreover, it must be observed for Las Casas that, though fervid in condemnation, he is not noted for inaccuracy or carelessness in his statements of fact.

There were, however, several other causes besides depopulation which served to hinder the good effect that might have been produced by the considerate legislation on behalf of the Indians which emanated from the court of Spain. The contest between the Spaniards and the Indians throughout the New World was not like that which the Spaniards themselves had waged with the Moors, when, after having been driven into a corner, as it were, of their country by the victorious Moslem, they had conquered their way back again, step by step, each step being marked by some heroic deed which formed a subject for heroic song. Neither was the contest like that between the Normans and the Anglo-Saxons, in which the latter offered a dull, stern, inert resistance to their conquerors, and succeeded in turning a conquest into an incorporation. Unfortunately, in the case of the Spanish Conquest in America, the conquered never possessed the respect of their conquerors. Throughout the New World, the laws, habits, manners, and customs of the natives were all defaced or set aside. Society was broken up. Few men think by what small and almost invisible ties society is kept together in any country, and how great a change even a small alteration of manners and customs may produce. But with the Indian, it was not a small alteration, but a total revolution.

It is not the Spaniards alone who have found exceeding difficulty in preserving nations, comparatively barbarous, whom they have subjugated. And it is admitted by all those who have investigated the subject that it would be one of the highest triumphs of civilization, and one of the foremost proofs of extraordinary vigor of government, if a conquering race were to succeed in subjugating, civilizing, and, at the same time, preserving the aborigines of any country that they may conquer. Of the importance of preserving them it is difficult to speak too highly, if they are regarded only as laborers, acclimatized and fitted to the soil—a conclusion which can not, with certainty, be pronounced of their conquerors until many generations have passed away.

There remains but one subject to be treated in order to explain how the inhabitants of the Old World settled down amid those of the New World, and that is the distribution of land. It may have been observed that hitherto mention has only, or chiefly, been made of the assignment of the conquered people to the conquerors. An *encomienda* conveyed only the services, or tribute corresponding to the services, of persons. But it was necessary also to distribute lands. This was done in two ways. First, wherever a Spanish town was founded, the land for building, as also some land for pasture, was set apart for the Spanish inhabitants of the town. But there was also a distribution of other lands, which were given in *Cavallerias* and *Peonias*. The *Cavalleria* was originally the land assigned to a horse-soldier; the *Peonia*, the land assigned to a foot-soldier.* It was decided that not more than five *peonias*, or three *cavallerias*, should

* From *Peon*, a foot-soldier, which also means a pawn at chess.

be assigned to any person. In the instructions given to Pedrarias Davila, the first governor of the Terra-firma, a *cavalleria* is defined to be a space of land in which two hundred thousand mounds (*montones*) could be set out; a *peonia*, that space of ground which contained a hundred thousand *montones.** This curious mode of apportioning ground had its origin in the island of Hispaniola, where the chief sustenance of the inhabitants was the plant named *yuca*, which was grown, as also was the potato,† upon artificial mounds. These mounds were a foot and a half high at the highest point, and from eight to ten feet in circumference.‡

Lands were also granted to those persons who wished to go from Spain to colonize in the Indies, and in that case they were not given by *cavallerias* or *peonias*. Finally, at a period about a hundred years after the conquest, the practice of selling land was the one chiefly adopted by the government. I have, however, no means of ascertaining the rate at which it was sold.

The principal circumstances connected with the settlement of the first colonists in the New World have now been stated. It only remains to be remarked that each colony had its own peculiar rate of progress, arising from the special circumstances of its conquest. While in one colony there was no such thing as slavery, in another, perhaps neighboring to

* "Cavalleria, dize, que es el espacio de tierra en que se pueden señalar ducientos mil montones: Peonía, la en que caben cien mil; de suerte, que dos Peonías hazian una Cavalleria."—ANTONIO DE LEON, *Confirmaciones Reales*, parte ii., c. 23.

† In a preceding volume (see vol. i., p. 251, note) an account is given of the mode of cultivating the potato.

‡ See OVIEDO, *Hist. Gen. y Nat.*, lib. vii., cap. 2.

it, the officers of government were battling hard to prevent the Indians from being made slaves. In one colony, while the Spanish lord was obtaining all that he could from his *encomienda* wthout law or limit, in another a fixed tribute had been appointed for each *encomienda.* Again, while in one colony personal services were rendered by the Indians, in another these services were totally abrogated. But the main current of legislation was such as I have described in the foregoing pages; and, ultimately, something like uniformity prevailed over the vast dominions of the Spanish crown in the New World. In this legislation the Protectors of the Indians took a large part. That the Indians were not entirely enslaved; that the *encomiendas* were not sold to the Spaniards; that a fixed tribute was assigned for each *encomienda;* that personal services were restricted or abrogated; that the natives were left subject to their own caciques, and not ruled over in their villages by Spaniards or negroes,* was owing to the unwearied labors of the Protectors of the Indians. Even in the distribution of lands among the Span-

* That the law forbidding negroes to live in the Indian villages was not merely passed by the home government, but that it was enforced by the local authorities, appears from the 126th article of the Decrees, promulgated in 1598, by the provincial council which had recently been held under the presidency of the Archbishop of Lima. Of these decrees there is a manuscript copy in my possession. The substance of the 126th article is, "*Que los negros, mestizos, mulatos, y otras misturas, no vivan entre los Indios.*"

In the proceedings of this council there is another article which deserves attention. It is directed against a practice in Peru, noticed by Las Casas (see *ante*, vol. iii., p. 412), of pressing the heads of infants into the shape of a cone. It orders that certain penalties shall attach to "the Indian man or woman who should mould the heads of infants in a certain form, which they call *Suytu uma*, or *Palta uma* [que amoldare las cabeças de los niños de cierta forma, que ellos llaman *suytu uma*, o *palta uma*]."—*Compendio de los Synodos Limenses*, MS.

iards a protector was found to protest against these grants as trespassing upon the property of the Indians. In fine, the result of the labors of these benevolent and watchful guardians of the Indians is to be traced to this day in whatever portion of wealth,* civilization, or prosperity of any kind is still enjoyed by the conquered race.

* Even Baron von Humboldt, who insists much on the general poverty of the Indians in Mexico, mentions that there were, at the time of his visit, some possessing large property. "Dans les intendances d'Oaxaca et de Valladolid, dans la vallée de Toluca, et surtout dans les environs de la grande ville de la Puebla de los Angeles, vivent quelques Indiens qui, sous l'apparence de misère, recèlent des richesses considérables. Lorsque je visitai la petite ville de Cholula, on y enterra une vieille femme Indienne qui laissoit à ses enfans des plantations de *maguey* (agave) pour plus de 360,000 francs."—*Essai sur la Nouvelle-Espagne*, tom. i., liv. ii., chap. 6.

BOOK XXI.

A GENERAL SURVEY OF SPANISH COLONIZATION IN AMERICA.

CHAPTER I.

INTERMIXTURE OF RACES.—MAIN LINES OF SPANISH DISCOVERY.

CHAPTER II.

THE MISSIONS OF PARAGUAY.

CHAPTER III.

THE CONQUEST OF BOGOTÁ.

CHAPTER IV.

THE DISCOVERY AND CONQUEST OF FLORIDA.

CHAPTER V.

STATE OF THE SPANISH COLONIES AFTER THE SEVERAL CONQUESTS.—CONCLUSION OF THE WORK.

CHAPTER I.

INTERMIXTURE OF RACES.—MAIN LINES OF SPANISH DISCOVERY.

TO explain and illustrate the dealings of the mother-country with the colonies; to show how the various provinces in America and the West Indies, that fell under the Spanish dominions, were in part dispeopled of the Indian natives, and peopled by Europeans and Africans—in fine, to describe how the Old World fastened itself upon the New, is a task which, fortunately, may be accomplished without narrating in full each individual conquest and discovery. As the foregoing results greatly proceeded from legislation, the history has merely had to follow the Spanish occupation of those countries where the events which occurred had the greatest influence in causing certain general modes of government to be adopted by the Spanish monarchs and their Council of the Indies. Moreover, it would naturally be from the earlier and the more important conquests that the Spanish Church and the Spanish government at home would form their ideas of the nature and capacity*

* It is very difficult to determine that capacity, and perhaps no one has decided that question better than a certain Father Ximenez, who has described them as "a people altogether in extremes: in labor most laborious; in idleness most idle; in eating most voracious; in not eating most abstinent;" and, in fact, like "children with beards." "Y para definir los Indios con definicion adecuada, es, definiendolos por contradictorias, porque es gente que en todo es extremos, y todos contrarios, y opuestos; al mismo método que lo que dijo Apiano, y

of the Indians; and these ideas greatly determined legislation. Again, it was from these earlier conquests that the Indians formed their opinions of the Spaniards, and learned, for the most part, to avoid their company with horror.

From what has been already narrated of the proceedings in the West India Islands and in Mexico, in Peru and in Guatemala, it is comparatively easy in the present day to ascertain why such violent contrasts are to be seen in the color and the race of the different inhabitants of various cities in the New World. At Lima, for example, negroes abound. The reasons for this are obvious. This city was not of Peruvian origin, but was founded by the Spaniards. The legislation which prevailed at the court of Spain soon after the founding of Lima forbade Indian slavery; discouraged, and finally prevented, the personal service of the Indians; and so ordered the *encomiendas*, by fixing the tribute to be levied upon them, as to produce a separation between the Spanish conquerors and the conquered natives. Meanwhile, however, the government placed no bar to the ingress of negroes beyond reserving the right of selling licenses for their importation. Very early in the history of the American continent there are circumstances to

prosiguiendo aquello digo: que es gente, en el trabajo fortisimos, en no trabajar peresosisimos; en comer voracisimos, en no comer parsisimos; en sus bienes requisimos y sumamente pobrisimos; y asi de todas las demas cosas suyas, y todo esto tan general, que lo mismo es uno que otro, el rico y el pobre, el que es Cacique ó Principal, como el mas igual: todos son iguales, y tan aniñados unos como otros, y así dijo bien el que los llamó *niños non barbos*, y á la verdad ellos son como muchachos en todo."—*Las Historias del Origen de los Indios de Guatemala, por El* R. P. F. FRANCISCO XIMENEZ, p. 143. Vienna and London, 1857.

show that negroes were gradually entering into that part of the New World. They constantly appear at remarkable points in the narrative. When the Marquis Pizarro had been slain by the conspirators, his body was dragged to the Cathedral by two negroes. The murdered factor, Illan Suarez, was buried by negroes and Indians. After the battle of Anaquito, the head of the unfortunate viceroy, Blasco Nuñez Vela, was cut off by a negro. On the outbreak of the great earthquake at Guatemala, the most remarkable figure in that night's terrors was a gigantic negro, who was seen in many parts of the city, and who assisted no one, however much he was implored. In the narrative of the return of Las Casas to his diocese, it has been seen that he was attended by a negro. And many other instances might be adduced, showing that, in the decade from 1535 to 1545, negroes had come to form part of the household of the wealthier colonists. At the same time, in the West India Islands, which had borne the first shock of the conquest, and where the Indians had been more swiftly destroyed, the negroes were beginning to form the bulk of the population; and the licenses for importation were steadily increasing in number.

While the negro element prevailed at Lima, the Indian element, then, as now, predominated in Mexico—a fact to be easily accounted for, when it is considered that Mexico was conquered and re-established by the wise Cortez; that there soon arrived in that capital large bodies of the Spanish clergy, who resolutely favored the Indians; and that, moreover, Mexico did not suffer from any civil wars among the Spaniards, but soon passed from a state of conquest to that of settled government, under the rule of the sagacious viceroy, Antonio de Mendoza. A similar course of investigation would explain the mixture of various races, or the predominance of one race, which may be noticed to this day in any town of Spanish America.

The Spanish possessions in the New World occupied an immense extent of territory, namely, from 40° 43′ south latitude, to 37° 48′ north latitude, the distances from the equator, on each side, being nearly the same. HUMBOLDT has observed that the Spanish territory in the New World was not only equal in length to the whole of Africa, but was also of much greater width than the Empire of Russia.* The most southern point was Fort Maullin; the most northern point, the Mission of San Francisco in New California, seven leagues to the northwest of Santa Cruz. Throughout this extent of territory, which is more than 6000 miles in length, that grand, forcible, and melodious language, in which Cervantes, Lope de Vega, and Calderon have written, prevails; and the adventures of Don Quixote have moved to sadness or to laughter thousands of persons from California to Chili.

It will be desirable to take a general survey of the spreading of the Spaniards over all the territories that they occupied in the New World. Their discoveries began at the small island of San Salvador, where Columbus first saw land. Thence they went to St. Domingo. From that island proceeded the expedi-

* "Cet espace de soixante-dixneuf degrés égale non seulement la longeur de toute l'Afrique, mais il surpasse encore de beaucoup la largeur de l'empire russe qui embrasse sur cent soixante-sept degrés de longitude, sous un parallèle dont les degrés ne sont plus que de la moitié des degrés de l'équateur."—HUMBOLDT, *Essai sur la Nouvelle-Espagne*, tom. i., liv. i., chap. i.

tions of Ojeda and Nicuesa. Venezuela was discovered and named by Ojeda in 1499, on that occasion when he had Amerigo Vespucci on board, who gave his name to the whole continent. In this voyage, all the coast from Surinam to Cape de la Vela was traversed. Nicuesa proceeded farther westward as far as the Boca de Chiriqui. In these voyages Darien was discovered and occupied; then Panamá was discovered; and Vasco Nuñez de Balboa was the first European to behold the South Sea.

From Darien it was that, in 1522, Gil Gonçalez Davila led the expedition that discovered Nicaragua. This branch of discovery, which may be called the southern branch, gave rise to the discovery of Peru; for Pizarro served under Ojeda and Vasco Nuñez, and, while in company with this latter commander, heard of the riches of the great Cacique Birú.

Cuba was discovered by Columbus in his first voyage. From Cuba proceeded the expedition of De Cordóva in 1517, and of Grijalva in 1518, by which Yucatan and some part of the coast of New Spain were discovered. From Cuba, in an expedition first planned to make search after Grijalva, Cortez led his Spaniards to the conquest of Mexico. Cuba may, therefore, be considered as the starting-point for the great northern branch of discovery, since the Spaniards discovered and spread from Mexico to California.* Nor were there wanting rumors in those days of the riches which have since been discovered in that part of America.†

* These discoveries include Mechoacan, Panuco, and all that country north of Mexico which is comprehended in the territories that were named New Galicia, New Biscay, New Leon, and New Mexico.

† "La presqu'île de la Californie a été pendant longtemps le *Dorado* de la Nouvelle-Espagne."—HUMBOLDT, *Essai sur la Nouvelle-Espagne*, tome ii., p. 422.

From Mexico discovery also proceeded southward, and in two directions. Cortez, in 1524, sent one of his captains to Honduras, and afterward proceeded thither himself; while Alvarado's conquest of Guatemala, combining with that of Nicaragua, formed a point of junction for the conquests of Cortez and Pizarro.

From Peru the Spaniards spread southward into Chili. Their occupation of this country was interrupted by constant misfortune. Almagro made no settlement in Chili. Valdivia, first sent by the Marquis Pizarro to undertake the conquest, and afterward by the President Gasca, succeeded in founding the town which bears his name, and also several others; but he was ultimately conquered by the brave Caupolican, the hero of the great epic called *The Araucana.* The English and Dutch, as well as the natives, were enemies with whom the Spaniards had to contend in Chili; and as late as the year 1598 the Araucan general of that day succeeded in destroying all the Spanish settlements in Araucana, and in putting the Spanish governor, Loyala, to death.* The Span-

---

"Cet Indien lui dit qu'il était fils d'un marchand mort depuis longtemps, que pendant son enfance son frère parcourait l'intérieur du pays pour y vendre les belles plumes d'oiseau qui servent à faire des panaches, et qu'il rapportait en échange une grande quantité d'or et d'argent, métaux, suivant lui, très communs dans ce pays."—PEDRO DE CASTAÑEDA DE NAGERA, *Voyage de Cibola* (1540), p. 1, 2. TERNAUX-COMPANS, *Voyages.*

"Solamente viddi dalla bocca della campagna sette villaggi ragionevoli, alquanto lontani, in una valle di sotto molto fresca e di molto buona terra, onde uscivano molti fiumi. Hebbi informatione che in quella era molto oro, e que gli habitatori l'adoperano in vasi, e palettine, con le quali si radono e levano via il sudore."—FRA MARCO DA NIZZA, *Relatione.* RAMUSIO, tom. iii., p. 357.

* "Asi quedaron destruidas, en el espacio de poco mas de tres años, todas las poblaciones que Valdivia y sus sucesores habian establecido

iards afterward re-entered the country; and there seems to have been constant war between them and the Araucans for ninety years, until 1773, when a peace was concluded, the Araucans retaining their independence. The Spanish dominion in this was bounded by the River Biobio.

The foregoing are the main lines of Spanish discovery and conquest; but there were minor ones which have not been recorded in this history, because the narrative, as far as regards Spanish legislation, remains complete without them. There are others which, for the same reason, have not hitherto been touched upon at all; but they can hardly be called minor conquests. These are now briefly to be considered. Such, for instance, were the conquest of Bogotá, the attempts at conquest in Florida, and the peaceful conquests accomplished by the Missions of Paraguay.

y conservado con tantas guerras en el vasto pais que yace entre *Biobio* y el archipielago de *Chiloe*, ninguna de las quales se ha podido hasta ahora reedificar, porque la que al presente se llama Valdivia no es otra cosa que una fortaleza ó un presidio."—Molina, *Historia Civil de Chili*, parte ii., lib. iv., cap. 6. Madrid, 1788.

CHAPTER II.

THE MISSIONS OF PARAGUAY.

THAT part of the country of Paraguay which was afterward reduced by the Jesuits, and called the Missions, was approached by the Spaniards from two opposite directions. In 1516, the Rio de la Plata was entered by the Grand Pilot of Spain, Juan de Solis, who had been sent upon a general voyage of discovery by Charles the Fifth. The unfortunate Juan de Solis was killed and eaten by the natives. The Portuguese afterward sent some explorers from Brazil to the confines of Peru, and in the course of their journey they must have passed through Paraguay.

In 1526, the celebrated Sebastian Cabot was intrusted by Charles the Fifth with an expedition which was to pass the Straits of Magellan, and to discover Tharsis, Ophir, and the imaginary Cipango. Cabot entered the Rio de la Plata, went up the river, and built a fort upon its banks, where the Tercero, descending from the Mountains of Tucuman, falls into the La Plata. It was Sebastian Cabot who gave the name to the river. As he found that the Portuguese were reconnoitring the country, he sent word of this to Charles the Fifth, and in two years afterward returned to Spain. He left in command of his fort an officer named Lara, who contracted an alliance with a neighboring cacique. But this chief, falling in love with a Spanish lady, surprised and massacred the garrisons, and burned the fort. In the encounter Lara slew the treacherous chief, but the lady and her companions were carried off by the victorious Indians.

In 1535 the Emperor fitted out a great expedition to the Rio de la Plata. It consisted of fourteen ves-

sels, and the command was given to Don Pedro de Mendoza, an officer of the Emperor's household. This governor founded Buenos Ayres. The expedition was very unfortunate, and Don Pedro de Mendoza died on his return to Spain. Before leaving the Rio de la Plata he had intrusted the chief command to a commander named Ayolas, who was at that time absent on a voyage up the River Paraguay. Two Spanish officers, who had been sent in search of Ayolas, founded the town of Assumpcion in the year 1538. Ayolas never received the news of his appointment, as he and his men were all slain by the Indians of Paraguay. A commander named Irala was then chosen by the Spanish soldiers as governor of the Rio de la Plata.

Meanwhile the settlement of Buenos Ayres had been most unfortunate. It had suffered the extreme of famine; and the first act of Irala's government was to abandon Buenos Ayres, and to concentrate all his forces at Assumpcion.

In 1540, Charles the Fifth, receiving no intelligence from Paraguay, and conjecturing that Ayolas was dead, sent out a new expedition under the celebrated Alvar Nuñez Cabeça de Vaca, who contributed eight thousand ducats toward the expense of the armament. He landed near the island of St. Catharine, and made his way across the country to Assumpcion, where he was received as governor. In the course of his journey across the country he was hospitably entertained by the natives, who were a branch of the Guarani Indians. They were not nomadic, but labored at their lands, cultivating maize, manioc, and potatoes. He found the country most fertile, and the people in a state of complete domestication,*

* "En todo este camino í tierra por donde iba el Governador í su gente, haciendo el descubrimiento, ai grandes campiñas de tierras, í mui buenas aguas, rios, arroios, í fuentes, í arboledas, í sembras, í la mas fertil tierra del mundo, mui aparejada para labrar í criar, í mucha parte de ella para ingenios de açucar, í tierra de mucha caça, í la gente que vive en ella, de la generacion de los Guaranies, comen carne

although, according to his account, they were cannibals.

After Cabeça de Vaca had taken possession of his government, he made wars and alliances with the neighboring Indians; sent an expedition to refound Buenos Ayres; and another, under the command of Irala, to prosecute discovery up the River Paraguay. Irala ascended the river as far as the Lake or Marsh of Xareyes.

On his return, Irala informed the governor that he had discovered a harbor, to which he had given the name of Los Reyes. It was resolved by the governor and a council that he summoned to choose this harbor as a starting-point for an expedition westward. The great desire of Cabeça de Vaca was to discover a route between Paraguay and Peru.

He commenced his expedition of discovery, ascended the river as far as Los Reyes, and then proceeded by land westward. After some days' journey he found the difficulties of the march very great, and his men very unwilling to prosecute the enterprise. He was, therefore, obliged to return to Los Reyes. The land in the vicinity of that harbor is, at certain seasons, flooded by inundations which cover an immense extent of country. Indeed, the waters of the marsh thus created afford a supply both to the Amazon and the La Plata; and were that territory occupied and subdued by civilized man, it would, perhaps, be the most admirable centre for a system of river navigation to be found in South America, or in the whole world.

While at Los Reyes, where he remained three

humana, í todos son labradores í criadores de patos í gallinas, í toda gente mui domestica."—*Comentarios de* ALVAR NUÑEZ CABEÇA DE VACA, cap. 10.—BARCIA, *Historiadores*, tom. i.

months, Cabeça de Vaca and his men fell ill of marsh fevers. He was compelled to abandon his enterprise altogether, and to return to Assumpcion. From the outset of his government his principal officers had intrigued against him, and he had been greatly unpopular with the troops. One of his chief faults in the eyes of his followers was that, acting in accordance with Charles the Fifth's instructions, he had protected the Indians, and, on his return to Assumpcion, had forbidden the Spaniards to carry away Indian women from Los Reyes. The royal officers conspired against the governor, whose continued illness prevented him from defeating their machinations. They seized upon his person, put him in irons, kept him in close confinement for nearly a year, and then sent him as a prisoner* in a vessel to Spain, together with some of their own party, who were to be his accusers at court. The process against him lingered on for eight years, when at last he was entirely acquitted,† but was not reinstated in his government. The chief authority in Paraguay thus again fell into the hands of Irala, who remained in power until his death, which took place in the year 1557.

The other direction from which the Spaniards approached Paraguay was through Tucuman. It is said that the first European who entered Tucuman was a soldier named Cæsar, who had been sent, with two or

* The unfortunate governor was still in such a state of ill health that, as his secretary says, he was as if he had the candle (placed in the hands of dying persons) in his hand—"*Casi la candela en la mano.*"

† In a narrative that was written by a German soldier named SCHMIDEL, who was in the La Plata expeditions, and was one of the malcontents, there is nothing to be found seriously inculpating Cabeça de Vaca.—See *Hist. y Descubrimiento del Rio de la Plata y Paraguay*, BARCIA, *Historiadores*, tom. iii.

three others, by Sebastian Cabot, from his fort, to make discovery in the direction of Peru. However that may be, it is certain that the Spanish conquerors in Peru soon became aware of the existence of this

province of Tucuman; for after the battle of Chupas, in which the young Almagro was defeated by the king's forces under Vaca de Castro, in the year 1542, that officer gave the government of Tucuman to a certain Diego de Rojas. Rojas entered the country accompanied by three hundred Spanish soldiers, but he perished in an encounter with the Indians. Other governors succeeded him; and in 1558 the town of New London was founded in Tucuman — the name of London being given in honor of Mary of England, the wife of Philip the Second. New London was afterward destroyed, and the spot where it stood in the valley of Conando is now occupied by a town called Fernando.

Buenos Ayres had been a second time deserted, and was not founded again until the year 1610. Tucuman, being colonized by the Spaniards, was made the seat of a bishopric. The third bishop, Francisco Victoria, finding that his diocese was in great need of spiritual assistance, wrote to the provincials of the Jesuits, both in Brazil and Peru, conjuring them to send him missionaries.* From both quarters the Jesuits came; and this was the beginning of the Missions in Paraguay. From Peru came Francisco Angulo and Alphonso Barsena. Of the five Jesuits that came from Brazil, one, Leonardo Arminio, was an Italian; another, Juan Salonio, was a Spaniard from Valentia; another, Thomas Filds, was a Scotchman; and the remaining two were Portuguese. For many years the Jesuits underwent the fate of most missionaries. Sometimes they were welcomed by the conquerors and colonists; sometimes they were indignantly

* "C'ést ce qui fit prendre à l'Evêque du Tucuman la résolution d'appeller dans son Diocèse le plus qu'il pourrait de ces Religieux, quoi qu'il lui en dût coûter. Il écrivit pour cela en même temps au P. Anchieta, et au Père Jean Atiensa, tous deux Provinciaux de leur Compagnie, le premier au Brésil, et le second au Pérou, et les conjura par les entrailles de Jesu Christ, de ne point lui refuser les secours qu'il lui demandoit."—CHARLEVOIX, *Histoire du Paraguay*, tom. i., liv. iv., p. 172. Paris, 1756.

rejected, especially when they sought to protect their Indian converts, and to abolish personal service. It would lead me beyond the bounds of this history to attempt to relate the proceedings of these individual missionaries, and I pass at once, therefore, to a period about twenty-five years later, when their efforts had become more consolidated, and were more steadily supported by the Spanish government.

The establishment of the Missions of Paraguay was a transaction very similar to the entrance by Las Casas and his Dominicans into the "Land of War." It is clear, from the peculiarities of the Indian character which have already been recorded, and from the breaking up of all government among the native princes, that it was possible for any body of monks, supported by Spanish soldiery occupying important neighboring towns, to civilize, Christianize, and rule over well-ordered communities of docile Indians.

To trace the history of the Jesuit Missions in South America, even after they passed from the domain of isolated enterprise and became part of a great system, would alone occupy a voluminous work; but some leading facts may be given, which will briefly indicate the spirit in which these missions were undertaken, and the results which were obtained by them. For this purpose, the instructions are here cited which were addressed to his brethren by a provincial of the Jesuits in South America, himself one of the early missionaries. These instructions are singularly sagacious, and are very comprehensive.

In the first place, the provincial commands his brethren to attend to their own salvation; "for," he says, "the more care we give to our own perfection, the more apt instruments we shall become for the salvation of the Indians." On that account the brethren must be very observant of the rules of the order, not omitting their religious exercises, and studying the lives of Ignatius Loyola and Francis Xavier.

Secondly. They must learn the Indian languages.

Thirdly. They must not go about singly, for the brother who is at hand to assist a brother is as the strongest tower to him.

Fourthly. They should not form a Reduction* with any settlement subordinate to it. It must consist of a single town. The object of this rule was to prevent the traveling about of the brethren, and to concentrate their attention upon one place.

Fifthly. Their object must not be to make many Reductions, but to give great labor to those of which they undertake the charge.

The provincial then defines their mode of procedure as respects the formation of Indian communities, and lays down the following rules for the brethren.

Before founding a town, they must consider well the site—that it should be in a fertile country, and out of the way of wars. The town must be carefully traced out beforehand, with a good arrangement for streets, and with room for each Indian to have his cottage and his little garden. The church is to be in the middle of the town. A convent must be built near it; and the cacique's houses are to adjoin these principal buildings. The brethren are to teach the Indians how to cultivate their land, and to assist them in doing so. Minute provisions are made for instructing the children, who are to learn how to read, to write, and to sing. The elder youths are to be taught apart from the girls; and the grown-up people are to

* *Reduccion* was the name given to a settlement of Indians reduced to the Christian religion, and taught to cultivate the arts of life.

be instructed with a special view to their being baptized.

Great prudence is to be shown in baptizing the adults. They must first be well taught and catechised, and they must give pledges that they will remain in the Reduction. The arrangements for religious service, by day and by night, are prescribed. Two of the company are to go about from time to time in the streets to check drunkenness. They are commanded never to chastise any Indian with their own hands, not even to give a boy a buffet.*

With "consummate care" they are to contrive not to become burdensome to the Indians. If they are obliged to ask them for any thing, it must be paid for. They are to live by the cultivation of their own lands.

They must show great prudence in dealing with the Spaniards. If these should come to the Reductions, they must be kindly received, but not allowed to stay many days. They must not be permitted to carry off Indians with them. If they attempt to do this, recourse must be had to the royal authorities.

A report must be made in each year to the superior of the order, residing at the town of Assumpcion, stating what has happened in the several Reductions.

As a final instruction, the provincial bids the brethren endeavor to maintain unity, remembering that which our Savior left as a testimony to his apostles, "This is my commandment, that ye love one another as I have loved you."

Such are the instructions given by the Provincial Diego de Torres, about the year 1612, to the Missions of Paraná, Guayrá, and Guaycurús. At that time

* "Ni aun dando á un muchacho un bofeton."—LOZANO, *Hist. del Paraguay*, tom. ii., lib. vi., cap. 1.

there were but three or four Reductions formed or in the process of formation. The first Reduction was established in the country of the Guaranis, and was called after "Our Lady of Loretto." The second Reduction was also founded in the Guarani country, and was called San Ignacio, after the founder of the Order of the Jesuits. There were afterward as many as thirty Reductions. It would be difficult to estimate the size of these Reductions, but they probably varied from three thousand to five thousand inhabitants.*

It now remains to be seen how the instructions of Diego de Torres, and of the provincial who succeeded him, were, in the course of time, fulfilled. At a much later period there is a description of the state of the Reductions, in which an account is given of "the temporal felicity of the New Christians of Paraguay."† The missionaries are described as vigilant and disinterested. The Reductions are like separate republics.‡ The Indians suffer very little from taxation. There are no slaves; there are no masters. The Indian caciques are in the place of *corregidors* to these republics. There is no ambition, and no desire for money. All possessions are proportioned to the capa-

* I observe that in a letter written by a young Italian Jesuit from a Reduction called Santa Maria, in Uruguay, he states that his audience, consisting of boys and girls, amounts to nineteen hundred and sixty-two. "Nè mi manca giammai numerosa Audienza; perchè secondo il Catalogo quì le Fanciulle sino à i quindici anni sono mille e due, e i Fanciulli novecento sessanta."—*Lettera terza del* PADRE CATTANEO.—MURATORI, *Il Christianesimo Felice del Paraguai*, p. 195.

† See the 17th chapter of *Il Christianesimo Felice del Paraguai:* "Della felicità temporale de' Paraguai."—*Descritto da* LODOVICO ANTONIO MURATORI. Venezia, 1743.

‡ "Quante Riduzioni, torno à dire, si contano in que' paesi, tutte sono altrettante Repubbliche."—MURATORI, *Il Christianesimo Felice del Paraguai*, cap. 17.

bilities of the family which has to cultivate them.* A certain portion of land is set apart, which is called *Tupambæ*, a word that means "the possessions of

* "Suol' essere ogni possessione proporzionata alle forze d'ogni Famiglia, e potrebbe anche maggiormente slargarsi, perchè loro non manca terreno; ma non si fa, perchè d' ordinario non v' ha che il Marito e la Moglie, o al più un Parente, che lavori quella terra, e non portrebbono farne di più."—MURATORI, *Il Christianesimo Felice del Paraguai*, cap. 18.

God." Of a morning, after they have recited their prayers and heard mass, all the Indian youths, in number perhaps four or five hundred, go and cultivate these common lands. The harvests are stored up in public magazines. From these stores the sick, the orphans, and the helpless are fed; and thus, too, provision is made for any exigency or any public calamity.

An historian of our own country has perhaps given the best account that is to be found of the Reductions in Paraguay.* After describing minutely all that took place from day to day in those Reductions, he says, "An Indian of the Reductions never knew, during his whole progress from the cradle to the grave, what it was to take thought for the morrow: all his duties were comprised in obedience. The strictest discipline soon becomes tolerable when it is certain and immutable; that of the Jesuits extended to every thing, but it was neither capricious nor oppressive. The children were considered as belonging to the community; they lived with their parents, that the course of natural affection might not be interrupted; but their education was a public duty. . . . . Man may be made either the tamest or the most ferocious of animals. The Jesuits' discipline, beginning with birth and ending with death, insured that implicit obedience which is the first duty of monachism, and was the great object of their legislation. Besides the overseers who inspected the work of the Indians, there were others who acted as inspectors of their moral conduct, and when they discovered any misdemeanor, clapped upon the offender a penitential dress, and led him first to the church to make his confession in public, and then into the square to be

* See SOUTHEY'S *History of Brazil*, vol. ii., chap. xxiv.

publicly beaten. It is said that these castigations were always received without a murmur, and even as an act of grace.

"Few vices could exist in such communities. Avarice and ambition were excluded; there was little room for envy, and little to excite hatred or malice. Drunkenness, the sin which most easily besets savage and half-civilized man, was effectually prevented by the prohibition of fermented liquors; and against incontinence every precaution was taken which the spirit of monachism could dictate."

The danger always to be apprehended from minute and despotic supervision, namely, that it obliterates character, represses free will, and enchains action, was no doubt fully manifested in these Reductions. But still the verdict of this historian may be acquiesced in when he says, "Europe had no cause to rejoice in the establishment of the Jesuits; but in Brazil and Paraguay their superstition may be forgiven them for the noble efforts which they made in behalf of the oppressed Indians, and for the good which they effected: the centenary of their institution could not be celebrated by these tribes with more gratitude and joy than were justly due."

The country of Paraguay seemed to be remarkably adapted for the peaceful missions which were beginning gradually to occupy it. It is inland and central, and yet most easily approachable by river navigation. The most important products of the world can be grown there—sugar, maize, tobacco, cotton—and it has peculiar products of its own, such as the Paraguay tea. It is not volcanic, and has not to dread the catastrophes which have often overwhelmed the Spanish cities on the other side of the Andes. It is not a country which requires extraordinary energy to penetrate and subdue it. Indeed, the province of La Plata consists chiefly of extensive plains. The most northern of them, named *El Gran Chaco*,* which is seen from the town of Assumpcion, extends over 120,000 square miles—a larger space than the total surface of the British Islands. In some parts this great plain is but a desert, but in others it is one of the most beautiful and productive countries in the world. It has lakes, rivers, and woods, and in the character of its scenery much resembles an English park.† It is rich in trees of every description—cedars, palms, balsams, aloes, cocoa-trees, walnut-trees, spice-trees, almonds, the cotton plant, the quinaquina that produces the Jesuits' bark, and another tree, of which the inner bark is so delicate and white that it can be used as writing paper.‡ There is also the ceyba-tree, which yields a soft woolly substance of which the natives make their pillows.

The fruits of this most fertile land are oranges, citrons, lemons, the American pear, the apple, peaches,

* This name is taken from the Kechuan word *Chacu*, which means the driving wild beasts into a circle to slay them (see *Die Kechua-sprache*, von J. J. von Tschudi, Wien, 1853); and as the Indians had hunted wild beasts in this manner, so now they were driven by the Spaniards from all quarters into these territories which lie between the Andes and the Rivers Paraná and Paraguay.

† "There is an indescribable wonder and awe to me about this Chaco which nobody seems to appreciate: there it lies, apparently a most rich alternation of woods and possible pastures—now probably rank long grass, full of tigers—looking exactly like a finely-cultivated country, with large tracts of waving corn and wood, yet without the faintest sign of any thing living."—*Paraguay, Brazil, and the Plate*, by C. B. Mansfield, Esq., M.A., p. 377. Cambridge, 1856.

‡ "Y otros árboles que tienen la corteza interior tan delicada y blanca, que alguna vez ha servido de papel para escribir."—Antonio de Alcedo, *Diccionario Geográfico-Histórico de las Indias Occidentales*, tom. i., p. 449. Madrid, 1786.

plums, figs, and olives. The bees find here their especial home; and twelve different species of them are enumerated, some of which form their nests in the trees in the shape of a vase The woods are not like

the silent forests of North America, but swarm with all kinds of birds, having every variety of note and feather, from the soft colors of the wild dove to the gay plumage of the parrot, from the plaintive note of the nightingale to the dignified noise of those birds which are said to imitate the trumpet and the organ.

A few Indians, rarely to be seen, and appearing like specks in the landscape, roam over this vast plain, which a modern traveler has well said might be "the cradle of a mighty nation."* It might have been thought that, far removed from the complex strife of European politics, and abundantly provided with all that can make life prosperous, the Jesuit missions would gradually have overspread this beautiful garden, or that in modern times it might have been adopted as one of the choicest spots for abundant colonization. That it may still become so is highly probable; but those European politics which seemed so unlikely to disturb remote Paraguay did not fail to suppress whatever good might have arisen from the untiring efforts of the Jesuit missionaries. In the latter half of the eighteenth century the Order of the Jesuits fell into disgrace with the governments both of France and Spain, and the most rigorous measures of suppression and banishment were adopted against them. The Jesuit Missions of Para-

* "One thing is abundantly clear to me, viz., that the Gran Chaco is the yet empty cradle of a mighty nation: it must be the theatre of a new era in history—it is *the* place. Just cast your eye upon the map; just see the tract of land, in length from Santa Fé ten degrees of latitude northward, and some six degrees of longitude in breadth from the Paraguay-Paraná toward the west, and consider if it be not a marvel. A splendid country, possessed by wild Indians alone, who live on nothing but wild beasts—men who, by their neglect of the earth, have forfeited their right to claim national property in it—a wild garden, surrounded on all sides by provinces occupied, or pretended to be occupied, by Spanish tribes, none of whom dare set foot in this territory, and yet have the impudence to claim it as their own—this territory is actually an undiscovered country."—MANSFIELD'S *Paraguay*, p. 354.

guay shared the fate of their order in the Old World; and thus, for the most part, was this magnificent territory abandoned to the tribes of wandering Indians, who here and there dot the landscape, but who can not, in any manner, be said to occupy the country. Paraguay remains for another peaceful conquest—not this time, perhaps, of a purely religious character, but more likely to be connected with some great schemes of colonization or of commerce.

CHAPTER III.

THE CONQUEST OF BOGOTÁ.

THE discovery and conquest of Bogotá were achieved by the Licentiate Gonzalo Ximenez de Quesada, acting as lieutenant for Don Pedro Fernandez de Lugo, the Governor of Santa Marta. This discovery was commenced in the year 1536; and Quesada was employed for several years in completing his discovery and consolidating his conquest. He conquered certain chiefs named Bogotá and Tunja. He founded the city of Santa Fé de Bogotá, and gave the whole province the name of "The New Kingdom of Granada." He had many hardships and perils to endure, and also difficulties to overcome from the claims of other conquerors, namely, Sebastian de Belalcazar and Federman, who advanced from other points upon the district that Quesada was conquering. But his adventures do not differ materially from many others of the same kind which have been already recorded in this history.

The people, however, whom he discovered and conquered deserve particular mention, for among them were found signs of considerable civilization, and even of scientific research. They were well dressed, having cotton clothes of various colors, and wearing garlands on their heads, in which were inserted artificial flowers. Their houses were well built. Busts and paintings were found in their houses. Their food was various, always a sign of civilization; and they manufactured salt. In some of their temples Quesada found emeralds, and also gold wrought into the shape of crowns, eagles and other birds, and animals.*

The mythology of the Muyscas (for this was the name of the Indians who inhabited the great plain of Bogotá) is very remarkable. All their knowledge and polity were brought to them by a mysterious stranger named Bochica, a bearded man. He taught them how to build, to plant, and to sow, and how to live in a commonwealth. This was in the days when the moon was not. Bochica was accompanied by a beautiful woman,† named Huythaca, not less malignant than beautiful. "By her skill in magic she swelled the river of Funzha, and inundated the valley of Bogotá. The greater part of the inhabitants perished in this deluge; a few only found refuge on the summits of the neighboring mountains. The old man, in anger, drove the beautiful Huythaca far from the earth, and she became the moon, which began from that epoch to enlighten our planet during the night. Bochica, moved with compassion for those who were dispersed over the mountains, broke with his powerful arm the rocks that inclosed the valley on the side of Canoas and Tequendama. By this outlet he drained the waters of the Lake Bogotá. Moreover, he built towns, introduced the worship of the Sun, named two chiefs, between whom he divided the civil and ecclesiastical authority, and then withdrew himself, under

* "Gonzalo Ximenez, visto que no havia podido dár con Sagamosa, bolvió por la Tierra de Duitama, í halló en unos Adoratorios hasta quarenta mil pesos de Oro fino, í baxo, con Esmeraldas, í alguna parte del Oro estaba en figuras de Coronas, Aguilas, í otras Aves í Animales."—HERRERA, *Hist. de las Indias*, dec. vi., lib. iii., cap. 13.

† Some say that she came afterward: she is represented as the principle of evil.

the name of Idacanzas, into the holy valley of Iraca, near Tunja, where he lived in the exercise of the most austere penitence for the space of two thousand years."*

I have elsewhere remarked that the number four was a dominant and important number in the New World. In the republic of Tlascala their chief city was divided into four quarters, ruled over by four chiefs. In the great city of Cusco the division was also into four districts, corresponding to the four divisions of the empire of Peru—Condesuyo, Collasuyo, Antisuyo, and Chinchasuyo. It was strictly ordered that all tribes coming to the city were to be attached to one or other of these divisions, so that the division into four was thus permanently maintained. And still farther south a trace of this division into four may be observed in the number of chiefs who ruled over the indomitable Araucans. Their number was sixteen,† a multiple of four, which exactly corresponds to the number in Guatemala. Among the Tultecas, the original inhabitants, or rather conquerors of Guatemala, there were four ruling families in four independent provinces, and in each province there were four persons designated to succeed to the royal authority. A similar mode of succession prevailed among the Mexicans. In the Quichean account of the creation of the world, which has come to

* HUMBOLDT'S *Researches*, vol. i., p. 74.

† "De diez y seis Caciques y Señores,
Es el soberbio Estado poseido,
En militar estudio los mejores
Que de bárbaras madres han nacido:
Reparo de su patria y defensores,
Ninguno en el gobierno preferido:
Otros Caciques hay, mas por valientes
Son estos en mandar preeminentes."

La Araucana de ALONSO DE ERCILLA Y ZÚÑIGA, canto 1.

light within the last few years, four men are created, and afterward four wives are given to them. Every fourth year in Mexico was a year of jubilee, and among the Appalaches of Florida there were four* great annual feasts.†

Bochica, before he disappeared mysteriously from the earth, settled the mode of election of the high-priest and king, which conjoint authority was to be conferred on one person, to be chosen by four chiefs or tribes. This great personage, like the Lama of Thibet, was secluded at an early age, and was not even permitted to see the sun until he should assume his rightful authority.‡

That the Muyscas had made some advance in science is proved by the fact of their having a lunar calendar with hieroglyphical signs, "representing the order in which the intercalations that bring back the origin of the year to the same season is made."§

* As another instance of a predilection for the number four, the Chibcas (a general name for the inhabitants of New Granada) divided the day and the night each into four parts. "*Los Chibchas dividian el dia* Sua, *i la noche* Za, *en quatro partes, á saber;* Sua mena, *desde el nacimiento del sol hasta medio dia;* Sua meca, *desde el medio dia hasta entrarse el sol;* Zasca, *desde que se entraba el sol hasta media noche, i* Cagui, *desde media noche hasta salir el sol.*"—EZEQUIEL URICOECHEA, *Memoria sobre las Antigüedades Neo-Granadinas*, cap. 3, p. 19. Berlin, 1854.

† See *Notes on the Floridian Peninsula*, by DANIEL G. BRINTON, A.B., p. 106. Philadelphia, 1859.

‡ This account is, in the main, confirmed by PIEDRAHITA, who made use of the MS. of Quesada, the conqueror of Bogotá: "Ultimamente afirman del Bochica que murió en Sogamoso despues de su predicacion; y que aviendo vivido alli retirado viente vezes cinco vientes de años, que por su cuenta hazen dos mil, fue trasladado al Cielo, y que al tiempo de su partido dexó al Cazique de aquella Provincia por heredero de su santidad y poderio."—LUCAS FERNANDEZ DE PIEDRAHITA, *Historia General de las Conquistas del Nuevo Reyno de Granada*, parte i., lib. i., cap. 3. Amberes, 1688.

§ "A stone covered with hieroglyphic signs of the lunar calendar,

Their laws of hereditary descent were peculiar, their estates descending to their brothers in preference to their own sons.*

They had some confused belief in the immortality of the soul, the resurrection of the dead, the reward of the good, and the punishment of the wicked, in a future state. They believed in a creator; but the chief divinities they worshiped were the sun and the moon. They had also idols who were considered as saints, and who were to intercede for them with the sun and the moon. They worshiped all stones, believing that these stones had formerly been men, and

and representing the order in which the intercalations, that bring back the origin of the year to the same season, are made, is a monument so much the more remarkable, as it is the work of a people whose name is almost unknown in Europe, and who have been hitherto confounded with the wandering tribes of the savages of South America. For the discovery of this monument we are indebted to Don José Domingo Duquesne of Madrid, Canon of the Metropolitan Church of Santa Fé de Bogotá. This ecclesiastic, a native of the kingdom of New Granada, and descended from a French family settled in Spain, was long the vicar of an Indian village situate on the plain of the ancient Cundinamurca. His office having enabled him to gain the confidence of the natives, who are descendants of the Muyscas, he has endeavored to collect all that tradition has preserved during three centuries concerning the state of those regions before the arrival of the Spaniards in the New Continent. He succeeded in procuring one of those sculptured stones by which the Muysca priests regulated the division of time; he acquired the knowledge of the simple hieroglyphics, which denote both numbers and the lunar days; and he has written a statement of the knowledge he acquired, the fruit of long and laborious researches, in a memoir that bears the title of *Disertacion sobre el Kalendario de los Muyscas, Indios naturales del nuevo Reyno de Grenada.* This manuscript was communicated to me at Santa Fé in 1801 by the celebrated botanist Don José Celestino Mutis."—HUMBOLDT'S *Researches*, vol. ii., p. 104.

* "No heredaban los Hijos, sino los Hermanos; í si no havia Hermanos, los Hijos de los Hermanos muertos: í á estos, como tampoco los heredaban sus Hijos, sino sus mismos Sobrinos, ó Primos, viene á ser todo una cuenta con lo de Castilla: salvo, que van por estos rodéos."—HERRERA, *Hist. de las Indias*, dec. vi., lib. v., cap. 6.

that there would be a resurrection in which these stones would be transformed again into men. They had another superstition of an almost incredible kind. In studying the religions of savages or of semi-civilized men, so strange are the objects of adoration that at last the student is scarcely surprised at finding any animate or inanimate object transformed by the power of imagination into a deity. The accomplished Egyptians worshiped as deities leeks, onions, cats, dogs, worms, and serpents. In eastern India the cow has been held sacred. It has been narrated how in Nicaragua toads were worshiped, and were occasionally punished by their worshipers if the weather was unfavorable. The earth, the elements, the sun, the moon, the stars, lightning, thunder, and the rainbow, have been common objects of adoration. But the Muyscas exceeded in the strangeness of their belief all other nations. They believed in their own shadows, and considered them to be gods. It was in vain that the Spaniards pointed out to these Indians what was the nature of a shadow, and how trees and stones had shadows. They could only reply that the shadows of the stones were the gods of gods. "Such," adds the historian, "was their stolidity and their misfortune."* They had also sacred lakes and consecrated groves. From the lakes no water might be

* "Adoraban tambien á su misma sombra, de suerte que siempre llevaban á su Dios consigo; y viendolo como hiziesse el dia claro, y aunque conocian que la sombra se causaba de la luz, y cuerpo interpuesto, respondian, que aquello lo hazia el Sol para darles Dioses: cosa que no estrañára oy la politica del mundo, sabiendo que los Ministros son las sombras de los Reyes, y que se alçan con la adoracion de Dioses, tanto mas grandes, quanto por mas retirada la influencia de la luz haze mayores las sombras: y si para convencer los les mostraban las sombras de los arboles, y de las piedras, nada bastava; porque á las primeras tenian por Dioses de los arboles, y á las segundas por Dioses de sus Dioses, tanta era su estolidez, y desdicha."—

taken, and in the groves not a tree might be cut down; but thither they went to make their offerings, which were gold and jewels. These they buried in the groves, or cast into the lakes. Their sacrifices were rarely human, except in the case of certain youths who were set apart in the Temple of the Sun, and who were worshiped and feasted until they arrived at the age of virility, when they were slain as an appointed sacrifice.

The foregoing account of the Muyscas shows the existence in South America of a considerable people, independent of the Peruvians, and yet having some points of resemblance with them. The Muysca language has perished; and it is very probable that the records of this people, as derived from the Spaniards, do not do justice to their advance in civilization. There can be no doubt, from what their conqueror, Quesada, saw, that they had attained to some knowledge of many of the arts of life. Their laws were good; and their punishments for breaches of the law were well proportioned, and not excessive.* Even with regard to human sacrifices, it is evident that these were comparatively rare; and that, in this respect, the Muyscas must be considered as far more civilized than the cruel Mexicans, with whom, as with the Peruvians, this singular people had some affinity.

PIEDRAHITA, *Historia General de las Conquistas del Nuevo Reyno de Granada*, parte i., lib. i., cap. 2.

* The Muyscas had a strange way of collecting debts. If a debtor did not pay his debts or his taxes, a "young tiger," or other wild beast, bred for the purpose, was tied to the door of his house, and he was obliged to maintain the animal and his keeper until the creditor was satisfied.

CHAPTER IV.

THE DISCOVERY AND CONQUEST OF FLORIDA.

THE history of Florida is, for the most part, an account of the misfortunes of individual commanders of expeditions much resembling those of Ojeda and Nicuesa. Hernan Ponce de Leon, in the search after the "Fountain of Perpetual Youth," first discovered Florida in 1512. He was wounded in an encounter with the natives, and died of his wounds in the island of Cuba.

In the year 1520, an auditor of St. Domingo, in the island of Hispaniola, a rich and learned man, formed a company, with six other inhabitants of that island, and went out with two vessels to capture Indian Caribs as slaves to work at the mines. This auditor's name was Lucas Vasquez de Ayllon. A storm drove the vessels on the east coast of Florida, and Ayllon entered the province of Chicora. This part of Florida was governed by a cacique named Datha, who was a giant. His gigantic stature had been artificially produced, for it is said that the Indians of those parts had a method of elongating the bones of children when very young, a practice which they applied to those of royal race.*

* "Porque, como referia el mismo Lucas de Ayllon, quando están mamando, los que han de Reinar, los Indios Maestros, de este arte, ablandan, como cera, los huesos del niño, con emplastos de ciertas yervas, y los estienden, hasta que dejan al niño como muerto."—*Ensayo Cronologico de la Florida*, por GABRIEL DE CARDENAS Y CANO (Barcia), p. 4. Madrid, 1723.

The simple Floridians at first fled from the vessels, thinking that they were new monsters generated by the sea. The Spaniards, however, succeeded in capturing a native, and, treating him well, attracted others to the ships. At last the cacique himself came, accompanied by numerous attendants. Ayllon allowed one hundred and thirty of them to enter his vessels, and then set sail, carrying them all off to the island of Hispaniola. In his voyage homeward he came upon those three unfortunate Lucayans who had made their escape from Hispaniola in the trunk of a tree.* The Lucayans had shown the most desperate aversion to servitude; and some had refused all sustenance, choosing death rather than slavery. The captured Floridians were of a similar disposition, and nearly all of them died from sorrow and home-sickness. Such an act of treachery as the above, perpetrated by a man of education and in authority, goes far to justify Las Casas in the defense which he made for the Floridian Indians in his controversy with Sepulveda, when that learned man referred to the martyrdom of Luis Cancér.

In 1524 Ayllon prepared another expedition, intending to conquer the province of Chicora, of which he had received a grant. He took with him the same pilot he had before; but this pilot was not able to discover the land where they had disembarked in the previous voyage, a circumstance which vexed him so much that he went mad and died. Ayllon, not being able to find his own province, landed on that part of the coast where it seemed most fertile. The Floridians received him in the most friendly manner; but, whether they had heard of his former exploit or not, their friendship was feigned. He sent, or himself

* See *ante*, vol. i., book iii., chap. ii., p. 220.

led, a body of two hundred men to reconnoitre a town about a day's distance from the coast. Here the Spaniards were feasted for four days, but were then attacked at night time, and were all slain. The same Indians then came down to attack the remaining Spaniards; but these, not without difficulty, succeeded in getting on board their vessels, and, after suffering many calamities, returned to Hispaniola. Some say that the commander Ayllon was among those who were slain in the night assault of the Indians. But if he returned, it appears that he did not long survive the ill success of his expedition, for in the next year, 1525, Charles the Fifth granted the conquest of Chicora to Ayllon's son. This man, not being able to furnish out an expedition, died of melancholy in the island of Hispaniola.

Afterward, in 1528, Pamphilo de Narvaez, the opponent of Cortez, led an expedition to Florida, where he perished miserably.

In this expedition, however, was a certain officer named Cabeça de Vaca, and his adventures in Florida form perhaps the most remarkable story of modern discovery. They serve to explain the mythical ages, for Cabeça de Vaca rose from being a prisoner to becoming a divinity; and, after reading his narrative, which bears every mark of truthfulness,* it is easy to

* I am well aware how much this narrative has been questioned. See an excellent work, published in 1859, by D. G. Brinton, entitled *Notes on the Floridian Peninsula*, in which (p. 17) he gives reasons for thinking that Cabeça de Vaca wrote his *Naufragios* in order to exculpate his former life, and to set forth to the world his steadfast devotion to the interests of the king. But Cabeça de Vaca had not to justify himself in respect of any thing but his government of La Plata; and how, except by some such story as his own, can we account for his journey of three thousand miles from Apalache to Mexico? His being able to accomplish such a journey, not his remaining uninjured for ten

understand the various traditions which were found current in the Indies, of remarkable strangers who had come among the natives, and had taught them new arts, new manners, and new laws.

Though the narrative of many of these minor conquests would not assist much in elucidating the main course of Spanish colonization and colonial legislation, yet there is generally something very notable in each conquest that stamps it with peculiarity. In that of Florida, for instance, this narrative of Cabeça de Vaca, showing how he and his companions were taken for supernatural beings, is so extraordinary that it deserves a place in any history of the Indies.

The Floridian Indians worshiped these Spaniards in so ample a manner that all the rights of property fell before their presence. The Indians who had charge of them did not take them to unfriendly tribes, because they were unwilling that their enemies should enjoy so great an advantage as to behold these new divinities. But, as they proceeded in their progresses, a general spoliation took place. Nothing was left in the houses of those Indians who were so fortunate as to receive the Spaniards. This practice scandalized and vexed the Spaniards; but they did not venture to prevent it; and even those Indians who were despoiled by Cabeça de Vaca and his companions begged them not to distress themselves about it, assuring them that they held the loss of their goods as naught in comparison with the pleasure of having beheld them—and besides, they would be paid by the spoil of other tribes. So the Spaniards moved on, accompanied by a multitude of Indians, who informed the new tribes they came among that these white men

years among the Floridians, is the wonder. I believe that his own account is substantially true.

were the children of the sun, who had power to heal the sick and to take away life, and that they should hide nothing from them, because every thing was known to these divinities. So great was the terror which their presence inspired, that, for the first few days upon their arrival at any new place, the inhabitants never stood before them without trembling, and did not dare to speak or to lift up their eyes. All that the Spaniards did by way of ceremonial was to make the sign of the cross over the natives, which was greatly desired by all who approached them.

The narrative may be summed up in the words of Cabeça de Vaca himself. "Among all these nations it was held for very certain that we came from heaven. While we went with them, we journeyed the whole day without eating until the evening, and we ate so little that they were astonished at observing it. They never perceived fatigue in us, for in truth we were so formed to labor that neither did we feel it. We kept up much state and gravity with them ; and, in order to maintain this, we spoke but seldom to them. The negro who was with us talked often to them, informed himself of the roads we wished to take, of the villages we should come upon, and of other things which we desired to know. We passed through a great number and diversity of tribes [*lit.* "languages"], and in all of them God our Lord favored us, for they always understood us, and we understood them. And we asked and responded by signs as well as if they could speak our language, and we theirs. For, although we knew six languages, we could not in all parts make use of them, as we found more than a thousand differences of language. Throughout all these countries, those who had wars with one another immediately made peace, in order to come and receive us; and so we left the whole country in peace. And we told them by signs, which they understood, that in heaven there was One whom we called God, who had created the heaven and the earth, and that we ourselves adored Him and held Him for Lord, and did what He commanded us; that from His hand came all good things; and if they should do as we did, much good would follow. We found such readiness in them to be converted, that, if we had had an interpreter, so that we could have made ourselves perfectly understood, we should have left them all Christians. We gave them to understand all this in the best way that we could; and from henceforward, when the sun rose, they raised their clasped hands to heaven with a loud shout, and afterward they spread their hands over the whole of their bodies. They did the same at the setting of the sun. It is a well-conditioned people, ready to follow any good thing well prepared for them."*

Cabeça de Vaca and his companions pursued their journey until they came into New Spain, and finally arrived at the city of Mexico in the year 1536.

* "Por todas estas tierras, los que tenian guerras con los otros, se hacian luego amigos para venirnos á rescebir, í traernos todo quanto tenian, í de esta manera dexamos todo la tierra en paz, í diximosles por las señas que nos entendian, que en el cielo havia un hombre que llamabamos Dios, el qual havia criado el cielo, í la tierra, í que este adorabamos nosotros, í teniamos por Señor, í que haciamos lo que nos mandaba, í que de su mano venian todas las cosas buenas, í que si ansi ellos lo hiciesen, les iria mui bien de ello; í tan grande aparejo hallamos en ellos, que si lengua hoviera con que perfectamente nos entendieramos, todos los dexáramos Christianos. Esto les dimos á entender lo mejor que podimos; í de aí adelante, quando el sol salia, con mui gran grita abrian las manos juntas al Cielo, í despues las traían por todo su cuerpo: í otro tanto hacian quando se ponia. Es gente bien acondicionada, í aprovechada para seguir qualquiera cosa bien aparejada."—*Naufragios de* ALVAR NUÑEZ CABEÇA DE VACA, cap. 31.—BARCIA, *Historiadores*, tom. ii.

Another Spaniard of mark, named Hernando de Soto, who was concerned in the capture of Atahuallpa, undertook the conquest of Florida in the year 1538. His expedition, like those of his predecessors, proved unfortunate, and he died in the course of it.

There were other fruitless expeditions of the Spaniards in the course of the ensuing thirty years. The French Protestants then entered Florida. Jean Ribault was sent thither by the celebrated Admiral Coligny. One of his officers, named René Laudonnière, founded Charlefort in 1562. But the French were cruelly massacred, not as being Frenchmen, but as being Lutherans, by Pedro Menendez de Avilés, who was commissioned by the court of Spain to undertake the reconquest of Florida. Avilés founded the town of St. Augustine; and, notwithstanding that the massacre of the French was revenged by a private French gentleman named Dominique de Gourgues, the Spaniards held possession of the country for nearly two hundred years, from 1567 to 1763, when it was ceded to the English.

The question will naturally occur, How it was that Spanish colonization did not spread farther northward, or rather northeastward, than Florida? Some would allege that the decadence of the Spanish monarchy gives an answer to this question. But perhaps it would be nearer the truth to say that the colonizing power of the Spanish people was exhausted. Each nation has but a certain amount of that power to make use of. In the early part of the sixteenth century the Spaniards had many outlets for the adventurous part of their population. A considerable element of the Spanish race was to be found in the populations of Italy and Flanders, as the cities of Milan,

Ghent, and Bruges could testify. Spain itself was certainly not an overpopulated country; and, moreover, it must be recollected that the regions already occupied by the Spaniards in the New World were more tempting to their fellow-countrymen than the colder climes of North America.

CHAPTER V.

STATE OF THE SPANISH COLONIES AFTER THE SEVERAL CONQUESTS.—CONCLUSION OF THE WORK.

IT is obvious, from a mere comparison of dates, that the history of Florida, however interesting in itself, could have had no bearing upon the main events of conquest and legislation in the Indies. The way in which the men of the Old World were to deal with the men of the New was mainly settled by what took place in the course of the early discoveries and conquests, and was comprised in the period during which Las Casas labored as Protector of the Indians, and when the Church and State of Spain were creating for themselves representatives in Spanish America.

This representation was, for the most part, exact and faithful. Corregidors, regidors, alcaldes, alguazils, procuradors, veedors, contadors, judges of *Residencia*, and all the officers usually to be met with in the various kingdoms of Spain, were transplanted into the Indies, and flourished there. The Church was fully represented in the New World by bishops, deans, priests, clerigos, and monks of every denomination. First came the Franciscans and the Dominicans; then the Fathers of Mercy and the Augustines. Lastly came the Jesuits, who, where they settled, maintained a hold upon the country greater than that of the other monastic orders, though all were far more active and busy than in Spain itself; and adventurous monks, who had pined in their convents at home for more work to do, found room for their energies in the New World, just as much as adventurous soldiers had done. In fact, there was an active emigration from the mother-country of many of its most energetic soldiers, citizens, and priests.

Again, the form of municipal government that prevailed in the cities of Spain was exactly copied in the Spanish colonies of America. Town councils were established in all the new cities, and were no doubt far more active and more powerful than such bodies in the old country. There is no precise account of how these town councils in the New World were created, but it is probable that the mode of their formation did not differ much from that adopted in the mother-country. In the town of Saragossa, for example, the mode of choosing the officers for governing that city was partly guided by considerations of fitness, and partly left to fortune. The names of the persons who were thought fit for any office were written on strips of parchment. These were inserted in wooden balls, and placed in a bag.* Afterward a child, who might not be more than ten years old, selected one of these balls, and the person whose name was found inside it had to fill the place in question.†

* "*Bolsa de Jurado Primero.* Item estatuimos, y ordenamos, que los nombres de los Ciudadanos, que de presente en la Ciudad son aptos, y suficientes para Jurado Primero della, conforme á las presentes Ordinaciones, sean escritos en sendas cedulas de pergamino, y cada una dellas puesta en un redolino de madera, los quales redolinos sean de un mismo peso, madera, color, y forma, puestos en bolsa cerrada, y sellada fielmente con el sello menor de la dicha Ciudad, y aquella intitulada con las palabras siguientes: *Bolsa de Jurado Primero.*"—*Ordinaciones de la Ciudad de Zaragoza*, p. 4. Zaragoza, 1693.

† "El dicho niño los rebuelva por debaxo la toalla, y saque de ellos un redolino, el que dicho niño publicamente ha de entregar al Secretario de la Ciudad, por el qual sea publicamente abierto el dicho redo-

However chosen, these bodies exercised considerable influence and authority, as has been seen in the history of Peru, sending their proctors to Spain, and making known their wishes and remonstrances very freely.

In the New World there were but two or three novelties as regards government and mode of life, which would strike a Spanish colonist as remarkable. In the first place, the householder of a town in the Indies, possessing Indians, was not allowed to be an absentee. Garcilaso de la Vega gives an exact definition of the meaning of the word householder, or neighbor, both of which senses are included in the Spanish word *Vecino*. "By neighbor is meant in the Indies he who possesses a *repartimiento* of Indians, and the word neighbor signifies this, because they are obliged to maintain neighborhood where they hold Indians, and they can not go to Spain without permission from the king, under penalty of losing their *repartimientos* if they should be absent from their neighborhood for two years."*

The second novelty in the Indies was the existence of *encomiendas;* for, though this word had been borrowed originally from the Spanish orders of knighthood, it bore a different signification now that it applied to a conquered race, with whom the conquerors were forbidden to have much communication, and

lino, y sacada la cedula de pergamino, que dentro de aquel será, la lea incontinente en alta voz."—*Ordinaciones de la Ciudad de Zaragoza*, p. 10.

* "Por vecino se entiende en las Indias el que tiene repartimiento de Indios, y esto significa el nombre vecino, porque estaban obligados á mantener vecindad donde tenian los Indios, y no podian venir á España sin licencia del Rey, so pena que pasados los dos años que no hubiesen mantenido vecindad perdian el repartimiento."—GARCILASO DE LA VEGA, *Hist. de Florida*, tom. i., cap. 2.

from whom they were merely to derive a settled tribute having the nature of a life interest.

The third novelty in the Indies was the existence of large bodies of negro slaves.

The kind of government which prevailed in the Indies has now been traced, and it has been seen how much it resembled that of the mother-country. There were, however, new products of the earth; new manufactures; an attention to mining such as did not exist in Spain itself; and also a new mode of life in respect of the large tracts of land which were occupied by the Spanish proprietors, and which naturally changed many of the owners from citizens into planters. The countries they colonized were too extensive for the colonists; and to this day a shrewd traveler will notice how a colonist may possess leagues of territory, and yet be a needy man.

Such a state of society was not likely to produce great results in the arts, the sciences, or in literature. There was, no doubt, a considerable amount of material prosperity among the Spanish colonists, but there was little of national growth; and so, when, in modern times, the colonies were released from the easy yoke of the mother-country, that release found them unfit for any settled polity, and left them a ready prey to civil discord and military turbulence.

The Indians, if they have not been highly civilized, have at least been somewhat Christianized; and all that is votive, festal, and devout in the religion they have been taught, has found a ready access to their minds.

Though much has perished of the early records of the New World, enough remains to throw great light, if carefully studied, upon the ancient history, religion,* and languages of the natives. Philology, archæology, and physiology may yet be greatly enriched from the early sources of American History. The natural history, too, of South America is, comparatively speaking, but little known, and a diligent investigation of the records of the Spanish Conquest would enable Europeans to direct discovery into the most profitable channels.

My attempt has chiefly been to describe the intermingling of races, the progress of slavery, the modes of Spanish colonization, and thus also to give some insight into the fate of the conquered people, and of that other race, the African, which fully partook the misfortunes of the native inhabitants of America. After many years of labor this attempt has been partially accomplished,† no one being more conscious than the author how many errors must have crept into a work of such great extent, and how many omissions there must be in a history where the materials are so abundant, and yet so difficult of acquisition.

The narrative extends over a period of one hundred and fifty years, in the course of which time the coast of Africa was mainly discovered, America rediscovered by Columbus, and the Spanish colonies brought into some form of law and order. The close connection of these two great events, the discoveries of Africa and America, has had the most remarkable

* In an Appendix will be given an account of the Quichean Cosmogony.

† I look forward with hope to some great historian arising who, devoting his life to the history of the New World, embodying in it the Spanish Conquest, and also giving a thorough account of the Indians in North and South America, of their relation to one another, and of their affinity with the nations of the Old World, will make all the other histories that have been written upon this subject appear poor and fragmentary.

and fatal results. The first negroes imported into Europe after the extinction of the old pagan slavery were brought in one of the ships of Prince Henry of Portugal, in the year 1442. There was, however, no regular trade in negroes established by the Portuguese; and the importation of human beings fell off,* while that of other articles of commerce increased, until after the discovery of America. Then the sudden destruction of multitudes of Indians in war, by unaccustomed labor, by immense privations, and by diseases new to them, produced a void in the labor market which was inevitably filled up by the importation of negroes. Even the kindness and the piety of the Spanish monarchs tended partly to produce this result. They forbade the enslaving of Indians, and they contrived that the Indians should live in some manner apart from the Spaniards; and it is a very significant fact that the great "Protector of the Indians," Las Casas, should, however innocently, have been concerned with the first large grant of licenses to import negroes into the West India Islands. Again, the singular hardihood of the negro race, which enabled them to flourish in all climates, and the comparative debility of the Indians, also favored this result. The anxiety of the Catholic Church for proselytes combined with the foregoing causes to make the bishops and monks slow to perceive the mischief of any measure which might tend to save or favor large communities of docile converts. Lastly, the evil of negro importation must have appeared, even to the wisest churchman or statesman, comparatively a small evil. The Indians at first numbered hundreds of thousands, to hundreds of the negroes. Any measure that tended to preserve the Indians would naturally ap-

* See *ante*, vol. i., book i., chap. ii., p. 87.

pear prudent and humane, even if it should involve suffering on the part of another inferior race, much fewer in numbers than the Indians. Taking all these circumstances into consideration, the gradual influx of a large black population into the New World is thoroughly accounted for.

I have chosen the middle of the sixteenth century as the term for concluding this History, because by that time* conquest was almost complete, and colonial organization was settled, or in the way of settlement. History, as it should have a marked epoch for its beginning, should have a definite epoch for its close. The stream of colonization and of conquest flowed on forcibly and uninterruptedly from the first voyage of Columbus to the reconquest of Peru. Then, like some mighty river, which, after its difficult outset in the mountains, has long sped impetuously onward, it at length attains a certain equable movement, not unprosperous, but somewhat stagnant, or, amid sandy and marshy tracts, loses its original grandeur and volume, divided into many minor channels,

* By the middle of the sixteenth century most of the chief historians and annalists had died, and the works of those who survived were not carried much beyond that period. Nothing more is to be gained from Peter Martyr, Oviedo, Bernal Diaz, Enciso, Las Casas, Garcilaso de la Vega, Cortez, or Gomara. Herrera, writing in another age, closes his decades soon after the reconquest of Peru. Remesal has nothing of any general interest to commemorate after narrating the death of Las Casas; and all such writers as Torquemada are merely interesting when they refer to the early periods of the Conquest. It is the same with the ecclesiastical historians, Davila Padilla, Fernandez, Gil Gonçalez Davila, Calancha, and Melendez. The lawyers, also, such as Antonio de Leon, and Solorzano, have comparatively little to relate after the time of Philip the Second; and the German and Italian writers, such as Benzoni, Gaspar Ens, and Levinus Apollonius, do not carry us farther in the main narrative than has been already recorded in this history.

as it makes its laboring way toward the end of its appointed course. It had better be parted from while it affords its noblest aspect to the beholder, and when it is perfectly clear whither it is tending.

The world still has, and long will have, reason to deplore that the efforts of the Spanish monarchs and of the other protectors of the Indians were not crowned with complete success; that the conquest of the New World was not achieved without such large destruction of the native people; and that the entrance into America of the civilized inhabitants of Europe should have been accompanied by the introduction of a subject race from another continent, whose enforced presence has since proved a dire obstacle to the maintenance of concord and to the growth of civilization. Possibly, what remedy remains for this great evil may yet be found in a diligent study of that humane legislation which attended the spread of the Spanish sway in the Indies. It is a page of her eventful history to which Spain may with just pride refer, as evincing a provident humanity which great nations in later ages have often failed to imitate, and as displaying the peculiar characteristics of the Spanish race—piety, loyalty, and chivalry—in their noblest forms.

He who has attempted to write a History of the Spanish Conquest may well look back with astonishment at the temerity which led him to undertake such a task, and with thankfulness at having been permitted in any way to bring his work to a completion—a privilege which literature laments to have been denied to so many of her worthiest sons. The subject of the history is, in its main outlines, unique. The triumphant march of Alexander, the rise and fall of Rome, the unintended conquest of British India, afford narratives to which the world will ever listen. But these have their parallels, and something like them may occur again. That one half of the globe should remain for ages ignorant of the existence of the other; that it should then be led by the insight and indomitable perseverance of one man to discover this long-concealed hemisphere; and that, in the short period of fifty or sixty years, the larger part of this New World should be subdued by a handful of men from the Old World, form a narrative of vast ends accomplished by the most scanty means, the like of which is not to be found in other annals. It is a tale which tells of deeds that no longer admit of imitation; which describes warfare resembling some strange, unequal conflict in fable or mythology, rather than the ordinary encounters of mortal men; and which, in the unrivaled nature of its picturesque and romantic incidents, lives only in the marvelous records of Spanish discovery, conquest, and colonization.

APPENDIX

THERE has recently been published, by the care of a learned German, Dr. Scherzer, the manuscript of a monk named FRANCISCO XIMENEZ,* which gives an account, translated from the language of Quiché, of the cosmogony which the Quicheans believed in. In parts it is very grand and touching; in others, and for the most part, it is puerile, and, as the monk who translates it says, it has neither hands nor feet.

In this Quichean cosmogony the creation is gradual and tentative. At first, beasts and birds are created by the formative gods. Then these creatures are bidden to speak out and praise their makers—not to keep on saying "Yol, yol." But they could only scream, and cry, and chatter. Then the formative gods created men out of wood, but they proceeded from their makers' hands without hearts and without understanding; and they, too, could not praise their makers. All the animals, great and small, and even sticks and stones, affronted these poor beings, and rebelled against them. The Heart of Heaven was consulted, and a great deluge came upon them. The monkey remains as a sign to men of the kind of man that was made of wood.

There are then two wonderful personages born in the obscurity of night, before there was any sun or moon, and they make a descent into Hell. They come to four roads—one red, one black, one white, one yellow; and the black road speaks to them, and tells them that it is the way to "the Lords of Hell." They pursue this way, and arrive before the thrones of these lords. They are invited by the infernal deities to take their place beside them; and, doing so, they find themselves sitting on burning stones; and the Lords of Hell laugh at their sufferings until their own bones come out of their skin for very laughter.

In this abode of Hell there are many houses of torment—the house of utter darkness; the house of insupportable cold; the house of tigers; the house of bats; and the house of sharp knives, which are forever making a noise, grating one against the other. These two

* *Las Historias del Origen de los Indios de Guatemala*, por El R. P. F. FRANCISCO XIMENEZ. London: Trübner and Co.

children of darkness are conquered in Hell, and put to death. Then there is a miraculous conception. Under a tree where the skull of one of these children of darkness had been placed, a virgin conceives, and afterward gives birth to two children, who also enter the infernal region; and they are victorious over all its terrors and torments.

Eventually man is created, but this time not of wood, but of yellow corn. Four men were created. The first man was named Balam-Quitze, which means the tiger with the sweet smile; and he invented human sacrifices. And the second man was called Balam-Acab, the third Mahucutah, and the fourth Yqui-Balam. And these men gave thanks to their creator (the singular is used here, though two deities are spoken of); but they saw every thing, the little and the great, the far and the near, even to the four corners of earth and heaven. This extent of vision did not please the formative gods; and a film was brought over the eyes of these four men by the Heart of Heaven, as when a mirror is clouded by being breathed upon, and then they could only see what was near to them, and what was clear. Four wives were given them, and their issue became a great people. "And not only were they four, but four only, the fathers of us, the Quicheans."

INDEX.

THE END.

www.ingramcontent.com/pod-product-compliance
Lightning Source LLC
LaVergne TN
LVHW021125110826
845150LV00005B/956

* 9 7 8 1 4 2 5 5 5 0 9 8 1 *